Adventures in Writing:
The Complete Collection
Melissa Donovan

Swan Hatch Press | San Francisco

Adventures in Writing: The Complete Collection

Copyright © 2014 by Melissa Donovan

First Edition, 2014

Published by Swan Hatch Press • Melissa Donovan

ISBN 978-0692205686

Adventures in Writing:
The Complete Collection

includes the following books:

101 Creative Writing Exercises
10 Core Practices for Better Writing
1200 Creative Writing Prompts

Table of Contents

Book One
101 Creative Writing Exercises

101 Creative Writing Exercises

.

Introduction

Writing is a way to communicate, but it is so much more than that. Through writing, we develop and share ideas and information. We express ourselves and make art.

Look around. The written word is everywhere. It's in books, movies, speeches, advertisements, and song lyrics. Writing is found on product packaging, computer monitors, smart-phone screens, greeting cards, and signs. Writing is all around us.

Writers are responsible for some of the greatest contributions to society and culture. We educate, entertain, sell, share, and make emotional connections.

The best writers make it look easy, as if the words roll onto the page with ease, but writing well requires tremendous effort. Our work demands concentration, patience, practice, and a willingness to experiment and take risks. Writers toil at the craft for years, building up an arsenal of tools, techniques, and skills.

Each writer comes to the craft for his or her own reasons. Some of us fell in love with magical tales and wondrous poems when we were children. Some of us are compelled to express our thoughts, opinions, and experiences. Some want to make art out of words. Some write for money. Some write for love.

There are a million reasons to write, and all of them are equally valid.

What You'll Find Inside This Book

The exercises in this book are designed to give you practical experience in writing across a range of forms and genres.

Some of these exercises provide tools and techniques that you can apply to your work. Other exercises inspire pragmatic writing projects that you may be able to submit for publication, such as stories, poetry, articles, and essays.

These exercises encourage you to explore the world of writing, help you build writing skills, and give you real-world experience and plenty of writing practice.

Exploring form, genre, style, and subject matter

Many writers are dedicated to one form or genre, and there's nothing wrong with that. This book is not going to try to convince a copywriter to become a poet or tell a novelist to start writing how-to manuals. But dabbling outside your favorite form or genre will strengthen your skills and equip you with effective methods and techniques that can be applied across all types of writing.

If you enjoy writing in different forms and genres, or if you haven't figured out what, exactly, you want to write, then these exercises will help you find your path.

Discovering tools and techniques (skill building)

You'll learn a lot by simply reading the exercises in this book. Each one includes a short introduction that presents literary terms, storytelling devices, and writing techniques that you can use in your own writing projects.

You'll learn about alliteration and assonance, the three-act story structure, and how to use metaphors and similes effectively. You'll experiment with writing by formula and writing in form. You'll also learn handy techniques that experienced and successful writers have been using for centuries, like discovery writing and outlining.

Creating fresh ideas and getting plenty of practice

Every exercise in this book is constructed so you'll learn something new about writing. These exercises are also designed to inspire you with fresh ideas for future writing projects. Many of the exercises in this book will help you develop projects that you can eventually polish, submit, and publish.

Through his research for the book *Outliers: The Story of Success*, Malcolm Gladwell established the 10,000-hour rule, which states that it takes ten thousand hours of practice to master any skill, craft, or trade. Many successful writers say you should never publish your first poem, short story, or novel. Instead, you should practice before you publish.

The exercises in this book give you plentitude and variety in your writing practice.

How to use this book

The exercises in this book are grouped by form, technique, and subject matter. One chapter focuses on poetry, while another emphasizes article writing. There's a chapter that looks closely at writing about people, both fictional and real, and another that promotes critical thinking.

You can work your way through the book from beginning to end, or you can choose exercises at random. You might select exercises that appeal to your mood, or you might choose chapters that address issues or problems you're having with your own writing projects.

You are encouraged, however, to step outside of your comfort zone. If you primarily write essays, then try a poetry exercise. You'll find that experimenting with one form of writing will reveal concepts and techniques that you can apply to another form. A blogger will learn a lot from doing storytelling exercises, and a fiction writer will learn how to better organize a story logically from the critical-thinking exercises.

Each exercise may include any or all of the following:

- introduction of a writing concept

- the steps or process for completing the exercise

- tips to make the exercise easier or clearer

- variations and alternatives to the exercise

- practical applications that the exercise offers, including its role in publishable projects

Some of the exercises are more challenging than others. You might spend several writing sessions on one exercise and finish another in just a few minutes.

Use this book and work through the exercises in whatever way feels most comfortable to you. Please make sure you also challenge yourself. If one exercise sounds hard, push yourself to work through it. If another seems dull, use it as an opportunity to develop discipline.

You'll also find that you can do almost all of these exercises over and over again. Each time, they'll come out different. Have fun and keep writing!

Chapter 1: Freewriting

Freewriting is one of the most creative and liberating writing exercises you can do.

Also called stream-of-consciousness writing, freewriting allows you to let your thoughts and ideas flow onto the page without inhibition. Anything goes. Turn off your inner editor and allow your subconscious to take over. The results can be inspiring, enlightening, and thought provoking.

Freewriting is ideal for daily writing practice. A twenty-minute freewriting session in the morning is an excellent way to capture your dreams or record your ideas before your head becomes cluttered with the day's activities. A nighttime session is perfect for clearing your mind of the day's clutter and for noting new ideas that have occurred to you throughout the day.

Guided freewriting is a bit different. As you write, you focus your attention on a specific idea, topic, or image. There are a number of variations on guided freewriting, which are explained in the variations section after the exercise.

With any kind of freewriting, you write quickly and let your thoughts flow freely. Remember, anything goes, even if it doesn't make sense. Thoughts that sound ridiculous as you're writing may gain meaning or clarity when you read it back later.

The Exercise

The process is simple. First, set a limit. Your limit is the minimum amount that you will write. Limits can be set in time, word count, or pages. Then write whatever comes to mind, no matter how outrageous. You will write up to your limit, and if you want, you can exceed it. In other words, if you set a limit of ten minutes, you must write for at least ten minutes, but you can write for longer if you want.

The first few times you try freewriting, you might find that your mind goes blank at different points in your writing session. When this happens, don't stop writing. Your pen should always be moving. If nothing comes to mind, write the word *nothing* over and over until your thoughts start flowing again. Just keep writing.

Tips: What limits should you set? If you have a timer, try setting it for twenty minutes, which is a good amount of time for any writing session. Or fill two pages in your notebook, writing in longhand. If you'll be writing electronically, then aim for five hundred words. You may want to experiment with how you set allotments for your freewriting sessions. Some writers find that anything beyond thirty minutes of freewriting becomes garbled; others find they hit their stride after the ten-minute mark.

Experiment with different writing tools. Many writers like writing in longhand for better creativity. If you write primarily on a computer, then give paper and pen a whirl for a few of your freewriting sessions.

Also, don't give up after your first attempt at freewriting. Most writers who are new to freewriting find that it takes a few tries to get the hang of it.

Variations: Below are a few examples of guided freewriting for creativity and problem solving:

Focused freewriting is writing around a certain idea or concept. If you're working on a novel, and your characters are stuck, a focused freewrite might help you break through the scene or move your characters to the next step. This is a bit like brainstorming, except you write freely and continuously, letting ideas stream instead of pondering them before committing them to the page.

Topical freewriting is writing about a specific topic or subject. If you're working on an essay, you might engage in focused freewriting about the subject matter. This allows you to explore your thoughts and feelings and figure out which ideas and aspects of the subject you want to examine or address.

Words and imagery freewriting is great for poetry writing and useful if you're writing *nothing* a lot in your general freewriting sessions. Choose a word or image and while you're freewriting, keep your mind focused on it. If your mind goes blank during the freewrite, come back to the word and write it over and over (instead of *nothing*). Some examples: *my body, apple tree, hummingbird, war, freedom, family,* or *library.*

Character freewriting helps you get to know your characters. There are two ways to do character freewrites. The first is to freewrite about the character. Write the character's name across the top of the page, set your timer, and then write whatever comes to mind about the character. The second method for character freewriting is to write in first person as if you are the character. This brings you inside your character's head to better understand his or her goals and motivations.

Solution freewriting is a technique for solving problems in your writing projects. Start by writing the problem across the top of the page. Try to form it into a question, and then write. Allow yourself to explore tangents and be emotional. You may find that you write yourself into a solution. Some examples include the following: *How can I explain the mystery I created for my story? What is missing from this poem? How can I better argue my position in this essay?*

Applications: Freewrites are perhaps best known for generating raw material that can be harvested for poetry. The nature of stream-of-consciousness writing lends itself well to poetry, because freewrites tend to produce unusual or vivid images and abstract ideas.

Freewrites are also perfect for daily writing practice, especially when you don't have a larger project underway or need a break from your regular writing routine.

Chapter 2: It's Personal

Personal essay, memoir, and journal writing exercises

2.1 Writer, Know Thyself

This exercise asks you to look in the mirror and ask yourself a critical question: Why do I write?

There are many forces that drive writers to the page. Some do it for love, for creative expression, or because writing is simply something they must do, a compulsion. Others do it for riches, for prestige, or to make a living.

It's not easy to succeed as a writer. Most writers have day jobs and write during their free time, chipping away at novels, drafting essays, articles, short stories, and poems. They spend their evenings polishing their work, and they spend their weekends submitting it to agents and editors. Some plan to self-publish. Many already have.

Writing professionally requires an immense amount of self-discipline, because in the early years, you're hustling. Trying to land gigs. Building up clips.

On top of self-discipline, writers are competing in a field that's saturated with dreamers and overrun with talent. Creativity is fleeting, gigs are scarce. Far too many novels end up half-finished and buried in a bottom drawer.

For those who intend to succeed, finish that novel, get that poem published, or earn a living wage as a freelance writer, staying focused is imperative.

Those who succeed are not the most talented or the smartest. They are the ones who refuse to give up. They have good writing habits; they are focused and motivated and consistently work toward their goals.

As a writer, it's important to know where you are in relation to your goals.

The Exercise

This exercise presents a series of questions about your goals and motivations as a writer. Your job is simple: Write a short paragraph to answer each question. Keep your answers concise and try not to go off on tangents.

You can revisit this exercise at least once a year to see how you're progressing, to stay focused and motivated, and to remember why you write.

If you are not ready to answer these questions, then set them aside and come back to them after you've worked through some of the other exercises in this book.

- What do you write, or what do you want to write? Think about form (fiction, poetry, memoir, etc.) and genre (literary, speculative, romance). Be specific.

- How often and how much do you write? Ask yourself whether you have enough time to write and whether you could make more time for your writing.

- What are your top three goals as a writer?

- Why are these three goals important to you?

- What is your five-year career plan as a writer? What do you need to do over the next five years to achieve one (or all) of your top three goals?

- In the past year, what have you accomplished in working toward your goals?

- What can you do over the next year to move closer to your top three goals and your five-year career plan?

Tips: Keep your goals separate and specific. If you want to publish a novel through legacy (traditional) publishing, you don't need an additional goal of getting an agent. Getting an agent is implied in the greater goal of legacy publishing.

If you have more than three goals, then list up to ten, but highlight your top three priorities.

If you're not sure what your goals are, then make goal-setting a goal. Give yourself some time to set goals (a few weeks or months).

Variations: Instead of answering all the questions in a single session, you can spread them out and answer one question a day. While concise answers will be the clearest, the first time you do this exercise, you might want to write a full-page response to each question. You can also use these questions as journal prompts and write your answers in your daily journal (see next exercise, "The 31-Day Journal").

Applications: These questions help you clarify your intentions. When you know what you want to accomplish, it becomes easier to attain. In addition, articulating your goals ensures that you can discuss them intelligibly, which comes in handy when submitting query letters, in meetings and interviews, and in discussions with other writers and professionals in the publishing industry.

2.2 The 31-Day Journal

Many journals follow a diary style for chronicling daily life, but a journal is also a space where a writer can explore ideas, work out problems, and reflect on themes and issues both real and imagined.

This exercise encourages you to try journal writing by experimenting with a few different types of journals. You can keep an idea journal for a week and then keep a reflective journal for a weekend. Or, rotate through the different types of journals for a few days each. Try all of them.

This is not only an exercise in exploring the many types of journals you can keep; it is also an exercise in discipline and building good writing habits through daily practice. As an added bonus, these journal-writing exercises also work as creativity boosters.

If you write for twenty minutes a day for thirty-one days, at the end of the month you will have developed a writing habit, and you will feel an impulse to write every single day. Try to keep your journal going past the thirty-one-day mark, but if you find that it doesn't benefit your writing or interest you, then move on and focus on daily writing through other exercises and writing practices.

The Exercise

Keep a daily journal for thirty-one days. Set aside a minimum of fifteen to twenty minutes each day for your journal-writing sessions. Over the course of the month, try each type of journal listed below. Make sure you try each one for at least a few days so you can truly get a feel for it.

Diary-Style: Diaries are recounts of the day's events. Some people keep diaries so they will remember their experiences later. Some hope their diary entries will eventually provide notes they can use in writing a memoir or autobiography. Many people keep diaries that they can pass along to their children, preserving their heritage. A few hope their diaries will become treasures for academics to sort through once they've made a literary mark by writing a prestigious novel or making a valuable contribution to society.

Diary writing helps you develop a daily writing habit. Keeping a diary also promotes memory and builds observation skills, which are essential for writers working in any field, form, or genre.

Self-Improvement: Nobody's completely satisfied with everything in life. There's always something else we want, whether it's a bigger salary, a smaller waistline, or the desire to write and publish a novel. A self-improvement journal is all about setting a single goal and then writing about your progress every day.

The fact that you're reading this book means that at the very least, you have some writing goals you'd like to achieve. You may want to find the form that's best for you, or perhaps you simply want to improve your writing skills. Pick any goal and write about your daily progress in a journal for a few days.

Reflective: Reflective journal writing falls somewhere between a diary and a personal essay. It weaves together a story from your life with your thoughts, beliefs, or lessons learned as they relate to that event.

Reflective journal writing goes beyond diary writing, because its intent is not to recount events but to put events into a context with deeper meaning.

Reflective journal writing requires that you pay attention to how you craft your sentences and paragraphs. You're telling a story and making thoughtful observations and conclusions about it. You are not limited to writing about the events of the day; you can reflect on any event or experience from your life.

Art Journal: Each day, try to experience some form of art or entertainment. Go to a museum and look at paintings and sculptures (or view them online). Listen to an album. Watch a foreign film. Try to experience a mixture of fine art and pop culture entertainment. Then, write about it.

Here are some questions to prompt your art journal entries: How did it make you feel? What did it inspire you to think about? How can one piece of art influence another? How do different mediums inform each other? How does what's happening in a culture inspire a novel or a poem?

Dream Journal: There's something mysterious and magical about dreams. In the dreamworld, anything is possible. Our deepest desires and greatest fears come to life. Whether they haunt or beguile, our dreams represent the far reaches of our imaginations.

Throughout history, dreams have often acted as catalysts for artists and inventors. You can use a dream as the foundation for a piece of writing. Your dreams can provide you with characters, scenes, imagery, and even plot ideas.

Keep a notebook by your bed for a few nights (or a few weeks, if necessary). As you're falling asleep, tell yourself that you will remember your dreams. As soon as you wake up, grab your journal and jot down everything you can remember.

Tips: Write in your journal at the same time every day. Wake up twenty minutes earlier so you can write, or take your journal to bed at night and do a twenty-minute session as a way to wind down from the day and get ready for sleep.

Variations: There are many more journals that you can keep. Some examples include gratitude journals, travel journals, and parenting journals. The idea is to write in your journal every day for thirty-one days and to write about yourself and your experiences.

Applications: There are two major benefits to keeping a journal. The first is daily writing practice, which is essential to any writer's development. Writing must become a habit, something you do as frequently and regularly as possible, regardless of how inspired you're feeling. Keeping a journal also promotes observation, self-awareness, and reflection, all skills that great writers must possess.

2.3 Making the Mundane Riveting

Every creative writer must learn to hold the reader's attention. There are many ways to do this. You can intrigue your readers with suspense or mystery. You can get them to become emotionally invested in characters. You can mesmerize them with dazzling language.

A true master can take something, anything, and make it interesting. In 1951, Ernest Hemingway published *The Old Man and the Sea*. Much of the story's narrative consists of an old man floating around in his boat, trying to catch a large marlin. Hemingway brought readers deep into the fisherman's life and turned what would, in most writers' hands, be a dull tale of description and introspection into a fascinating and gripping read.

Of course, what's riveting to you might make someone else fall asleep. A book that wins the Pulitzer Prize might bore you, whereas someone else thinks it's a rapturous work of art. Beauty has always been in the eye of the beholder, which is something to keep in mind as you tackle this exercise.

The Exercise

Take some event from your life and make it riveting. Tell it in a way that captivates readers. You can use an event that actually was exciting—an adventure or crazy experience you've had—to make the exercise a little easier. To truly challenge yourself, choose something relatively ordinary, such as a day at the office or a family holiday. Stick to the truth—in other words, don't fictionalize it. Write it as a story with a beginning, middle, and end. Aim for about fifteen hundred words and write it in first person (from your perspective).

Tips: Many students are given the following assignment: write about a memory from your childhood. Their papers are often boring recounts: *One year my family went to Disneyland. The plane ride was scary, but the rides were fun. We stayed in a big hotel.* That's boring! Think about how the story unfolds for the reader. Think about word choice: *My childhood dream was to visit*

Disneyland, but I thought it would never happen. We didn't have much money. So when my parents loaded us into the car and said we were going on vacation, I figured it was another trip to my grandparents' house—until we pulled into the airport.

Variations: Write your story in third-person narrative.

Applications: Many literary journals and magazines accept personal essays. Many others accept short stories. This exercise has the potential to turn into a piece that you could submit for publication. It could also act as the foundation for a memoir, which is a focused narrative about an author's real-life experience.

2.4 Show Some Appreciation (or Emotion)

One of the most popular forms of personal writing is a gratitude journal. These journals are hailed for helping people maintain a positive attitude and stay focused on what matters.

Writers have to face extraordinary challenges that many other professionals never have to deal with: working for free to build skills and gain experience, piles of rejection slips, and the hassle of writing query letters and sending submissions. Most other professionals merely send a resume and cover letter and then go for an interview.

It's easy to get discouraged and stressed out. When life as a writer brings you down, gratitude can lift you up.

However, this exercise has other benefits. Are you prone to writing dark or sad poems or stories? Many young writers say the only thing that inspires them is heartache. Appreciation writing teaches you to write about joy, too. This comes in handy whether you're writing a self-help article for a magazine or creating a character with a positive attitude.

The Exercise

Start by writing a list of all the things in life for which you're grateful. These can be big things like family, home, and food, or little things like your favorite book, a sunny day, or a stranger's smile. Your list should have at least twenty-five items on it, but feel free to write as many as you can think of. When you're done, choose one item and write a short piece (500–750 words) about it. Try to answer all of the following questions:

- What am I grateful for?

- How does it make my life better?

- What would my life be like without it?

- How do I show my appreciation?

When you're done, reread the piece and polish it. Whenever you're feeling down, revisit the piece you wrote, or do this exercise again for a lift.

Tips: You can include appreciation-journal writing in your existing journal. Just write a short list of things you're grateful for every morning when you wake up. This starts your day on a positive note. You can also keep a journal that is strictly for gratitude. Instead of listing what you're grateful for, write a little bit each day about one thing that makes you feel appreciative.

Variations: This exercise is not limited to gratitude. In fact, you can tweak it for any emotion imaginable. You can write about things that make you mad, sad, confused, excited, hopeful, or inspired. Whatever emotion you choose, try to select words that are infused with that emotion. When writing about gratitude, use positive language and avoid negative words.

Applications: Writing is a great way to explore your emotions. Experience will teach you to write in a way that is emotionally appealing to an audience. When readers connect emotionally to something you've written, you've hooked them. Learning to deal with emotion in your writing is therefore an extremely valuable skill that can be applied across all forms of writing.

2.5 *Your Bare Essentials*

You can take a story or an event and strip it down to its most basic elements in order to examine its core ideas and subject matter. There are a number of techniques that you can use to accomplish this: lists, outlines, mind maps, and storyboards.

Sometimes our writing goes off on tangents. It wanders away from the core subject matter or theme. If we sit down to write a persuasive essay on the health benefits of drinking plenty of water, we might wander off into a tirade on the unhealthy quality of soda pop. In a story, we might follow a supporting character into a tangential series of actions that are loosely relevant, but not essential, to the plot.

The best writing stays focused on a core idea or message. If we use discovery writing (writing without a plan), we may realize ideas we otherwise wouldn't have imagined. On the other hand, we might find ourselves straying from the heart of what we're writing. Learning to stay on message takes practice and planning.

The Exercise

Choose a real-life experience you've had, and pare it down to its core elements by writing an outline.

Here are some suggestions: your earliest memory, most embarrassing moment, an ordinary day in your life, a vacation, adventure, losing a loved one, or falling in love.

Choose something concrete, and make sure it's something you remember well.

Write an outline detailing your event. In a sense, you're creating a timeline. Start by making a list of everything that happened. If you're writing about a vacation, the first item on the list would be when you initially had the notion to take that vacation. The second item would be when you bought tickets and reserved a hotel room. The third item might be packing.

Then review your list and add anything you might have left out. If you're listing a sequence of events related to a vacation, you might recall a conversation you had with someone who had taken a similar trip. Add it to the list.

Finally, go through your list again and highlight the most interesting events and actions, the ones that would warrant inclusion in an essay or story about your experience.

Tips: Use roman numerals (I, II, III) to list the main ideas or actions. Use capital letters for supporting ideas and numbers for details. Here's an example:

I. Made Reservations

    A. Airline tickets

    B. Hotel reservations

1. Hotel offers rental cars and free shuttle service

Variations: Draw a mind map. Write the core event in the middle of a piece of paper and draw a circle or box around it. Then write all the related actions and events around that bubble, and connect them to the main idea with lines.

Applications: Outlining streamlines the writing process. If you plan ahead, then you will spend less time revising. Many writers simply start writing about that vacation. Once the piece is complete, they might realize they left out a whole day or some funny thing that happened. You don't have to outline everything you write, but an outline often minimizes the number of revisions required in order to polish and fine-tune a piece.

You can use the outline you created to write a story or essay. Focus on making it engaging and entertaining.

2.6 Silver Lining

This exercise encourages you to think about lessons and messages in your writing. These shouldn't be obvious. In fact, stories that blatantly build up to a lesson or I-told-you-so moment usually fall flat with readers, because they come across as preachy or dogmatic.

Lessons and messages work best when they are subtle. Readers want to use their minds, so make them think about what the underlying themes of the piece are.

On a more personal level, this exercise asks you to look at your own life experiences in a new way. This thinking exercise challenges you to reevaluate cause and effect.

The Exercise

Think about an event in your life that was unpleasant. It could be the loss of a loved one, your first heartbreak, an illness, or any other trauma or malady. It can be something serious or a minor disappointment. It has to be something that, at the time, was a negative experience.

Your challenge is to find the silver lining. What good came out of your terrible experience?

Keep in mind that most negative experiences carry great lessons. They are also links in the chain of life that, if broken, may change or affect everything that has happened since.

Tips: Write about the painful event and transition into its silver lining without being obvious about it. Focus on telling your story as somewhat of a tragedy. Avoid hinting at the good that came from it until it actually comes. Or focus on the silver lining, and use flashbacks to demonstrate that the joys of today are built on the pains of yesterday.

Variations: Instead of finding the silver lining in a negative experience, write about something bad that came out of something that initially appeared to be a blessing.

Applications: Lessons and silver linings are almost always woven through stories, fictional and true. Understanding chains of events and how the balance of good and bad experiences shapes our lives is essential to good writing. You can use this exercise to write a personal story or essay in the style of a memoir that you can submit or publish.

2.7 *Report It*

Is your life newsworthy? Have you ever witnessed, committed, or been the victim of a crime? Have you ever participated in a protest or a performance? Have you ever had an odd or unusual experience?

Traditionally, professional journalism adheres to a set of ethics, focusing on the facts and details of the story and presenting those facts thoroughly and objectively. The traditional journalist does not inject his or her feelings or opinions. Journalists and reporters inform readers by revealing the who, what, where, when, why, and how of a news story.

Journalists are human. The news media in general is increasingly accused of using a variety of creative tactics to spin the news in favor of its own religious, political, or financial agendas. For example, in a report, a journalist should not badmouth a suspected criminal, but that journalist can include a quote from a witness who has badmouthed the criminal while intentionally not including a positive quote from some other witness.

Journalists can pick and choose quotes, facts, and even which stories to report.

Journalists and reporters are responsible for feeding us information about what's going on in the world. Yet considering that they are mere human beings, flawed, emotional, and opinionated just like the rest of us, one can only begin to imagine how spun the news actually is.

The Exercise

Revisit your past and write a news report about something you experienced firsthand.

The rules are simple: straight journalism. Refrain from including your personal feelings or opinions and don't take sides.

Write about the event as if you are a reporter looking in on your life from the outside. Answer these six questions: who was involved, what happened, where did it happen, when did it happen, how did it happen, and why did it happen?

Make sure you include a headline that will attract readers.

Tips: To get a feeling for how journalism is written (its tone and style), visit a reputable news site and read a few articles. As you do this, keep an eye out for reports and articles that are infused with the journalists' opinions or personal views. How easy are they to spot?

Variations: Instead of reporting a story, write a gossip piece: Were you spotted while out on a hot date? If you're at a loss for subject matter, get creative and write a fictional news story; make something up, change something from your past, or better yet, write a news story from your future (maybe you win the Pulitzer Prize in ten years).

Applications: The most obvious application is that you could, someday, become a journalist or a reporter. Journalism is an objective style of writing (at least, it's supposed to be). This exercise encourages you to write about something you care about while refraining from including your feelings or personal views.

2.8 Reader Response

There is nothing that will teach you more about writing than reading. Although books on the craft of writing are extremely helpful, reading novels, poetry, memoirs, and other published works regularly and frequently will enhance your writing skills faster and more fully than anything else you can do.

Reading will strengthen your writing; taking time to generate a thoughtful response to what you've read will strengthen it even more. Every writer should keep a reading journal. It's a place to note and explore thoughtful responses to what you've read and will help you gain a deeper understanding of your reading material. This kind of insight is invaluable for a writer.

The very act of writing promotes critical thinking. When we write, we are forced to clarify our thoughts. Often, through this process, our ideas crystallize. We may realize something about a story we've read that was not immediately obvious, but upon reflection, becomes integral to helping us understand it.

This deeper level of understanding benefits our own writing immensely, which is why writing critically about material we read is one of the best practices for building comprehensive writing skills.

The Exercise

Write a reader response to a single piece that you've read. This exercise will be more beneficial if you explore a full-length book: a novel, a memoir, or a collection of poems or essays. If you're strapped for time, you can choose a short story or a single poem or essay. Don't retell the story; just share your reaction to it. You are encouraged to build on this exercise and make a habit of thinking critically about your reading material by keeping a reading journal.

Tips: Here are some questions and prompts to get you started:

- How did the book make you feel? Were you sad? Scared? Intrigued?

- What was it about the story that evoked an emotional response from you? The characters? The plot? The subtext or themes?

- Did you feel more like an observer, or were you pulled into the story, more like a participant?

- How did the author build tension? Write down each pinnacle or event that led to the final climax.

- Was it a page-turner? What were the hooks or cliffhangers that made you want to keep reading?

- What was uniquely likable about the protagonist? What made the antagonist bothersome or despicable?

- How would you describe the tone of the narrative? Was the prose flowery or poetic? Vulnerable or stoic?

- Did the cover and title make you want to read the piece? How do they represent the book and compel readers?

- How was the book structured? Did it have chapters? Were they numbered or named? Was there an introduction, prologue, or epilogue? A table of contents? To whom was the book dedicated? Who is the publisher? Whom did the author thank in the acknowledgments?

Variations: You can also apply this exercise to a film, album, or art collection. View the work with a writer's eye and compose your response as both an analyst (so you can cull writing techniques from it) and as a reader or member of an audience.

Applications: A good story analysis and response can be repurposed into a book review or an essay that deconstructs the work. There are plenty of literary journals and blogs that accept submissions of this nature.

2.9 *Reflections*

A memoir is a book-length autobiographical narrative that is almost always written in first person. Unlike a regular autobiography, a memoir is not a life story. It revolves around a particular theme, idea, event, or experience.

Memoirs are similar to personal essays or reflective writing. However, memoirs tell a story. A memoir may contain a message or lesson, but this is not mandatory.

Memoirs often take a reader inside unique lifestyles or experiences. Examples include being a prisoner of war, coping with illness, and achieving personal or professional success; there are also adventure or travel memoirs. Stephen King's book *On Writing* features a memoir about King's journey to becoming a wildly successful author followed by his recommended writing techniques.

The Exercise

Think about an experience you've had or an aspect of your life that readers might find interesting. Perhaps you spent a year living in another country. Maybe you held an unusual job or had some other unique experience.

Instead of writing a full memoir (that would be quite a feat for one writing exercise), write a synopsis for your memoir.

A synopsis is a summary of the book designed to interest readers. A synopsis doesn't give away the ending; it highlights key elements within the narrative.

Tips: Don't stray from the theme. If your memoir is about your life as a dog walker, leave out the story about the time you fell off the slide and had to have fifteen stitches (unless, of course, this event is somehow tied directly to your life as a dog walker). Using questions in a synopsis can be effective: *Ever considered your own dog-walking business?* To prepare for this exercise, read the synopses of a few memoirs (check the back covers).

Variations: If you're inclined, go ahead and write your memoir, or write the first chapter and see if it works as a personal essay. If you're struggling to come up with a concept for your memoir, you can instead write a synopsis for a memoir you've recently read.

Applications: This writing exercise is good practice if you intend to write a book someday. If you plan to take the traditional publishing route, you'll have to write synopses for agents and editors and try to convince them to read the rest of your manuscript. If you self-publish, then your synopsis will be one of your most important marketing tools. This exercise also encourages you to think about a broad topic (your life) through the lens of a single theme.

2.10 *Your Author's Bio*

If you ever get your own website or blog or publish a book, article, or pretty much anything else, you will have to write your author's bio.

You should know ahead of time that almost all writers despise writing their own bios, but it's something that has to be done. For published authors, a bio is especially essential, because it will be used as part of your press kit. Whenever someone reviews your work or interviews you, they're going to look at your bio to get some basic information. Your most loyal fans will also want to read your bio to get to know you better.

Why do authors find this process so tedious? Well, we have led full and complex lives. A bio asks us to distill our life into a page (or less). If you have tons of writing credits, you might be forced to squeeze some out. If you don't have any, you'll be pressed to fill out your bio adequately.

Of course, one of the best ways to get ideas for how to construct your bio is to visit other authors' websites to see how they've composed their own bios.

Many bios will briefly mention the writer's other hobbies or interests, but these should be kept to a minimum. A bio should focus on who you are *as a writer*. However, the last paragraph or sentence of a bio often states where the author lives and whom he or she lives with (spouse, children, pets).

The Exercise

Spend some time looking at professional authors' bios, and then write your own. It should be approximately 250–350 words, written in third person, and it should focus on who you are as a writer. Take your time and go over your bio several times, editing and polishing it.

Tips: Try to make your bio as clear and concise as possible. Would you send this to a newspaper or magazine? If not, keep working on it.

Variations: Write a 140-character bio for Twitter (this should be in first person). Try writing a short fifty-word bio (about the length that appears in article bylines and "About the Author" boxes on blogs and in newspapers).

Applications: You can use your bio on your blog or website. You'll also find that you can extract excerpts from your bio to fill out profiles on various social media websites, especially once you get active with marketing and promoting yourself as a writer.

Chapter 3: People and Characters

Individuals and group dynamics

3.1 People Are People

People and characters are among the most important elements in a piece of writing. In nonfiction, you need to treat subjects fairly, and in fiction, you need to make your characters believable.

To create the effect that a character, a made-up person, is real, a writer must have a deep understanding of people. What motivates them? What are their fears? What are their strengths and weaknesses?

Writing about real people presents its own set of challenges. If you're writing about someone whom you adore or respect, how do you deal with their flaws, mistakes, and weaknesses? If you are writing about someone you despise, how do you treat them fairly or objectively?

When you're telling someone else's story, you take on a huge responsibility. Whether the people you write about are real or imagined, it's a tough job.

The Exercise

Choose a real person and write a short story from that person's life. This piece will be nonfiction, written in third person. Your mission is to tell a story rather than write a biographical piece. Use the prompts below if you need ideas:

- Some relationships are complicated: siblings who don't speak to each other, couples who sleep in separate rooms, exes who still come to holiday dinners.

- Choose a celebrity or historical figure to write about. It can be someone living or dead. Do a little research about the person and then write a short piece telling a part of his or her story.

- There's always a bad apple in the barrel: the bully on the playground, the snitch in the office, and the drama queen who stirs up trouble at every opportunity. They have stories, too!

- Authority figures: parents, bosses, and government officials. You know them; they're in charge of the world. What's their story?

- Bonus: for this prompt, you get to mix in a little fiction. Everybody loves a mysterious stranger. The cute barista. The handsome doctor. The eccentric woman who sits on the park bench every Thursday afternoon. Think of an interesting stranger you've seen around and concoct his or her story.

Tips: To add realism to your story, use dialogue, mannerisms, and gestures. Don't spend too much time on physical descriptions; a few, choice details will suffice. Focus on revealing the inner conflict and struggles of your subjects through their words and actions.

Variations: Instead of writing a nonfiction piece, write fiction, but use a real person as inspiration for your main character.

Applications: If you can tell a good story about someone, you can probably get it published, whether it's fiction or not.

3.2 We Are Family

They say you can pick your nose and you can pick your friends, but you can't pick your family. In this exercise, you can pick anyone you want, but it has to be someone you know personally.

As a writer, you will find that you are occasionally called upon for obligatory writing duties. A friend might ask you to proofread her wedding announcement. Your mother might ask you to write your grandfather's obituary. Requests for birth announcements, speeches, and eulogies may land on your doorstep with astounding frequency. After all, you're the token writer among your friends, family, and coworkers.

This exercise will teach you how to write a piece that is personal and emotional while also respectful and somewhat formal.

The Exercise

Draw upon your inner circle of family and friends, and write one of the following:

- birth announcement
- obituary or eulogy

- wedding announcement, or best-man or maid-of-honor speech

- graduation (or valedictorian) speech

- retirement speech

Tips: Consider your tone carefully. An obituary or wedding announcement is formal and respectful. Eulogies and wedding speeches can be tender or humorous.

Variations: Write a news profile, such as one you'd see if someone was running for office and was profiled in a local newspaper.

Applications: Writing pieces with this level of importance can be intimidating. For example, writing a speech that you'll have to deliver might be so terrifying that you just can't think of anything appropriate to write. Writing an obituary or eulogy for a loved one can be painful. These are important documentations of our lives and our loved ones' lives, and writing these pieces is an honor. This exercise gives you practice writing in a private but formal manner and also gives you experience in dealing with emotional subject matter.

3.3 Biography

Often, in studying another person closely and listing their most significant accomplishments and life events, we gain a deeper understanding of them.

We can learn a lot from other people. We study the lives of great leaders, celebrated artists, and innovators who have contributed to our cultures in meaningful ways. Put simply, the biggest human interest is other humans.

A biography is nothing more than all the facts about a person's life arranged into sentences and paragraphs that are organized and interesting. It sounds easy enough, but you'll find that there are hurdles to overcome in biography writing.

For example, do you humanize a serial killer by mentioning his beloved childhood pet or the charity work he did in college? Do you include your favorite politician's extramarital affair from thirty years ago? Which facts are objective and relevant?

In a well-written bio, facts are not overlooked or selected to give the subject a slant of the author's choosing. A good biography is honest and objective. However, in reality, biographies are often biased (or spun). If you were on a politician's campaign, for example, you'd write a spin piece and leave out all the negative information. But if you were on the opponent's campaign, you'd probably spin it the other way and make it all negative. And if you were an objective journalist, you'd simply look for the truth.

In a short bio, you can't include every detail. You're going to have to choose which facts from the subject's life are relevant.

The Exercise

Most biographies are about famous people. However, there are already enough of those biographies occupying shelves in libraries and the servers that hold Wikipedia. In this exercise, you'll write a biography of someone you know.

You can use a fake name, but you have to stick to the facts. Before you start, decide whether you'll do a spin piece or an objective piece.

Tips: Identify your target audience and a publication for the piece. This will help you narrow your focus. For example, you might write a bio about your mom in the context that she is running for president. You might write a piece profiling your best friend as a local small-business owner. You could also write a Wikipedia-style article about anyone you know, but try to emphasize their greatest achievements (good or bad) to justify their presence in an encyclopedia.

Variations: If you're up to the task, write one spin piece and one objective piece. Write both about the same person. As another alternative, write a detailed outline for a book-length biography about someone you know.

Applications: This exercise comes in handy if you ever write an article or essay about a famous or historical figure, or if you ever need to write your own biography. It's also a great starting place for coming up with characters.

3.4 Character Sketch

Creating characters is one of the most exhilarating exercises that a writer can work through. You get to make a person! And you can make that person out of nothing, you can base the character on someone you know, or you can combine ideas from your imagination with traits and qualities of real people.

If you write fiction long enough, you'll find that some characters arrive fully formed in your mind. Others are shy; they take a while to get to know. You know their names but can't picture their faces. You know their professions but can't put a finger on their goals. Their strengths are obvious, but surely they have weaknesses too!

Yet the biggest challenge in creating a character is making the character realistic. Your reader has to believe this character is a living, breathing person, even though he or she is just a figment of your imagination. If you can create a believable character, you're a skilled writer indeed.

The Exercise

A character sketch is a lot like a bio except the person is made-up, not real. For this exercise, you'll write a bio for a person you've invented. Here are some bits of information that you should include:

- Name and physical description: What does your character look like? How does he or she dress? Try to come up with one unique identifying feature, like a mole or birthmark, a twitch or limp, freckles or bitten fingernails.

- Family background: Where did your character grow up? What were the character's parents like? Don't go into too much detail about your character's family but feel free to include a few simple details.

- Education and career: Is your character educated? Intelligent? What does he or she do for a living? How many jobs has your character held?

- Significant relationships: Is your character married? A parent? Who are the important people in your character's life?

- Personality traits: Is your character moody or laid back? Shy or outgoing? Passive or aggressive? How does your character behave in public? In private? What are your character's goals and motivations? Strengths? Weaknesses?

• General history: What significant experiences has your character had? These could be anything from a traumatic event in childhood to losing a loved one as a young adult.

Tips: If you think you might use this character in a piece of fiction, then write the sketch right up to the point in your character's life when the story starts. For example, if your story features a character who is thirty-two years old, then your character sketch should cover the first thirty-one years of your character's life. Remember, a sketch is all about the highlights—don't write the story; just sketch the character.

Variations: For an extra challenge, write a sketch for a character who is nonhuman or create a cast of characters.

Applications: Character sketches are great warm-ups for writing short stories and full-length novels. You can also use your character in a fictional role-playing game.

3.5 The Bad Guy

Some writers excel at crafting villains. Others struggle because villains have to do cruel things to the other characters. Villains are mean. If you're a good person, you might find it hard to get into the mind of someone who is unsavory or downright evil. If you want to write good fiction, you have to be able to wiggle into a lot of different minds, many of which bear no resemblance to your own.

There are several types of villains. Lord Voldemort from the *Harry Potter* series is an absolute villain who is truly and totally evil. You never see him doing anything nice.

There are also sympathetic villains who are a little more human. Yeah, they're bad guys, lowlifes, or jerks, but they also have redeeming qualities. Hannibal Lecter from *Silence of the Lambs* was a psychopath, but he never hurt Clarice. He must have had some good in him, right? These villains tend to be a little more believable and a lot more sympathetic, because absolute villains are actually pretty rare in real life, if they exist at all.

Another type of villain is the uncertain or perceived villain. These are characters who appear to be threatening to a protagonist (the hero or main character in a story), but we're not sure about their true nature. They are classic *others*, characters who are perceived as enemies because they are the ones causing conflict. However, we don't know their motives or whether they are good or evil. Sometimes they're both or neither.

In fiction, an antagonist doesn't have to be a villain at all. The character who provides a source of conflict for the protagonist can be good, evil, or neutral. For this exercise, we'll focus on the evil variety of antagonists.

The Exercise

Write a short scene in which a protagonist first meets or learns about a villain.

Tips: In some stories, the moment when the protagonist and antagonist meet is climactic. In other stories, the antagonist isn't apparent as an opposing force until the story unfolds. Before starting this exercise, think about some of your favorite stories and recall the hero's interactions with the villain. The best insight into storytelling often comes from simple observation.

Variations: Try doing a character sketch for a villain (see exercise 3.4).

Applications: Every story needs an antagonist, and villains are always up to the task of antagonizing a hero. If you decide to write a short story or a novel, you can use the villain you've created and the scene you've written.

3.6 Getting into Character

In fiction writing, authors are like actors. While writers don't physically act out every scene, they certainly play the scenes out in their minds. To do this, a writer has to get into the characters' heads, just like actors do.

Unlike an actor, a writer doesn't have the leisure of occupying a single character for the duration of a story. A writer must be all of the characters, all of the time.

One minute you're in the mind of a gang leader, and the next minute, you're in the mind of a small child. A few minutes later, you're a bartender, and then you're a bum. While these constant shifts can be exciting, they are also challenging.

The good news is that it gets easier with practice. Start slowly, with one or two characters. Once you get the hang of it, you can bring more characters into the fold. This exercise is a good starting place, because it forces you to become someone other than yourself for a few pages.

The Exercise

You can use a character you've already created, or you can create a new one. You can also become someone you know from real life or choose someone famous. Your job is to write a two-page monologue in the character's voice (first person).

Before you start the exercise, make sure your character or subject has something to say. He or she should be talking about something specific, preferably something dramatic. A great approach is to have the character either relate a story from personal experience or reflect on his or her thoughts and feelings about a significant event.

Tips: You might want to do a little research to help you get into your character's mind. For example, if you've chosen a celebrity, you can watch interviews to see how he or she behaves and thinks.

Try to capture the voice of your character. The most vivid characters can be identified through distinct dialogue (phrasings and figures of speech), physical mannerisms, and gestures.

Watch out for filler words and phrases. Since the character is speaking, the audience knows whatever the character says represents his or her thoughts, feelings, and beliefs. Avoid phrases like *I think, I feel, I believe,* or *I wonder.*

Variations: As an alternative to writing a monologue, write a few diary-style journal entries as your character.

Applications: Monologues are quite common in plays and films. They also appear in stories and can be turned into pieces of performance art.

3.7 Character Study

Nobody's perfect, but in fiction, we tend to idealize characters. Have you ever noticed that lots of heroes always do the right thing? Villains will be mean just for the sake of being mean, even when they don't gain anything by it.

The same thing happens in nonfiction writing. Often, an article or biography has a specific purpose—to promote or smear someone. Just read any political article or glance at a gossip rag, and you'll see that most writers overtly fawn or frown upon their subjects.

The most interesting pieces of writing give us characters and people who are complex. They have respectable attributes, but sometimes they make mistakes. They have secrets. Under the right circumstances, they will take the heroic route. On a bad day, they could easily take the villainous path.

One of the best ways to learn how to create a realistic character is to study great characters from your favorite stories and interesting people from the real world. Observe their actions, choices, and words.

The Exercise

First, you'll need to choose a character from a story that you're well acquainted with. You can choose a character from a movie, television show, or book that you know intimately. If you need to watch or read again, do so (this is why a movie might be the best choice for this exercise—you can watch it and then do the exercise, whereas it will take you longer to watch a TV series or read a novel). Choose a character who is interesting, puzzling, or mysterious. The more complex, the better.

Your job is to write a character study. A study is different from a sketch because you're examining a character, whereas in a sketch, you're creating a character. It's different from a bio, because you're not merely highlighting significant events and accomplishments in the character's life. You're goal is to get inside the character's head.

Start by listing the basic facts: name, age, physical description, occupation, etc. Then dig deeper and ask some probing questions about the character you've chosen:

- When the character makes a choice, what are his or her prime motivations behind that particular decision?

- What mistakes has the character made?

- What are the character's secrets?

- Look for moments where the character's words or actions could be interpreted in more than one way.

- You may view the character one way, and the other characters may have their own perceptions of the character, but how does this character see himself or herself?

- What significant events shaped the character's personality?

- Where are the character's loyalties? Why does the character possess these particular loyalties?

- How does one action or decision that the character makes set off a chain of events?

- Think about the character in terms of mind, heart, and spirit. What makes this character tick?

Tips: Look for subtleties. In a way, you are psychoanalyzing this character. Even a top-notch psychiatrist will not know every aspect of a patient's mind and heart. Often, the greatest insight we gain into people (real or made-up) happens in minor moments that could just as easily go unnoticed.

Variations: Try this exercise with a real person instead of with a character.

Applications: There is no better way to learn about people and characters than by simply studying them. This exercise helps you develop a writer's eye for how you view people in real life and characters in existing stories. Continue to look closely at characters and people. Think about the things they say and do, and ask why they are the way they are.

3.8 Nothing is Absolute

Story elements are often absolute. The villain is 100 percent evil; the protagonist and his or her friends are pure, good, and innocent. The world is dystopian or utopian. It's the best day ever or the worst day ever.

A lot of writers lean to extremes and polarities, which can make a story more exciting and dramatic. In some cases, absolutes make a story more effective. For example, it's a lot easier to blow up the enemy camp when you believe everyone in it is evil.

However, absolutes in stories are unrealistic. Readers actually become a lot more emotionally invested in a villain who is potentially redeemable. The reason for this is simple: we're all fallible, we've all made mistakes, and we're all imperfect. Redeemable villains and heroes who make bad choices appeal to us because see ourselves in them. And we want to believe that we can be redeemed, too.

The Exercise

The most popular science fiction, fantasy, and superhero stories feature absolute villains and heroes.

Find five heroes and five villains who are not absolutely good or evil. They can be real people from history or current events, or they can be characters from fiction (TV, movies, and books). For each one, write a short paragraph describing his or her good side and another short paragraph describing his or her bad side.

Tips: Choose a mix of characters, including supporting characters and sidekicks. Are main characters more or less likely to be absolutely good or evil?

Variations: You can turn this exercise on its head and look instead for absolutes. Make a list of villains who didn't possess any redeeming qualities and a list of heroes who were not flawed in any way. Then hand your lists to a friend and see if they can find the villains' redeeming qualities and heroes' flaws.

Applications: This exercise teaches you to see characters in their entirety. When you can see the good, the bad, and the ugly in real people (and other writers' characters), your own characters and subjects will be more believable.

3.9 Animal House

Not all characters in a piece of writing are people. Writers often have to decide how to handle animals and other nonhuman entities. In fiction, nonhuman characters often seem human. Animals, robots, vehicles, and even houses all become important characters if you anthropomorphize them.

The Exercise

For this exercise, you'll do a character sketch for a nonhuman character (see exercise 3.4 for tips on writing a character sketch), but you'll take it a step further and also write a scene. Your job is to make a nonhuman feel human to the reader.

Tips: The scene is more important than the character sketch, so if you have to cut corners, skip the sketch. Invest your time and energy into writing a scene that brings this character to life.

Variations: If you don't have time to make up a character, write a scene starring your pet. If you don't have a pet, write a scene starring one of your favorite nonhuman characters from the world of fiction.

Applications: Bestowing human qualities on animals and inanimate objects is an especially useful skill for anyone who wants to write for children or in genres such as science fiction and fantasy. However, this technique comes in handy in other ways, too. A human character might perceive or treat an inanimate object as if it's a person. We've all seen characters who name their cars or computers. We may even know people in real life who do such things. These are great quirks that make characters more realistic.

3.10 Your Gang

Writing about one or two people in a story or piece of nonfiction isn't too hard. Even a scene with three or four characters can be well executed by a beginning writer. When you start approaching casts and ensembles with seven, eight, nine primary characters, you risk turning your story into a riot. Everybody gets out of control.

Ensemble stories in fiction tend to be epics; they span long periods of time (sometimes several generations). Often in these stories, there are many main characters but only a few are in focus at any given time. You're more likely to find a good ensemble on television or in a movie than in a novel. But in all mediums, there are great stories about groups and families.

Writing a true ensemble piece requires considerable mastery in writing. As the author, you have to constantly keep all your characters in play, rotating them and managing their complex personalities. You can't forget about any of your characters, and you can't let any of them hog the spotlight. It's a balancing act.

The Exercise

Choose an existing ensemble from a book, movie, or TV show and write a long scene or a short story featuring all of the characters. Don't retell some story about the characters from the source material. Take the existing characters and make up your own story or scene for them.

As an added challenge, relocate the characters to a different setting. For example, take the cast from a book and put them in the setting of a movie.

The minimum number of characters you should work with for this exercise is six. Aim for eight.

Tips: You can write big scenes with all characters present (a dinner party would be a good setting for this). You can also put the characters in different locations and write a series of scenes that take place in these various locations. One example would be a huge family gathering for a holiday weekend. The characters will disperse to different rooms. You have to move through the house showing the reader what everyone is doing, and it all has to tie together in a meaningful way.

Variations: Come up with your own ensemble. Write a series of short character sketches and establish a setting in which these characters would be thrown together. They could be family, coworkers, passengers on a subway, or students in a classroom. You can also attempt this exercise with real people and write a scene from a real-life experience or make up a scene featuring your friends and family (a holiday gathering, school field trip, or work meeting). Make sure you give all the characters equal weight. Remember, it's an ensemble.

Applications: If you can write an ensemble scene, you might be suited for television writing!

Chapter 4: Speak Up

Dialogue and scripts

4.1 Basic Dialogue

Relationships are established, in large part, through conversation. Our verbal exchanges with others lead to friendship, romance, and conflict. Good dialogue does the same thing. It moves the action of a story forward. It reveals truths about the characters in the story. Most importantly, good dialogue feels real, even if it's not.

If you transcribe a natural conversation between two or more people, place quotation marks around their comments, and add a few dialogue tags, your narrative will fall flat on its face. That's because good written dialogue feels like real speech, but it's all an illusion. If you read dialogue closely, you'll realize that people just don't talk that way. We talk in bits and fragments. But our true, natural speech doesn't translate well to writing, so we improvise. We writers work our magic to make dialogue feel genuine.

Even in nonfiction books, such as memoirs, the dialogue is rarely (if ever) presented word for word as it was originally spoken. While many memoirists keep journals, and a few may have even recorded key conversations, they have to do their best to recall what was said, and many of them are open about the fact that the dialogue represents their best recollections.

It's worth noting that most dialogue, and certainly the best dialogue, is interwoven with action. As they speak, characters do things. They open the fridge and grab a beer. They fiddle with their shoelaces. They make faces and gestures. Not all communication happens verbally, and we rarely sit still when we talk to other people.

The Exercise

Write a scene that centers on a conversation between two people or characters. You can write fiction or nonfiction. If you're writing nonfiction, then recall an important or memorable conversation you had or overheard and re-create it. If you're writing fiction, then get a couple of your characters together for a discussion.

Tips: Make sure you punctuate your dialogue correctly. Don't get too creative with dialogue tags. In other words, stay away from tags like *he retorted, she muttered, he whispered, she stated.* Nothing beats the tried-and-true *he said* and *she said.*

Variations: As an alternative, test the claim that real conversation does not translate to good dialogue. Record a conversation (or find one that has already been recorded) and then transcribe a page or two. Make sure you use an actual conversation, not an interview. Read the piece aloud and observe why it does not work as narrative. When you're done, try reworking it into a good piece of dialogue.

Applications: Dialogue is present in most forms of writing. It even occurs in journalism, although in that form, dialogue is technically called "quotes" and must adhere strictly to what a person actually said. In stories (true or fictional), dialogue adds realism and encourages the reader to engage more closely with the narrative, because they feel like they are in on the conversation.

4.2 The Silver Screen

In some ways, a screenplay is easier to write than a novel. Screenplays tend to be shorter and more concise. They are usually around 120 pages (one page for each minute of film). A screenplay is highly condensed and doesn't require a lot of description. The writer doesn't have to worry about prose and voice because a screenplay is comprised of setting, action, and dialogue.

On the other hand, a screenplay has to be tight and as close to perfect as possible, and screenplay formatting is notoriously strict. If you don't follow proper formatting, nobody in the film industry will look at it.

If you see stories in your head as a series of moving pictures (rather than hearing stories as words), then screenwriting might be for you. If you struggle with complex grammar and long sentences or descriptions, or if you prefer to tell a story simply and straightforwardly, then screenwriting just might be your thing.

The Exercise

Keeping in mind that in a screenplay, one page equals one minute, write a five-minute script. It can be part of a greater story, or it can be a short film. It can even be an advertisement.

Tips: Before you start, take a quick look at screenplay formatting. A quick search online will bring up formatting rules and examples of screenplays that are properly formatted. Learning proper screenplay formatting is beyond the scope of this exercise, but you should certainly be aware of it.

Variations: If you're struggling for ideas, then try writing a script based on a scene from your favorite book or short story. This is called an adaptation.

Applications: There are many opportunities in the world of writing scripts. Movies and television shows are the most glamorous options, but some scriptwriters make commercials, promotional videos, or tutorials. With videos and film getting cheaper and easier to make every day, good scriptwriters are going to be in increasingly high demand.

4.3 Body Language

Sometimes what people say without actually speaking tells us a whole lot more than what comes out of their mouths. Using body language to communicate is natural. We all understand it intuitively—some better than others.

As a writer, you can closely observe people's body language and learn how humans speak without words, so you can bring unspoken communication into your writing.

Imagine two characters, a man and woman who are complete strangers, both shopping in a bookstore. You wouldn't write *Their eyes locked. They were instantly attracted to each other.* That would be boring and unimaginative. Instead, you would let the scene unfold and describe it to the reader—how their eyes met, how he gulped and she blushed, how they both suddenly felt warm, how the two of them slowly worked their way toward the center of the store until they finally met in the horror section.

The Exercise

Write a scene between two (or more) characters in which there is no dialogue, but the characters are communicating with each other through body language. You can also write a nonfiction piece. Surely you have experienced nonverbal communication. Take that experience and describe it on the page.

The scene should comprise at least two pages of interaction without dialogue, showing two or more characters engaging with each other. Here are a few scene starters:

- A cop, detective, or private investigator is tailing a suspect through a small town, big city, mall, amusement park, or other public area.

- Strangers are always good sources for ideas about communicating with body language. Think about where strangers are brought together: public transportation, classes, elevators, and formal meetings.

- Kids in a classroom aren't supposed to be speaking while a teacher is giving a lecture, but they always find ways to communicate.

Tips: What if one character misinterprets another character's body language? That could lead to humor or disaster. Maybe the characters are supposed to be doing something (like in a classroom where they're supposed to be listening to the teacher), but instead they're making faces and gestures at each other. Don't tell the reader what *he thought* or *she wondered* as these constructs are thought dialogue.

Variations: As an alternative, write a scene in which one character speaks and one doesn't: an adult and a baby, a human and an animal.

Applications: There are depictions of nonverbal communication in almost all types of storytelling from journalism and biography to memoir and fiction.

4.4 Love Scenes

Love is the most sought after of all human emotions. We have tons of clichés to express our love of love: it makes the world go round, it lasts forever, and it keeps us together. In songs, movies, poems, films, and novels—the most popular central theme is love.

Love scenes can be cheesy, mechanical, tender, or passionate. One thing is certain: nothing captivates a reader like a well-written love scene. It doesn't matter if the people in the scene are having a one-night stand or are long-lost lovers. If it's well written, your readers will respond to it.

Sex: it's what people do. Single people, married people, young people, and old people. Sex is an inherent component in many love scenes, and often, it's central to a love scene.

However, love scenes are not always about sex. In fact, love scenes aren't always between lovers. Love can be romantic, familial, fraternal, or patriotic. A love scene can be a first kiss or a last kiss. It can be a tender moment between friends or relatives. In fact, sweet, emotional exchanges are some of the best love scenes.

The Exercise

Write a love scene that demonstrates two people expressing their love and adoration for each other. Make sure the scene includes dialogue and action. Use an experience from your own life as inspiration or make one up.

Tips: The magic word is *love*, not *sex*. There's a genre for fiction that is sexual in nature: erotica. The idea here is to show two people expressing their love for each other through intimate words and actions.

Variations: Some people have a lot of love for inanimate objects. People love their cars, gadgets, clothes, and other possessions. It's not uncommon for people to express love for objects with sentimental value. As an alternative, write a scene depicting a character who loves an inanimate object.

Applications: Love happens all the time, every day. It's all around us. Unless you're writing scientific textbooks, there's a good chance love will enter the equation of your writing at some point. You need to know how to depict it.

In stories that aren't romance or love stories, readers enjoy a taste of affection between characters. Think of the best action, science fiction, fantasy, mystery, and horror stories. Love may not be the focus of the plot but it's there somewhere.

4.5 Multiple Speakers

It's hard to manage a crowd. When you have an ensemble of characters, and everybody's in the room at once, the narrative can be a nightmare to keep organized. If such scenes are not well executed, they can be impossible for readers to follow.

Sometimes it's necessary to write a scene that has a bunch of people all talking at once. This happens at meetings, family gatherings, in classrooms, and on public transportation.

It's critical in scenes like these to keep your narrative clear and organized. You cannot let the reader get confused about who's sitting where or which character is speaking.

The Exercise

First, you'll need to choose a situation in which there are several characters in one place. You should have at least six characters in play. Write out the scene, making sure each character gets at least two lines of dialogue and a few actions or gestures. Also, try to give the scene some purpose. In other words, don't simply transcribe what happened at your last office meeting if it was just another boring and meaningless meeting. But if it was the meeting where they laid off an entire department, then it will probably inspire some good storytelling.

Tips: The scene should be entertaining or meaningful, and in a novel, every scene should be relevant to the plot. One of the easiest ways to develop an entertaining scene is to turn an otherwise insignificant event into a major drama: a family is eating in a restaurant when one of them suddenly has a heart attack between the appetizers and the entrées.

Variations: If writing the scene in prose gets confusing, use a simple script format.

Applications: If you can manage dialogue between a group of characters in a single scene, you've got serious writing chops. Group scenes are among the most challenging to execute clearly and effectively.

4.6 He Said, She Said

Have you ever been reading a story and got so lost in the dialogue that you didn't know which character was speaking? Have you ever lost track of which character the pronoun referred to? For example, you're reading a story about three women who are best friends. Sometimes when the narrative refers to *her* or *she*, you're not sure who it's supposed to be.

In scenes with lengthy conversations between characters, the dialogue tags (*he said* or *she said*) can feel monotonous to the writer. It's tempting to start using creative tags: *she uttered, he mentioned,* or *she retorted.* These rarely enhance the narrative; usually, they are a distraction.

Readers are trained to the whole *he said* and *she said* dialogue format. They know these are cues that tell them who's saying what. They don't really register in the reader's mind as part of the story. So while they feel repetitive as you're writing, they're actually not.

However, there are instances in which it's better to use *she asked* or *he replied.* If a character screams or shouts, then you might want to specify that in the dialogue tags; you can also use exclamation marks.

Note that in dialogue tags, *he* and *she* will often be replaced with character names: *Tom said, Jane said.*

The Exercise

Write a dialogue scene with at least three characters having a conversation. It could be three coworkers, three kids playing in the woods, or three members of a family. Make sure the scene takes place in a setting where the characters can simply talk. In other words, they shouldn't be running through the jungle or anything like that. The objective is to make the dialogue smooth. It should always be clear who is speaking.

Tips: Since you have three characters, two will be of the same gender, so you have to watch your pronouns. Use character names in dialogue tags, but not exclusively; alternate between character names and pronouns. Also, note that the subject comes before the verb and the person opens their mouth before they speak: it's *Jane said, Tom said*, not *said Jane, said Tom*. Also, you're writing a scene, so intersperse the dialogue with action. Show the characters doing things while they're talking. One might get up and pace the room. Another might sweep her hair out of her eyes.

Variations: If three characters are too many and you're getting hung up on pronouns, then scale it back to two characters of the same gender. Try three later. If three characters are easy, add more.

Applications: Clarity is essential. The reader must always know which character is acting or speaking. This applies anytime you write dialogue, whether in a biography, a memoir, or a novel.

4.7 Quoteworthy

One of the greatest achievements a writer can make is writing prose that is quoteworthy. Many great lines and slang words or phrases have come to us from plays, books, poems, and movies.

In *Star Wars*, every so often, one of the characters says, "I've got a bad feeling about this." Every time someone says that, they're about to face a conflict. Those characters are awfully intuitive! This line caught on with the public. *Star Wars* fans grew up and became writers, and in tribute to their favorite movie, they might have one of *their* characters say, "I've got a bad feeling about this" right before something bad is about to happen.

Every generation has its memorable quotes. In the nineties, *Forrest Gump* told us, "Life is like a box of chocolates: you never know what you're going to get." In the eighties, *Top Gun* gave us "the need for speed." Even today, most people are familiar with a quote from the 1939 film *Gone with the Wind:* "Frankly my dear, I don't give a damn."

Quotes from novels are less likely to become famous than quotes from movies, probably because we'll watch a good movie over and over (heck, it's only two hours), many more times than we are inclined to read a book— even a book we love. Yet hundreds of years after his death, Shakespeare's most memorable lines are widely known:

- Romeo, Romeo, wherefore art thou Romeo?

- What's in a name? That which we call a rose / By any other name would smell as sweet;

- Parting is such sweet sorrow...

These are all from just one play by William Shakespeare (*Romeo and Juliet)*.

The Exercise

Come up with a list of three to five catchy and memorable lines or bits of dialogue. Wait—that's not all. You also have to provide context. It's not enough that Rhett Butler says "Frankly my dear, I don't give a damn." What matters, what makes the quote so memorable, is that he says it as he walks away from the woman he loves, and in that line, Rhett has finally given up on her (and given her up). It's a *moment.* Your quoteworthy lines have to be placed in pivotal moments.

Tips: Context is everything. If you establish a situation before you develop your quoteworthy lines, this exercise will be much easier. Start the exercise by placing your characters in a situation.

Variations: If you find yourself sitting there for over an hour, and you haven't come up with anything you think is quoteworthy, do not give up! Instead, set a goal to *find* three to five quoteworthy lines in the next few novels you read.

If that proves to be too much, then look for quoteworthiness in movies and TV shows. However, don't include quotes that are already famous.

Applications: The purpose of this exercise is not to push you to write dialogue that everyone runs around quoting and repeating. The purpose is to think about dialogue as an opportunity to 1) give your characters strong and memorable voices, and 2) make the narrative punchier and more captivating.

4.8 Character Chat

If you write fiction, your characters might occasionally behave like bratty, stubborn children who refuse to cooperate. Oh sure, you created the characters, so you think you have full control over them. But you will quickly learn that characters have minds of their own.

Your intention was for Charlie and Emily to fall in love, but Emily keeps looking at Josh with goo-goo eyes. *Cut it out, Emily! That's not the guy for you!* But she insists. Or you have a character who's supposed to save the world, except he's kind of a jerk and definitely a loser, and there's no way readers will believe this guy's going to risk himself to save anyone.

It's a bizarre phenomenon. But we are not puppeteers pulling our characters' strings. Well, actually, we can be. There's a word for writing like that: forced. When you try to cram a square character into a round mold, it feels unnatural. Readers pick up on that stuff, and it doesn't do you or your story any good.

So what do you do when your characters are committing anarchy?

Well, you could try talking to them.

The Exercise

You're going to have a little chat with one of your characters. Just open a document or pull out a sheet of paper. Say hello to your character, and then write the character's response. Keep going back and forth. Model the conversation after an Internet chat.

Tips: This is a good way to get to know your character before you start writing a story. If you can relax and get into a creative, Zenlike state, your character will, in fact, talk to you.

Variations: You might not want to speak directly to your character. Okay, fine. Instead, do a script-style dialogue between your character and some other character. This exercise happens outside of your manuscript or draft. In other words, it's not intended for publication or inclusion in your story. It's a getting-to-know-you exercise, and it will work if you simply write a scene between two characters or talk directly to them yourself.

Applications: You can use this exercise anytime your story or your characters are stuck.

4.9 Distinct Voices

Writers talk a lot about voice as an element of writing, and what they mean is the writer's voice or the style of the prose. In college-level literature courses, you might be asked to identify an author from a short excerpt. You're not expected to have memorized the author's entire repertoire. You are supposed to have read the author's work closely enough that you can recognize his or her voice.

Some writers and teachers say that voice cannot be taught. It comes with experience. The more you write, the more your voice will emerge.

Voices emerge from characters, too, except they emerge quickly, and if they don't, you have to find their voices or maybe give them their voices. One character might speak with a lot of slang while another uses quaint words and phrases. How your characters speak will depend on where they grew up, how educated they are, and what class or culture they belong to.

Geography, education, and culture aside, we all have our own way of speaking—that little special something that is uniquely ours. If you can give your characters unique voices, then you will be a master of dialogue.

The Exercise

Write a dialogue scene with two or more characters. Your objective is to give each character a distinct voice. In other words, if you remove all the surrounding narrative and dialogue tags, a reader will be able to identify who is speaking.

Tips: To test your exercise, remove everything from the scene except the dialogue. Take out the action, the descriptions, and the dialogue tags. Now, read it aloud. Can you tell which character is saying what? Give it to a friend to read. Can your friend identify two voices?

Variations: As an alternative, take a dialogue-heavy scene out of a novel or script and test it for yourself. Are the characters' voices distinct? If not, tweak them until they are.

Applications: Writing distinct dialogue adds to the overall voice of a narrative but more importantly, it makes characters more realistic.

4.10 Internal and External Dialogue

Some narratives tell us what characters are thinking. In a first-person narrative, the entire story is told by one of the characters, from his or her perspective (the viewpoint character is referred to as *I*). In a third-person narrative, the story is told by a narrator who is not a character in the story (all characters are referred to as *he*, *she*, or *they*).

Third-person point of view gives the author the most flexibility because the camera can see all the characters equally and objectively. In some cases, the narrative might get closer to certain characters and bring the reader inside those characters' thoughts. In these instances, it's like the camera is sitting on those characters' shoulders.

Narratives often share characters' thoughts with the reader. This is called thought dialogue:

- I know, she thought, I'll write a book.

- He thought she was talented.

Thought dialogue can be formatted in different ways. Traditionally, all spoken dialogue is placed in quotation marks, and thoughts are italicized. Some authors forgo punctuating and formatting dialogue and thoughts altogether, but the narrative has to be extremely clear and concise to pull this off without confusing readers with regard to who is thinking or speaking.

The Exercise

Write a scene in which three characters are having a conversation. The scene will be written in third person, but it will go inside one of the characters' heads and include that character's thought dialogue. That character will participate in the conversation through spoken dialogue, but the narrative will also give readers that character's inner thoughts via thought dialogue.

Tips: Use conventional punctuation and formatting: quotation marks for dialogue and italics for thoughts.

Make sure the thought dialogue is relevant to the scene or essential to the story.

Variations: Write the same scene in first person or use third person but include thought dialogue for all three characters. This is difficult to pull off, because you'll have three characters who are all talking and thinking at the same time.

Applications: Some writers avoid thought dialogue because it gives certain characters an advantage, and in third-person point of view, thought dialogue can feel like a cheat. Instead of showing the reader what is happening, thought dialogue often tells the reader by revealing what characters are thinking. However, it can be used effectively. When you've completed this exercise, review the scene you've written and decide whether the thought dialogue enriches or weakens the scene. Revise accordingly.

Chapter 5: Fiction

Making it up

5.1 World Building

In order for readers to visualize a piece of writing and put it in context of the world they know and understand, you, the writer, have to fully realize the story's setting. Does it take place in a metropolis or the countryside? Are the characters inside some virtual reality or on a distant planet? Does this tale take place a long time ago or in the far-off future?

The setting could be a real city (maybe the city in which you live) or it could be a made-up town or village. It can occur in the past, present, or future.

In historical fiction, we don't build worlds, but a historical setting requires research for accuracy. Writers must have a thorough understanding of the geography, culture, and significant events surrounding the time and place in which a story is set.

World building is when we invent our own setting.

Consider classic fantasies like *Alice in Wonderland* or *Peter Pan*, and the necessity for world building becomes clear. In speculative fiction, which includes science fiction and fantasy, world building often requires elaborate planning.

The Exercise

Create a world from scratch and write a one-page description for a speculative fiction story setting. First, you'll need to decide whether your story takes place in the past, present, or future. Next, determine how your world is different from the real world in which you're currently living. Is it populated with mythological creatures, like trolls, unicorns, and fairies? Are there aliens? Is your world a metropolis or a desolate, distant planet?

Tips: Here are some elements to include: geography and landscape, climate, culture, economics, trade, social (class) structure, and government systems.

Variations: Write a one-page overview of an existing fantastical world. You could describe Wonderland, Neverland, the Matrix, or the faraway galaxy from your favorite science fiction story. As another alternative, you can work on a historical setting. Historical fiction requires solid research, so make sure you get your facts right.

Applications: Setting is one of the key elements in fiction. It can also be important in nonfiction writing, especially when writing a memoir or any nonfiction project that deals with geography, ecology, or the environment.

5.2 Yourtopia

This exercise builds on the previous world-building exercise by asking you to go to extremes in creating a setting for your story.

Dystopia is a type of world that is dark and miserable. Humanity is suffering en masse. Dystopian fiction is often marked by disease, oppression, war, overcrowding, and human enslavement. Utopia is the opposite of dystopia. It's a world in which life is ideal. These worlds are somewhat subjective. One person's dystopia might be another person's utopia.

Exploring and inventing such worlds requires using your imagination and thinking in extremes. You're basically creating a world in which the worst possible scenario—or best possible scenario—has arisen. In these stories, the scales are tipped to good or evil.

The Exercise

Write a two-page overview of a dystopian or utopian world. For this exercise, you will create a future on earth, so your overview should include a brief history explaining how the world reached this dystopian or utopian state, as well as descriptions of the social systems and cultural structures.

Tips: Remember that the key to a dystopian—or a utopian—world is its extreme nature. One way to develop a dystopian setting would be to consider the harshest situations that humanity has endured throughout history and then bring them all together into a single world. Look for periods of enlightenment and prosperity, and combine those for a utopian setting.

Variations: If creating an entire world seems overwhelming or intimidating, try creating a smaller setting—a town or an island. As an alternative, make a list of fantastical worlds you've seen in fiction, TV, and movies. Then list elements of the world that are positive and negative.

Applications: Inventing such worlds is good practice in creating environments and for developing ideas for conflict and resolution. If the world itself naturally provides struggles for the characters, you've just found a good source of conflict.

5.3 Setting as Character

Does a place have personality? Is a city alive? Can it speak to us? Does it feel or think? How does a story's setting affect the characters?

Anthropomorphism is the practice of humanizing an inanimate object. Dancing teacups and talking appliances are examples of anthropomorphism in fiction. Humanizing a place is usually subtle. It doesn't dance, sing, or talk. When settings are humanized, they don't act as backdrops for a story; they act as characters. Such settings have personality and attitude.

In Anne McCaffrey's popular science fiction series, *The Dragonriders of Pern,* a group of humans find themselves establishing a colony on an unfamiliar planet. While the planet doesn't talk or take action (and the characters don't believe it can do these things), it is given a clear personality.

Writers often characterize their settings, attributing traits to them that are normally reserved for people or characters. A city is mean, a house is friendly, a street is lonely.

The Exercise

Choose a setting for a story. It can be a room, a building, a town, or an entire planet. It can be a real place or a place you've made up. Next, write a character sketch for this place.

Tips: Review exercise 3.4 for tips on creating a character sketch. Use those tips to give your fictional setting human traits.

Variations: If you'd rather write a bit of narrative instead of a sketch, then write a short scene in which the setting of your story is the central character.

Applications: Setting as character is actually pretty rare, but when it's executed well, it captures readers' imaginations. If you've ever read a story about someplace and wished you could go there, then you know how a powerful setting can engage and inspire readers.

5.4 Fictionalize It

Real life gets fictionalized all the time. When people tell stories, they often embellish to make the events in their stories more exciting. A feral cat becomes a bobcat. A five-foot drop becomes a twenty-story fall. And a bad day becomes the worst day ever.

Sometimes we fictionalize real life by accident. In the game of telephone, all the players sit or stand in a line. The first person writes down a statement and then whispers it into the next person's ear. Each person whispers the statement to the next person in line, and when it gets to the last person, he or she says aloud whatever was whispered into their ear. It never matches what was originally written down.

Rumors and legends are often the result of accidental games of telephone. Something happens, and people start talking about it. As they spread the word, they misinterpret or misunderstand what they originally heard, and eventually, the story loses its accuracy.

Sometimes we fictionalize reality on purpose. If you've ever read a book or seen a movie that was "based on a true story," you saw real life fictionalized. These stories use real events but embellish them to make the tale more interesting.

The Exercise

Think about a significant event that you experienced. It could be the day your parents came home with a baby brother or sister or the time you won the school spelling bee. Write a short outline of what happened, and then make some sweeping embellishments. The goal here is to make drastic changes: alter the setting, characters, plot, or sequence of events. Instead of a baby brother or sister, maybe your parents came home with triplets. Instead of taking place in the school's gymnasium, the spelling bee was held someplace exciting, like a theme park or a national monument. Update your outline with the embellishments you've made.

Tips: As you write your outline, focus on listing the actual actions and events that occurred. You wake up, take a shower, have breakfast, and then go to the spelling bee. But there's more to it than that. When you wake up, you also turn off your alarm clock. Instead of simply taking a shower, you undress, wash, dry off, and then dress. You must prepare breakfast before you eat it. And what do you do with your breakfast dishes? Focus on the little steps that comprise each action in the sequence. Often that is where embellishments work best. An alarm that doesn't go off or a broken dish can make a story more realistic and more interesting. These details can also lead to story developments. For example, an alarm clock that doesn't go off might cause you to be late.

Variations: As an alternative to using a day in your life, look to the news or a documentary for a real event that you can fictionalize by embellishing details.

Applications: Many fiction writers base stories or characters on real life and then get overly attached to reality. Why write fiction at all? These stories often end up feeling forced or contrived. The beauty of fiction is in finding the truth rather than telling it. Real life is a wondrous source of inspiration; embellishments make fiction writing delicious.

5.5 It's All in the Details

When you're writing, one simple detail can tell a reader more than a full page of dull, drawn-out description. This is especially true in fiction, where you're working with made-up material and need to get the reader to believe in it.

Detail is important on every level. Whether you're introducing a character, describing a setting, or going through an action sequence, the little things will give your story much needed realism.

For example, you can write a lengthy description of a character's appearance and include descriptions of hair color, skin tone, facial shape, eye color, physical build, and each article of clothing the character wears. By the time the description is complete, the reader is fast asleep. It's more effective to use a few, key details that are unique to that character and are the most memorable things about his appearance:

Greasy strands of black hair hung around his scrawny, pockmarked face. His teeth were yellow and crooked, and he wore a stained tee shirt with a picture of a beer bottle on it.

The Exercise

Choose a character and a setting and write a scene in which both are revealed through descriptive detail.

The scene should not be a long description of your character or setting; rather, it should be a scene with action, dialogue, and purpose, but in which vivid, meaningful details about your character and setting are revealed.

Tips: Use clear, interesting, and sharp descriptions. Keep these descriptions to a minimum, but use rich details so that they are clear in the reader's mind. When you've completed your draft, revise and edit it to make the details in the piece as clear and memorable as possible.

Variations: Instead of writing a scene, develop a character or establish a setting with an emphasis on detail.

Applications: Knowing which details to include in a piece of writing can be tricky. Writers and readers have different preferences for how much detail they want. Working closely with the details and descriptions in a story helps you become more aware of what works (or adds to the story) and what doesn't.

5.6 Fan Fiction

All around the world, there are fan communities comprised of people who are totally obsessed. Some are obsessed with rock stars and sports celebrities. Others are obsessed with products. (Surely you've met an Apple user?) As you have probably guessed, we're concerned with fans who are obsessed with stories.

When fans write fiction set in a famous or popular story world, it is known as fan fiction. Most fan fiction is found in science fiction and fantasy, but it is found in other genres, too. Fan fiction is more popular for works that appeared in film and television, but novels have also spawned fan fiction.

For the most part, fan-fiction writing is a hobby. It's almost never published commercially. And before you write fan fiction, you should know a few things about copyright law.

You can, of course, write whatever you want privately. You can rewrite the ending to a movie that disappointed you or make the lead character in your favorite romance fall in love with someone else. What happens in your notebook is not subject to copyright law, but as soon as you share, distribute, or publish your fan fiction, the law becomes relevant.

When an author writes a novel, the world and characters of the story become that author's intellectual property. Story elements in a movie or TV show are also owned by some entity, usually the network or studio that produced it. Basically, the story, plot, and characters all belong to somebody.

Some intellectual property owners are strictly opposed to fan fiction. If they find fan fiction being published in any way, shape, or form, they might take legal action. Others are lenient. In many cases, as long as fan fiction writers are not making money off the work, they'll let it slide. A few might pick and choose. If you take their heroes and turn them into serial killers, you could get a letter from their lawyers.

Fortunately, most intellectual-property owners embrace fan fiction. They understand that fan fiction celebrates and pays tribute to their work, and they also realize that fan fiction is a form of free publicity.

The Exercise

Think about one of your favorite stories. It can be a movie, television show, or novel. Now, write a scene set somewhere in that story's world. For this exercise, do not change anything that happened in the original story.

Tips: In fan fiction, there are no rules. You could rewrite some part of a story, but most fan fiction explores the existing story further, instead of trying to change what already happened. In some fan-fiction communities, changing the canon is frowned upon. For this exercise, you can use existing characters and write a scene that takes place after the story ended, or you can create new characters and set them in the world of the story (this works well for science fiction and fantasy).

If fan fiction intrigues you, search for fan fiction communities online.

Variations: Instead of writing a single scene, write an outline for a longer story. What will the next installment of your favorite series look like?

Applications: Fan fiction is great for beginning fiction writers, because most of the story elements are provided for you: the world, the characters, and a history are already established. This allows you to practice writing dialogue and action without worrying about creating characters and worlds.

Be aware that fan fiction is not likely to get published, but there are a few exceptions. Sometimes, an author will team up with fans who are writers and publish collaborative stories. And you never know—if you make it big or get lucky, you could write the next story in your favorite franchise.

Fan-fiction communities help you improve your writing, network with other writers, and connect with fans of a work you admire—people like you.

5.7 Symbols and Symbolism

In *Alice and Wonderland*, a white rabbit appears, and Alice follows him down a rabbit hole that leads to Wonderland. In the story, the white rabbit is a herald—a character archetype that signifies the first challenge or the call to adventure. This is the change in the main character's life that marks the beginning of the story.

The white rabbit became so widely known that it eventually evolved into a symbol. Because it's white, it can symbolize purity. Because it's a rabbit, it can symbolize fertility. But because it was the herald that called Alice to her adventure, the white rabbit is often used as a symbol to represent change. Sometimes, it's simply used as a herald.

The white rabbit appeared in *The Matrix,* an episode of *Star Trek,* and in several episodes of *Lost.* In *Jurassic Park*, a character finds a file labeled "whiterabbit.obj" and in Stephen King's *The Long Walk*, a character refers to himself as "the white rabbit type."

The white rabbit can function as a traditional symbol or as a reference to *Alice in Wonderland.* Such is the case with the song "White Rabbit" by Jefferson Airplane.

Symbolism occurs whenever one thing represents something else. For example, a book could represent knowledge. A caged bird could represent oppression or imprisonment. In a story, the repetition of a symbol (every time the book or caged bird appears) can have significance to the story. Maybe every time a character fails because he doesn't know enough, there's a book in the scene. Or perhaps a person who is oppressed keeps a caged bird but doesn't recognize the irony (that he is imprisoning a living creature while suffering his own oppression).

The Exercise

Develop a list of five to ten symbols. Invent your own symbols rather than using ones that commonly appear in fiction. If you're working on a story or novel, make a list of symbols that you might use in your project. Symbols are often linked to big themes: love, revenge, sacrifice, redemption, narcissism, etc.

Tips: You might find it easier to choose a theme or issue and then look for a symbol that represents it. On the other hand, if you have an interesting image (a red scarf, a snow globe), you might find a way to turn it into a meaningful symbol.

Variations: Choose one symbol and write a list of ways that it can be used throughout a story. How many ways could you bring a white rabbit into a story? It could be seen in a pet store. It could be somebody's pet. It could be in a science lab. It could be part of a magic show. Make sure you don't give the symbol more importance than the plot or characters. A symbol is present to add depth and give the story greater meaning. It's an accent to the story, not the central focus of it.

Applications: Symbols enrich a piece of writing, adding layers to the themes and meaning of the piece.

5.8 Unbelievable!

Fiction writers often ask readers to believe the unbelievable. Even stories that are not fantastical contain elements that are so unlikely, most people won't believe it unless the piece is deftly written.

For example, in sitcoms, it's common to use a misunderstanding as a comedic device. Two characters who are married to other people are seen coming out of a hotel together. A third character happens to be driving by and immediately concludes they are having an affair. The third character then struggles with whether to confront them, tell their spouses, or mind her own business. Laughs ensue because the audience is in on the joke: the two characters were planning a surprise party for one of their spouses and had rented a ballroom inside the hotel.

In real life, such misunderstandings may happen occasionally, but usually they get worked out without a bunch of comedy and drama. If the third character is close enough to the others to be concerned, she would normally know about the surprise party and would therefore know why the two were at the hotel together, or the third character would realize that what she saw may not mean they are having an affair, so she would do a little checking before drawing conclusions about what's really going on.

In fantastical fiction, writers convince readers of extremely farfetched notions: zombies, wizards, aliens, fairies, vampires, time travel, and unicorns, to name a few.

Some fiction doesn't require readers to suspend disbelief. In fact, some stories are so easily believable that they could just as well be true. For this exercise, you'll stay away from stories like those.

The Exercise

Come up with an unlikely scenario, something that most people would roll their eyes at and say *yeah, right.* In the case of a misunderstanding, we often think the third character is silly, stupid, or not thinking clearly, because she made such a shortsighted assumption based on what she saw.

Come up with a scenario that's as unlikely as possible. It can be as simple as a misunderstanding, or it can be as elaborate as an alien race living in the New York sewer system.

Once you have your scenario, write a short scene. This is where you should focus on making readers believe the unbelievable.

Tips: One way to make the impossible seem believable is through detail. It's hard to believe there are aliens living in the New York sewer system, but if you can explain what they look like, how they live, and where they came from, then you just might be convincing.

Variations: If you can't come up with an unbelievable scenario or premise, borrow one from a famous story. Instead of writing a scene, examine the piece you've chosen and identify the details and techniques the writer used to make it believable.

Applications: It's hard enough to convince the public of the truth, thus the saying: truth is stranger than fiction. A writer who can convince readers to suspend disbelief for the duration of a story has acquired one of the most magical skills that any writer can possess: the ability to create illusions.

5.9 *Potter Wars*

A lot of artists struggle with the desire to write original material. Of course we all want to be original, but is that even possible?

Some say there are no new stories, just remixed and rehashed versions of stories we're all familiar with. When we say a piece of writing is original, a close examination will reveal that it has roots in creative works that preceded it.

Most of us writers have had ideas that we shunned because we thought they were too similar to other stories. But just because your story idea is similar to another story, perhaps a famous one, should you give up on it?

Look at this way: everything already exists. The ideas, plots, and characters—they're already out there in someone else's story. Originality isn't a matter of coming up with something new, it's a matter of using your imagination to take old concepts and put them together in new ways.

To test this theory, see if you can guess the following famous story:

> *A young orphan who is being raised by his aunt and uncle receives a mysterious message from a stranger. This leads him on a series of great adventures. Early on, he receives training to learn superhuman skills. Along the way, he befriends loyal helpers, specifically a guy and a gal who end up falling for each other. Our hero is also helped by a number of nonhuman creatures. His adventures lead him to a dark and evil villain who is terrorizing everyone and everything that our hero knows and loves.*

If you guessed that this synopsis outlines *Harry Potter*, then you guessed right. But if you guessed that it was *Star Wars*, you're also right.

This shows how two stories that are extremely different from each other can share many similarities, including basic plot structure and character relationships, and it proves that writing ideas will manifest in different ways when executed by different writers.

If it's true that originality is nothing more than putting together old concepts in new ways, then instead of giving up on a project that you think has been done before, you should simply try to make it your own by giving it a new twist.

The Exercise

Use the synopsis above to write your own short story. However, do not write a space opera or a tale about wizards.

Tips: One of the key differences between *Star Wars* and *Harry Potter* is the setting. One is set in a galaxy far, faraway; the other in a magical school for wizards. One is science fiction; the other is fantasy. Start by choosing a completely different genre and setting, and you'll be off to a good start. For example, you could write a Western or a romance.

Variations: Instead of writing a short story, write a detailed outline for a novel or novella.

Applications: This exercise is designed to demonstrate the following:

- It's not unusual for two writers to come up with similar ideas.

- A vague premise or concept will be executed differently by different writers.

- Instead of worrying about original characters and plots, focus on combining well-known elements in new ways.

5.10 The Elevator Pitch

If you want to pitch your fiction to a publisher or an agent, then you need to be convincing and concise. And if you want to pitch your fiction to readers, you have to make it sound captivating. You have to entice everyone.

In describing your fiction, you must first be aware of genres in publishing, and you should be able to place your work in appropriate categories.

Some writers loathe the genre model, and with good reason. Genres are confining. What if you want to write a story about aliens that explores the human condition and is written in verse? Is it literary fiction, science fiction, or poetry? Where would your story be shelved or categorized?

On the other hand, genres make it easier to market fiction, and they help readers find the types of stories they like best. If you love fantasy but dislike romance, you know which section of the bookstore to visit. Without these labels, finding good books to read would be a hassle.

The Exercise

Choose a story you've written or one of the exercises you've completed in this book, and write a short pitch for it with a focus on genre. Read aloud, your pitch should be about thirty seconds long (the length of an elevator ride). Make sure you identify the genre and include a brief description of your story's premise. Focus on making your pitch enticing. Don't include any major spoilers. In other words, it should make people want to read your story, without giving too much away.

Tips: Be as specific as possible. For the story you choose, list all of the genres that apply to your story. If necessary, conduct research about bookstore categories and genres in literature. Then, choose the single best genre or category for your story. If necessary, you can also identify a subcategory or two.

Variations: If you don't have a project to use for this exercise, then write a pitch for your favorite book.

Applications: If you write fiction and intend to get your work published, you'll have to pitch it at some point. There's no way around this, and the better you can sell your stories, the more of your stories you'll be able to sell.

Chapter 6: Storytelling

Once upon a time, someone, somewhere lived happily ever after

6.1 The Three-Act Structure

Every good story has a beginning, middle, and end. In the beginning, we meet the characters and learn about their problems. In the middle, those problems persist as the characters struggle through ongoing conflict. At the end, the main conflict is resolved. That's storytelling in a nutshell.

While there are other models that can be used in storytelling, the three-act structure is the simplest and most common. It is broken down as follows:

Act 1: Introduction or setup
Act 2: Rising action (conflict)
Act 3: Resolution

The three-act structure is used in writing novels, movies, plays, and all other forms of storytelling. It helps writers make sure they have the essential elements in their structure and provides a framework through which we can discuss, evaluate, and analyze a story.

The classic example of a three-act story is boy meets girl:

Act 1: Boy meets girl (setup)
Act 2: Boy loses girl and tries to get her back (rising action)
Act 3: Boy gets girl back (resolution)

This is the foundation of almost every romance and love story, and there is an infinite number of variations.

The Exercise

Using the boy-meets-girl model as a starting point, write five to ten ideas for stories based on the three-act structure. You do not have to write romance, but be sure to include a beginning, middle, and end (setup, rising action, and resolution).

Tips: Avoid going into too much detail. You don't need to create character sketches, outlines, and scenes. Keep it as simple as possible.

Variations: Choose five to ten books and films and break them down into their three-act structures. This forces you to whittle your favorite stories down to their bare bones.

Applications: The three-act structure is used in storytelling for all mediums and also in discussing and analyzing a story comprehensively. It is, perhaps, the most important foundation in storytelling that all writers should be familiar with.

6.2 *The Hero's Journey*

The hero's journey is complex enough to provide fodder for an entire book of fiction and character-writing exercises. It is essentially a formula for storytelling that was not developed but discovered.

Acclaimed mythologist Joseph Campbell discovered that across all cultures throughout history, there are specific plot points and character archetypes that occur in the greatest myths, legends, and other tales. These comprise the hero's journey, which is also sometimes called the monomyth.

The original structure has seventeen stages, and many variations have been culled from Campbell's discovery. For this exercise, we'll work with one of the most widely used variations, a twelve-stage structure developed by Christopher Vogler. This variation started as a memo that made its way around Hollywood.

Here's an adaptation of Vogler's twelve stages of the hero's journey:

- **Home or starting place:** We are introduced to the hero in his or her home or starting place.

- **Call to adventure:** The hero's world undergoes a dramatic shift, either by an external force (the villain) or by some change within the hero's heart or mind.

- **Refusal of the call:** The hero resists the call to adventure or refuses to accept a role in the forthcoming challenge.

- **Meeting the mentor:** The hero meets someone with knowledge or experience and receives training or supplies that will be required for the adventure.

- **Acceptance of the call:** The hero finally accepts the call and resolves to leave home to embark on the adventure, entering a new space or state of mind.

- **Friends, foes, and tests:** The hero acquires allies or helpers. Foes are established, and allegiances are determined. The hero is tested.

- **Approaching the underworld:** The hero and his or her helpers get ready for the first big challenge.

- **Ordeal in the underworld**: The hero enters the underworld and faces death (this can be symbolic), but will emerge reborn or with a new understanding or purpose.

- **Reward:** There is a reward for overcoming the ordeal and surviving the underworld.

- **Preparing for the return:** The hero prepares to return home; the last leg of the mission lies ahead. The tension is reaching its peak.

- **Climax:** There is a final obstacle or challenge at the climax. The stakes are higher than ever. The hero makes a sacrifice, suffers a loss, or undergoes another death and rebirth.

- **Resolution and return:** The conflict is finally resolved. The hero returns home (this can be a symbolic homecoming), having grown and bearing knowledge or items (treasure) that will change the world for the better.

You can read the full twelve stages from Christopher Vogler's memo by visiting www.thewritersjourney.com.

The Exercise

Give the hero's journey a spin. You don't have to write a full manuscript; just outline twelve movements for a story adhering to the formula above. It can be a novel, short story, play, or movie.

Tips: If you want to master the hero's journey, pick up a book or research it online. Wikipedia lists the full seventeen stages from Campbell's original work.

Variations: As an alternative to creating your own outline based on the hero's journey, read a book or watch a movie, and list the stages of the hero's journey for that story. Some suggested stories and films for this exercise: *Star Wars, Harry Potter, The Wizard of Oz, The Matrix, Titanic, Robin Hood.*

Applications: While some writers think formulaic writing is too commercial or contrived, formulas and structures are useful for writers. Writing a novel or a full-length movie is an incredibly involved process, and any help is good help. Formulas can ensure that your story is not missing something essential. It also helps you create a story with familiar patterns that resonate with audiences.

In terms of formulas, the hero's journey is unique, in that it was discovered in cultures across time and space, which means it is a foundation for writing a story that is timeless and universal.

6.3 Narrative and Point of View

The simplest definition of narrative is only one word: story. Narrative is the text of the story (words and sentences), as well as the setting, characters, dialogue, and plot. It's the sequence of events. Narrative is the whole shebang.

A good narrative is structured. It has a beginning, a middle, and an end. It also has a point of view, which is the perspective from which the story is told. The two most common points of view in narrative are first person and third person.

A first-person narrative is told from the perspective of a person or character inside the story. It's easily identifiable because there is an "I" or speaker relaying the story. First-person narrative is popular because it takes readers into the mind of the character whom the story is about. One of the most famous novels written in first person is *The Catcher in the Rye* by J. D. Salinger:

> If you really want to hear about it, the first thing you'll probably want to know is where I was born and what my lousy childhood was like, and how my parents were occupied and all before they had me, and all that David Copperfield kind of crap, but I don't feel like going into it, if you want to know the truth.

Third-person narrative offers a broader perspective and feels more like an outside observer is relaying the story. Many writers prefer third person because the perspective does not rely on any single character. Therefore, third-person point of view is more flexible.

Third-person narrative can be further classified into two axes:

- The first axis is the subjective/objective mode. The subjective mode describes characters' thoughts and feelings, whereas objective mode does not.

- The second axis is omniscient/limited. The omniscient point of view indicates a narrator that has full knowledge of all events, places, and time. A limited point of view is closely connected to a particular character in the story and cannot provide information or details about events or actions that the focal character is unaware of.

The Exercise

Choosing point of view for a story is a big decision. Some writers get several chapters into a book and then decide they need to change the point of view. That requires a lot of rewriting. You can do a quick exercise to experiment with point of view. Choose a story or piece of writing that you have completed. You'll work with the first page (or a one-page excerpt). If it's in third person, rewrite it in first person. If it's first person, rewrite it in third person.

Tips: You may find that changing the point of view requires revising the entire tone of the story. Changing point of view often changes the amount of information that the reader has access to. Does this help or hurt your story?

Variations: If you don't have a piece of writing that you can use for this exercise, then choose a short story or novel that you are familiar with and rewrite a scene. Try writing the scene in both axes and all four modes.

Applications: When we're writing a story, we can become so focused on plot and character that we forget to think carefully about how we style the narrative and which point of view is best for the story. This exercise requires that you deliberate on point of view and experiment with it to see how different points of view affect narrative.

6.4 Starting in the Middle (Nonlinear Storytelling)

Any decent narrative has a beginning, a middle, and an end. But here's a little storytelling secret: you can start your story in the middle of the action.

The premise of the television show *Lost* was that a plane crashed on an island. The show is the survivors' story. Many writers would be inclined to start the story either while the passengers are boarding the plane or while they're in the air, before the aircraft goes down.

The show's creators had a better idea. Start the story with a man waking up in the jungle *after the crash*. He's dazed. He gets up, stumbles around, and then runs out of the jungle to the beach, where the plane wreckage is burning and people are running around screaming.

The audience is thrust right into the middle of the action. *Lost* also used flashbacks to take the audience further back in time so they could experience the flight and the crash as well as the characters' distant pasts.

The lesson is that the beginning of your story may not be the same point where you actually choose to start telling it. Starting in the middle won't always work, and in truth, every beginning can be traced back to some other, previous beginning. The trick then is choosing the right moment in your story to introduce your setting, characters, and conflict.

The Exercise

Come up with a simple story (or use one you've already written). Write a short timeline detailing the chronological sequence of major events. This might be a list of scenes that comprise the story. Then write an outline, synopsis, or overview showing how you can start your story by jumping into the middle of the action. Now that the beginning has been lopped off, provide an explanation for how you will reveal it to readers.

Tips: Use note cards to organize and reorder your scenes.

Keep in mind that nonlinear storytelling doesn't always work. Avoid using it just for the sake of being creative.

Here are a few ideas to get you started:

- **Murder mystery.** Start the story when the detectives are already conducting the investigation rather than the standard, which is to start it when they get a call to the scene of the crime.

- **Love story.** Romances have become increasingly formulaic. The characters meet, fight their feelings, and then finally fall in love. Rearrange the order of events. Can you tell a love story that starts at the wedding and is told backward?

- **Hero's journey.** Exercise 6.2 outlines one variation of the hero's journey. Can you tweak the sequence and tell the story out of chronological order?

Variations: Use a story from a book, TV show (episode), or movie that you know well. Start by writing a list of key scenes. Then, rearrange the scenes and add transitions or additional scenes that help tell the story nonlinearly. You don't have to write out the narrative; an outline or synopsis will show you how nonlinear storytelling might work.

Applications: Nonlinear storytelling adds complexity and depth to a story. It's not for everyone and isn't appropriate for every story, but experimenting with it will show you how difficult it is to execute. You will also see what a useful device it can be and how severely it fails when used inappropriately.

6.5 Discovery Writing

Some writers swear by their outlines. If they know every twist and turn their story will take, they can focus on the details in the prose, dialogue, setting, and characters.

Other writers use discovery writing (which is often called pantsing, as in *writing by the seat of your pants*) because if they know where the story is going, they become too bored to bother writing it.

Discovery writing is the process of letting the story unfold as you're writing it. You start with a few characters and a setting, and you just start writing.

The characters take over, and you just follow along. Magically, a plot emerges.

Discovery writing may not work for all writers and may not be the best technique for all genres. For example, it might be difficult to write a good murder mystery if you don't start out knowing who did it. How will you plant clues and red herrings?

Even if you're the kind of person who works better with a plan, you should give discovery writing a try.

The Exercise

Choose a few characters (you can create new ones or use characters you've already created) and pick a setting. Do not plan any plot or action for your story—just start writing. Try to make your story at least three pages, but feel free to follow it for as long as necessary to get to the end.

Tips: There's no law that says you have to exclusively use outlining or discovery writing. In fact, you can use outlining to plan major milestones in your story and then use discovery writing to find your way to those milestones. There's no universal technique that works for all writers. Your best bet is to experiment with both outlining and discovery writing and figure out what works best for you. Most writers find that some combination of discovery writing and outlining is ideal.

Variations: If discovery writing stumps you or causes you to write in circles, then try establishing the ending and write toward it. If you're still stuck, then use the three-act structure (see exercise 6.1) and discovery write your way through those three acts.

Applications: Experimenting with different techniques is the only way you'll find the method that works best for you.

6.6 Chekhov's Gun

Chekhov's gun is a literary device in which an element is mentioned in a story and its purpose or significance becomes clear later. For example, early in a story, the narrative mentions that the protagonist carries a knife.

Later, she uses that knife to defend herself in a fight. If the knife hadn't been mentioned earlier, it might feel like an object of convenience. On the other hand, if the knife is mentioned, but she never uses it, the reader might feel cheated after anticipating a good knife fight.

The real purpose of Chekhov's gun is to remind writers that they have an obligation to fulfill all promises made to readers. If the narrative mentions that the protagonist carries a knife, the reader expects that she will, at some point, use it. If she doesn't, the writer has failed to fulfill a promise. In other words, don't pepper your story with unnecessary, insignificant, or meaningless elements. Make everything count!

The term "Chekhov's gun" comes from a letter from Anton Chekhov to Aleksandr Semenovich Lazarev (also known as A.S. Gruzinsky) in which he said, "One must not put a loaded rifle on the stage if no one is thinking of firing it."

The Exercise

Write a short scene and introduce two objects at the opening of the scene. Make sure one of the objects is used later in the scene, but leave the other object unused. Note that these objects will not be part of the descriptive content. For example, if the scene includes a description of a room and mentions a chair in the corner, you don't have to use the chair later because it is part of the setting description.

Let your scene sit overnight, then read it back the next day. Notice how the unused object lingers in the reader's mind in an unpleasant way. Once you're done, feel free to revise and edit out the unnecessary object, or add action in which it becomes significant.

Tips: Differentiating between what constitutes a necessary or unnecessary element can be tricky. In some cases, a knife that is mentioned may not need to be played later (for example, a knife might be mentioned in the context of one of the characters eating). In other cases, a chair that is mentioned will need to be played. A woman might carry a purse, but that doesn't mean she needs to retrieve anything from it, because most women carry purses. On the other hand, if she's carrying a file marked TOP SECRET, the reader expects to eventually be let in on the contents of the file.

Variations: Go through a story you've already written, and look for instances in which you included unnecessary or misleading elements.

Applications: The difference between excellence and mediocrity in storytelling often lies in the details. Chekhov's gun is one of the many details that could cause a story to lose credibility with readers. Therefore, checking your narrative for unnecessary or irrelevant elements will strengthen and improve your work.

6.7 Oh No He Didn't!

Plot twists, cliffhangers, and page-turners. Oh my! These are the sneaky techniques writers use to keep readers captivated. And we've all been there. *It's late, and I'm tired. After this chapter, I'm going to bed.* Then there's a cliffhanger—a shocking development in the story. *Forget sleep! I have to find out what happens next!*

Some writers are criticized for overusing these devices or for planting twists that are contrived or forced. A good plot twist or cliffhanger is natural to the story and doesn't feel like the writer strategically worked it in.

Some stories feature major twists in the middle of chapters. It's placing such a twist at the end of a chapter that turns it into a cliffhanger. Soap operas and television dramas are known, loved, and loathed for their application of these devices. It's how they hook viewers, and it's a way you can hook readers.

Each writer has to decide whether to use these techniques in storytelling. You might think they're too strategic or rob your story of its artfulness. Or maybe you like the exciting edge that a good twist or cliffhanger brings to a story.

The Exercise

Write an outline for a scene or chapter that ends on a cliffhanger. Approach the cliffhanger by building tension to the moment:

The bad guys are chasing the good guys and gaining on them. They're getting closer. One of the bad guys draws his gun, lifts it, cocks it, and aims it at our hero. He pulls the trigger. See you next week!

You can also plant a cliffhanger that comes out of nowhere. The chapter is winding down, everything is moving along as expected. Suddenly a character walks into a room and tells her ex-lover that she's pregnant—and he's the father. *Uh-oh!*

Both types of cliffhangers work equally well.

Tips: The best cliffhangers leave huge questions hanging in the air. Who did it? What just happened? Will they survive? How is that possible? What will happen next?

Variations: You can expand on this exercise by fleshing out a scene that ends on a cliffhanger (instead of outlining). To expand further, write the follow-up scene and satisfy the reader's curiosity by answering the big questions raised by your cliffhanger.

Applications: If you want to be a commercially successful author, you will probably find that mastering the cliffhanger is a huge asset to your writing skills. The cliffhanger is almost mandatory in horror and mystery genres, so if that's what you want to write, you'll need to be able to execute a good clincher.

6.8 Danger and Conflict

Lots of writers complain about the horrible things they must do to their characters. You create them and develop a special affection for them. They're practically your children. And you pretty much have to torture them.

Characters must suffer. Otherwise there's no sense of overcoming obstacles. There's nothing to resolve. That means there is no story.

There can't be a resolution if there is no conflict. Conflict is generally unpleasant. So unpleasant, in fact, that many writers are completely derailed from writing fiction because they can't stand hurting their characters.

Suffering is part of life. Great fiction mirrors life, which is why we so often hear that not only is truth stranger than fiction, fiction often holds greater truths than reality. When your characters agonize over their circumstances, they are tested. They might lose something (or someone), but they might gain something greater.

We could talk for days about clouds with silver linings and how it's darkest before the dawn. These clichés only serve to remind us that life is what we make of it. Sometimes, what is more important than the danger or conflict is how your character reacts to it. Consider the following scenarios in stories where parents lost a child:

- One father founds a nonprofit organization dedicated to finding missing children.

- One mother fights off depression for over a decade until she finally seeks help and learns to rebuild her life.

- One couple divorces. The husband sinks into alcoholism. The wife spins into self-destruction.

The way we react to a crisis is based on our personalities, philosophies, and the way we were raised. Keep this in mind as you rake your characters over the coals.

The Exercise

You can create a new character especially for this exercise or use a character you have already developed. Decide what is this character's greatest fear. Then make it happen by writing a riveting scene packed with tension and conflict.

Tips: If you can't think of something that would terrify your character, look up phobias on the web and make one of those phobias your character's biggest fear.

Variations: You can sketch a scenario instead of writing out the narrative. For example, a character with a mortal fear of drowning survives a helicopter crash that leaves him floating in the middle of the Pacific Ocean.

Applications: This is a basic tenet of storytelling. Anytime you write a story, there must be conflict. It's not always the character in a deathly situation or facing his or her greatest fear, but it is always unpleasant. In other words, if you can't make your characters suffer (or at least make them extremely uncomfortable), you're going to have a hard time writing stories that resonate with readers.

6.9 Plots

In his book *The Seven Basic Plots: Why We Tell Stories*, Christopher Booker claims that there are only seven different plots in all of storytelling.

Booker's argument sparked much discussion among writers and readers, and a great debate ensued. Is it true? Are there only seven plots? And if so, how could any story written after the first seven be original?

You can have a lot of fun trying to categorize your favorite fiction into one of Booker's seven plot categories:

- Tragedy

- Comedy

- Overcoming the monster

- Voyage and return

- Quest

- Rags to riches

- Rebirth

Booker's concept of limited possibilities within fiction is not a new idea. Joseph Campbell dissected the major elements of narrative and produced the monomyth (or hero's journey) in *The Hero with a Thousand Faces*, which identified the core plot elements of successful storytelling (see exercise 6.2). Campbell's ideas have been applied, tested, dissected, rearranged, and resurrected by writers, filmmakers, and literary analysts.

Another common breakdown of plot boils them all down to three possibilities:

- Man against man
- Man against nature
- Man against himself

And we wonder why it seems like everything's been done.

The Exercise

Choose ten stories that you have read. You may also use stories from film or television, but make sure at least half of your stories come from good old-fashioned books. You'll need a piece of paper (or electronic document) with three columns. List the story titles you've chosen in one column. In the second column, assign each of the stories to one of the three plots listed above (man vs. man, man vs. nature, man vs. himself). In the third column, assign one of Christopher Booker's seven plots to each of the stories you've chosen.

Tips: The main plot centers around the core climax and resolution, which occurs at or near the end of a story. All other plots are subplots.

Variations: For this exercise, you are asked to identify the main plot. As an alternative or bonus exercise, you can also assign each subplot from a story to a plot type.

Applications: Plot and character are two of the core elements in any story. Therefore, every writer benefits from mastering these elements first as a reader, then as a writer. As a storyteller, you should be able to identify the different types of plots in any story you read or write. Additionally, many writers suffer from lack-of-originality syndrome. They feel that every idea they have has already been done, so why bother writing anything at all? This exercise shows you that there are no new ideas, but you should forge ahead anyway.

6.10 Subplots

Subplots enrich a story. They give it layers so that it feels more like real life.

Think about your life and the events happening around you at any moment in time. There is never just one thing happening. There are many things going on. Some of them are not related to each other; others are closely intertwined. That is the reality in which we all live. For a story to feel real, whether it's based on true events or is completely imagined, it must mimic the complexity of real life.

One story's subplot may be another story's main plot. In a romance novel, the main plot is about the two main characters coming together and falling in love. But subplots abound: problems at work, conflict with family, surviving a disaster. In another genre, the romance might be a subplot, while another plot takes the main stage. A story about a broken family trying to survive the aftermath of a tornado might include a subplot wherein one of the characters falls in love.

A story can have one or two subplots, or it can be dense with them. Some subplots occur in sequence: one after another. Others are woven throughout the entire narrative. A master writer can introduce a wide range of subplots to the extent that the reader often focuses on them, rather than on the main plot.

The Exercise

Start by coming up with a few characters and a main plot, which will span the entire length of your story. Now, decide how you can weave three to five subplots throughout the main plot. Write an outline and notes about how the plot and subplots will be intertwined. Building a timeline can also be helpful.

Tips: Many novels are structured so that there is one main plot plus several subplots. The subplots can be threaded through the story or they can occur in single chapters or scenes. Set up at least one of your subplots to reconcile in a single scene or chapter early in the story, and set up at least one that will thread to the end.

Variations: Practice identifying subplots in some of your favorite books and movies. Use the plot types listed in exercise 6.9 as guidelines.

Applications: When writing a story, there is a lot to manage. The more characters a story has, the more plots and subplots it will have. At times, a complex story can feel unmanageable. Practicing on a small scale will help you see how to keep elaborate stories, plots, and subplots organized.

Chapter 7: Form Poetry

Working within a framework

7.1 Couplets and Quatrains

Poetry may not be the most widely read or published form of writing these days, but it's probably the most widely written.

Despite the lack of enthusiasm for the form among readers and publishers, poetry still has a traditional place in our culture. You'll hear poetry read at most significant events, such as weddings, funerals, graduation ceremonies, and presidential inaugurations. Poetry is the foundation for most children's books, and it's so closely related to songwriting that in many cases, it's hard to tell the difference between a poem and a song lyric.

Couplets and quatrains are two of the most basic building blocks of poetry.

Couplets

A couplet is a pair of lines in a poem. The lines usually rhyme and have the same meter or syllable count. Contemporary couplets may not rhyme; some of them use a pause or white space where a rhyme would occur.

Couplets can be used in a number of ways. Some poems are simply a couplet. Other poems are composed of a series of couplets. Stanzas can end with a couplet, or an entire poem can end with a couplet.

Quatrains

A quatrain is either a four-line stanza within a poem or a poem that consists of four lines. Many modern song lyrics are composed of quatrains.

A quatrain may contain one or two couplets. The nursery rhyme "Humpty Dumpty" is a quatrain of two couplets:

> Humpty Dumpty sat on a wall,
> Humpty Dumpty had a great fall.
> All the king's horses and all the king's men
> Couldn't put Humpty together again.

The Exercise

This is a three-part exercise. First, write a couplet (two rhyming lines with the same meter or number of syllables). Then, write a quatrain (it doesn't have to include meter or rhymes). Finally, write a quatrain that consists of two couplets.

Tips: Keep your language and subject matter simple. Aim for catchy language and vivid imagery.

Variations: Mix it up—write a poem that consists of a couplet followed by a quatrain and then another couplet. Try using couplets and quatrains to write a song lyric.

Applications: Couplets and quatrains have an infinite number of practical applications for a writer. Couplets are ideal for writing a children's story, because kids gravitate to simple language and rhythmic rhymes. You can also use couplets and quatrains in songwriting and greeting-card poetry.

7.2 Iambic Pentameter

If you chat long enough with a poet, eventually this term is sure to pop up in the conversation. Iambic pentameter is, historically, the most common metrical line used both in poetic verse and in verse dramas.

An *iamb* is a type of meter (in poetry we call it a foot, which is a unit of poetic measurement). It is an unstressed syllable followed by a stressed syllable: da DUM. Words that are iambs include the following: conCERN, eVOLVE, aMEND, eLUDE, toDAY.

A *pentameter* is five units (or five feet).

Therefore, *iambic pentameter* is a line of verse that is five iambs:

da DUM da DUM da DUM da DUM da DUM

Iambic pentameter can be used throughout an entire poem or just in certain lines or stanzas. Here is a couplet written in iambic pentameter:

I walked across a meadow in the rain
I danced beneath a starry summer sky

Iambic pentameter can take on a singsong quality or a brooding tone. It's quite musical, and its emotional quality depends largely on the flavor of words and images used.

While not in heavy use nowadays, except in songwriting, iambic pentameter has been quite popular throughout history. William Shakespeare used it in his plays and sonnets.

The Exercise

Write a poem in iambic pentameter. It can be a short poem, but make it at least four to six lines long. The lines don't have to rhyme, but rhymes will give your poem a nice musical quality.

Tips: Pay special attention to the stressed syllables, remembering that the first syllable is unstressed and every alternating syllable after that is stressed.

Variations: Iambic tetrameter is four feet of iambs: da DUM da DUM da DUM da DUM. Iambic trimeter has three feet of iambs: da DUM da DUM da DUM. As you can imagine, iambic meter ranges from one to ten (or more) feet of iambs per line. Write a poem in one of the other iambic forms.

Applications: As with so many poetic forms, iambic pentameter is ideal for children's stories and verses. It's also a useful tool in songwriting.

7.3 The Sonnet

The sonnet is the most well-known poetry form, largely because the most famous English writer of all time, William Shakespeare, had a penchant for writing sonnets. That was about four hundred years ago.

Today's poets tend to prefer free-form poetry, often without any rhyme scheme or discernible pattern. So why should we study outdated forms like sonnets, and why should we experiment with them?

Sonnets, along with all other literary forms and genres, make up our collective literary history. It is beneficial for writers to be familiar with the literary canon, which is the foundation upon which the entire writing profession is built.

Writing in form (even if just for practice) provides rules and boundaries. If you can learn to write well within form, then you will write even better outside of it.

When you practice writing in form, you face a specific challenge within a framework. If you write an English sonnet, each of your lines must be ten syllables. While this sounds limiting, it provides boundaries that you can work within. Sometimes too much freedom is overwhelming. Most writers have felt intimidated by a blank page. Form provides a structure that often makes writing easier.

Form also allows a writer to expend more creative energy on a poem's content. There is much to balance when writing a poem—language, rhythm and meter, word choice, subject matter, imagery. With rhythm and meter out of the way, you can concentrate on other aspects of the poem.

What is a Sonnet?

A sonnet is a fourteen-line poem that follows a strict rhyme scheme and focuses on a single thought, idea, or emotion. Most sonnets are found in lyric poetry, which conveys personal feelings and is sometimes set to music.

English sonnets are among the most famous types of sonnets, thanks to William Shakespeare. He wrote 154 of them, which is why English sonnets are also sometimes called Shakespearean sonnets. They are fourteen lines, and each line consists of ten syllables written in iambic pentameter (see exercise 7.2 for more information on iambic pentameter). The structure of an English sonnet is a set of three quatrains (four-line stanzas) followed by a rhyming couplet (two lines). The final couplet usually summarizes the entire poem. The rhyme scheme is ABAB CDCD EFEF GG.

Below is an English sonnet written by Shakespeare, annotated to show the rhyme scheme. Keep in mind that English pronunciation back in the sixteenth and seventeenth centuries differed from today's pronunciation. When this poem was composed, words like *temperate* and *date* would have been spoken in strict rhyme.

Sonnet 18: "Shall I Compare Thee to a Summer's Day"

William Shakespeare

(A) Shall I compare thee to a summer's day?
(B) Thou art more lovely and more temperate.
(A) Rough winds do shake the darling buds of May,
(B) And summer's lease hath all too short a date.
(C) Sometime too hot the eye of heaven shines,
(D) And often is his gold complexion dimmed;
(C) And every fair from fair sometime declines,
(D) By chance, or nature's changing course untrimmed.
(E) But thy eternal summer shall not fade
(F) Nor lose possession of that fair thou ow'st;
(E) Nor shall death brag thou wand'rest in his shade,
(F) When in eternal lines to time thou grow'st,
(G) So long as men can breathe or eyes can see,
(G) So long lives this, and this gives life to thee.

The Exercise

Write an English sonnet.

Tips: Make sure your sonnet focuses on one theme, subject, or idea. Part of the appeal of a sonnet is its subject matter, which is usually personal or intimate. Also, double check your rhyme scheme and meter (syllable count).

Variations: While sonnets are all fourteen lines long, the structure varies. In addition to English sonnets, there are Italian sonnets, Occitan sonnets, Spenserian sonnets, and modern sonnets. Each of these sonnet forms sets forth structural rules; for example, the Italian sonnet includes an eight-line stanza (octave) followed by a six-line stanza (sestet). Additionally, there are variations within each group. You can find a host of sonnet forms by doing a quick search on the Internet. Spend some time studying these forms and experimenting with them.

Applications: Many literary journals and poetry magazines accept poems for submission, and most will welcome a sonnet.

7.4 Haiku

Although haiku appears to be one of the simplest poetry forms, it's actually quite complex. To truly understand haiku, you need to know a little bit about the Japanese language, or more specifically, some key differences between Japanese and English. Also, traditional haiku adhere to strict rules regarding form and content.

A haiku consists of seventeen *mora*s or phonetic units. The word mora can be loosely translated as *syllable*.

A haiku is a seventeen-syllable verse. Traditionally, haiku were written on a single line, but modern haiku occupy three lines of 5-7-5 syllables.

Haiku also use a device called *kireji* (cutting word). This word breaks the haiku into two parts that are distinctly different but inherently connected. The kireji is not a concept used in English, so poets writing haiku in English often use punctuation marks instead of kireji, usually a hyphen or ellipsis.

The kireji provides structure to the verse and emphasizes imagery used on either side. It may not always be easy to identify the kireji in a haiku, but if you look for a word or punctuation mark that abruptly breaks the train of thought and severs the haiku into two parts, you've probably found it.

Another basic element of haiku is the *kigo* (season word). A true haiku is set in a particular season and is fundamentally concerned with nature. The kigo might be an obvious word like *snow* (indicating winter), or it could be vague as with a word like *leaves* (which can be present in any season).

Contemporary Haiku

There is much debate (and some controversy) over what technically qualifies as a haiku. Some poets merely adhere to the 5-7-5 syllabic and line structure and disregard the kireji and kigo elements. Purists insist that a poem is not haiku if it does not meet all of the traditional requirements.

Additionally, many modern poets do not write haiku that exclusively focus on nature. Contemporary haiku explore just about any subject imaginable.

The Exercise

Try your hand at writing a few haiku. For this exercise, focus on writing a poem that is seventeen syllables on three lines with the following meter: 5-7-5.

Tips: The most captivating haiku are quite lovely and use imagery that is almost tangible. Many haiku have an element of surprise or use turns of phrase that are clever, reminiscent of puns.

Variations: Write a few haiku that follow stricter, more traditional rules. These haiku are concerned with nature and include the kireji (cutting word) and kigo (season word).

Applications: Haiku remain popular and can be found in literary and poetry journals. They are also ideal for social media (especially Twitter) and are fun and quick to write. They promote clear, concise writing and can help you cultivate the art of using vivid imagery.

7.5 The Double Dactyl

It sounds dangerous and threatening, but the double dactyl is actually harmless.

A dactyl is a trisyllabic metrical foot composed of one stressed syllable followed by two unstressed syllables. That sounds confusing, but just think of a dactyl as a three-syllable word or phrase in which the first syllable is stressed. The word *poetry* (*PO-et-ry*) is a dactyl. So are the words *blueberry* (*BLUE-ber-ry*) and *fantasy* (*FAN-ta-sy*).

A double dactyl is exactly what it sounds like: two consecutive dactyls. Therefore, *blueberry fantasy* is a double dactyl.

However, the term double dactyl also refers to a form of verse poetry. In informal settings, it might be referred to as *higgledy piggledy*, which is itself a double dactyl.

A double dactyl poem has two stanzas. Each stanza has three lines of double dactyls and a fourth line that includes one dactyl plus a single-syllable accented word. The fourth lines might be something like *blueberry pie* or *fantasy sky*. Here are a few more specifications:

- The last lines of the two stanzas have to rhyme with each other.

- The first line of the first stanza is nonsense. For example, *higgledy piggledy.*

- The second line in the first stanza is the poem's main subject and should be a proper noun and a double dactyl. For example, *President Washington.*

- At least one line in the second stanza has to be a single six-syllable word that is a double dactyl. For example, *agoraphobia.*

Originally, there was also a rule that any six-syllable word used in a double dactyl should never be used again in the same poem.

Because the rules are so detailed and specific, double dactyls are challenging to write, but they are also a lot of fun, and children love them because they are silly.

The Exercise

Write a double-dactyl poem.

Tips: There is a template you can use on the following page.

Variations: As an alternative, try to come up with a list of ten words that are dactyls and ten words or phrases that are double dactyls. Finally, come up with five proper nouns (names) that are double dactyls. After that, you might be more inclined (and prepared) to write a double-dactyl poem.

Applications: There will be times when you're writing and need to make words or sentences fit a certain space or rhythm. Writing form poems like double dactyls helps you build skills for such tasks. They also make great children's poems.

Double-Dactyl Poem Template

LINE		STANZA
1	Double-dactyl nonsense	First stanza
2	Double-dactyl proper noun and subject of poem	
3	Double dactyl	
4	One dactyl plus a single-syllable accented word	
5	Double dactyl	Second stanza
6	Double dactyl	
7	Double dactyl	Use at least one six-syllable word that is a double dactyl in any line of the second stanza.
8	One dactyl plus a single-syllable accented word; must rhyme with final line in first stanza	

7.6 Get Your Writing in Shape: The Lanterne

Shape writing is a fun exercise in fitting words into a defined space.

Like haiku, the lanterne form of poetry is from Japan. In this form, we write a poem that has a distinct shape—the shape of a Japanese lantern.

A lanterne has five lines. The first line consists of one syllable. The second line contains two syllables. The third line contains three syllables. The fourth line contains four syllables. The fifth line is a single syllable: (1-2-3-4-1). Each line must be able to stand on its own, so words and ideas cannot be started on one line and completed on the following line.

Some lanternes use a title to form a sixth line, which also functions as part of the poem.

One

dancing

in a crowd

people moving

still

Sometimes, poems accidentally form a shape. Poets may also intentionally fit a poem into a shape that is related to the poem's subject or provides extra insight to the poem.

The Exercise

Write a lanterne.

Tips: The ideas in each line can be connected but they also have to stand alone as separate ideas.

Variations: Pick some other shape and write a poem to fill it. Make sure you type it to see how it looks in print.

Applications: Writing a predetermined number of words, characters, or writing to fill a specific allotment of space is an excellent skill for any writer to possess. Sometimes you'll use these skills in poetry, fiction, and other forms of prose or narrative. If you're editing a paragraph with sentences that are all roughly the same length, you may need to create some rhythmic balance, so you'll want to revise some sentences to make them shorter, which is essentially the same as writing to a specific word or syllable count. If you write copy for a newspaper or magazine, you will often be given a space limitation.

7.7 Doggerel

Poets have a special term for poetry they find distasteful or unrefined. A doggerel is a poem that is considered to have little literary value. If a poem is called doggerel, it's basically being referred to as trash.

Doggerel breaches the rules of refined poetry; sometimes it does this intentionally. Poems that are dripping with sentiment to the point of preciousness are doggerel. So are poems that contain clichés. If the meter is broken, it's doggerel. If a haiku fails to meet the standards of the form, it could be considered doggerel. Other violations that mark a poem as doggerel include misordering words to fit a metrical or rhyme scheme, writing about a trivial or shallow subject, or handling subject matter ungraciously or poorly.

Doggerel is usually the result of incompetence on the part of the poet. However, doggerel is not just a word we use to label bad poems. Some poets intentionally write doggerel, and in doing so, they turn their noses up at sophisticated or academic poetry. These rascally poets breach the conventions of good poetry writing, thus creating doggerel, but they do this by writing poems that are witty, clever, and entertaining. One such application of doggerel would be to use it for a parody piece.

They say that to become a great writer, you first must write badly. Nobody knows for sure who "they" are or why "they" seem to know everything about everything, but "they" are usually right. So for this exercise, you're going to try to be bad.

The Exercise

Write a doggerel. Your poem should be at least eight lines long, and it should contain at least three of the following poetic violations: overbearing sentimentality, clichés, broken meter, bad rhymes, misplaced or disarranged words to make the lines fit the meter or rhyme scheme, and trivial subject matter.

Tips: Make your poem as bad as possible, and when you're done, have a good laugh at yourself.

Variations: If doggerel comes easily to you, then write a doggerel that parodies a famous work (a story, poem, or other piece of art) or a doggerel that is satirical.

Applications: Writing is rather serious business, unless you're a comedian, which most of us are not, especially those of us perusing books of creative writing exercises. Sometimes we need to lighten up a little and remember not to take ourselves too seriously. This exercise should help you do that.

7.8 Found Poetry

Writers worry too much about being original. They write a poem and throw it away, because some other poet already has already done the subject justice. They write a story and crumple it up, because the premise or the plot have been done before. Characters are too familiar. Stories are too formulaic. The words have all been used too many times.

Tue originality isn't about making something new. It's about taking what's out there and seeing it from a new perspective or combining existing ideas in fresh ways.

That's what found poetry is all about. You take an existing text and mold it into a poem. It's a collage with words instead of pictures. A found poem follows these rules:

- It is made up exclusively of existing texts.

- The words are not changed.

- There are few additions or omissions.

- Line breaks are imposed by the poet.

- The poet may work the text into a form.

They are called "found poems" because they are discovered rather than made. Surely, you've read a passage in a textbook or newspaper article and thought that there was a poem in there somewhere. Well, you just found a poem!

The best source texts for found poems come from prose that is not meant to be poetic: speeches, news articles, and textbooks. However, found poems can come from other poems, song lyrics, and stories. Lots of stories probably have poems hidden within.

The Exercise

This exercise might prove to be a bit of a treasure hunt. Peruse some source material in search of a hidden poem. Flip through newspapers and textbooks, or search online for texts of speeches, reports, and official documents. As you read through your source material, look for interesting images and metaphors or compelling language—words that pop. Keep the original text mostly intact, using line breaks and spacing to convert it into a poem. Go light on making changes, additions, and omissions.

Tips: A good place to start your search would be the Internet, because you can easily copy and paste the original text into a document and then work with it. Wikipedia is packed with articles on almost every subject imaginable. Search there for topics that interest you; it's a great resource for this exercise.

Variations: As you can imagine, poets like to break the rules and get creative. Some poets mix different texts together, changing and adding words and lines as they see fit. You can, too. You might also nestle some found poetry into a larger poem that you're writing.

Applications: The main purpose of this exercise is to promote creativity and learn how to turn something old into something new. This exercise also shows you how to see existing texts in new ways.

7.9 Serious Form: Rondeau, Rondel, Rondelet

Some poets refuse to write in form; they see it as old-fashioned or limiting. But others swear by form, insisting that within form, there is actually more room for creative thinking to blossom.

Your position on the matter should only be decided after you've experimented wholeheartedly with a variety of forms.

Most studious young and new poets throughout history have had to write in form before they were given a blank page and invited to try their hands at free verse. This is in keeping with tradition in studying the arts. A young singer who is not a songwriter doesn't get her own songs; she sings someone else's. A young painter first copies the masterpieces, then makes his own. Poetry is no different.

Let's look quickly at three different forms, all hailing from France.

Rondeau

A rondeau is fifteen lines long. It has three stanzas: a quintet (five lines), a quatrain (four lines), and a sestet (six lines), with the following rhyme scheme: AABBA AABR AABBAR. Note that R stands for refrain, which is a repetition. In the rondeau, the refrain is a short phrase taken from line one and repeated on lines eight and fifteen. Every line other than the refrains should have the same meter.

Rondel

A rondel is thirteen lines. It has two quatrains (four lines each) and a quintet (five lines), with the following rhyme scheme: ABba abAB abbaA. All the capital letters indicate refrains, which are repeated lines.

Rondelet

A rondelet consists of a septet (seven lines) with two rhymes and a refrain: AbAabbA (capital letters indicate refrains). The refrain is four syllables (tetrasyllabic) and all other lines are twice as long: eight syllables (octosyllabic).

The Exercise

Write a rondeau, rondel, or rondelet.

Tips: Before you begin, prepare your document by marking off the rhyme scheme and stanzas. See exercise 7.5 for an example showing how to construct a form poetry template. Make notes where you'll have to count syllables and place refrains. Stick to the form you choose, and focus on tight, concise word choices. Avoid any unnecessary or superfluous words. Also, search online for any of these three poetry forms and you'll find plenty of rondeaus, rondels, and rondelets that you can use as examples.

Variations: Instead of choosing one of these forms, write one poem in each of these forms. That way, you get more for your money (three writing exercises in one!).

Applications: There are many literary publications that accept form poetry. You may be able to get your rondeau, rondel, or rondelet published.

7.10 *Invention of Form*

Who came up with the sonnet or the haiku? How did certain forms of poetry become so popular? Why are some forms so unpopular? And how many forms have been left by the wayside, ignored by poets?

Here's a more interesting question: how would you like to become an inventor?

The Exercise

Invent your own form of poetry. The form you develop should have all of the following guidelines:

- How many total lines will the poem have?

- How many stanzas?

- How many lines in each stanza?

- How many syllables should the lines have?

- What is the rhyme scheme?

- Will any lines be repeated as refrains?

Finally, give the form a name and write a poem in it.

Tips: To approach the exercise tactically, create a template for your poem (see exercise 7.5 for a template example).

Variations: You can always combine two (or more) other forms. What if a form started with a haiku followed by quatrain? Think about ways you can combine and tweak existing forms.

Applications: While existing forms of poetry are useful for creating a framework in which you can make poems, developing your own form gives you practice at building your own structure.

Chapter 8: Free Verse

Language and literary devices

8.1 Growing Vocabulary

A writer's vocabulary is paramount. Yet many writers use the same commonplace words over and over again. Repetition is rampant in writing, even though we have a vast language full of interesting and meaningful words at our disposal.

There's no excuse for using weak and tired words. After all, tools like the thesaurus and dictionary are easy to use and freely available on the Internet.

Writers often focus on technical elements of the craft, such as grammar, spelling, and punctuation. We also spend a lot of time thinking about structure, setting, plot, and characters. However, word choice is what makes our writing distinct. It's where we develop a voice and how we take a line drawing and fill it with color. When your vocabulary is robust, your writing shimmers.

Word choice can mean the difference between a decent piece of writing and a fantastic piece of writing.

The Exercise

For this exercise, you'll need the following:

- a poem (this can be a poem you wrote or a poem by another author)

- writing tools (word processing software or pen and paper)

- a thesaurus

You can do this exercise on paper or electronically, but you'll need to make copies of the poem you've chosen to work with. An electronic format will be easier, since you can copy and paste with relative ease.

Step One: Nouns and Verbs

Go through the poem and highlight all the nouns and verbs. You can use bold, underlining, or italics. When you're done, work through the poem and replace each noun and verb with another word that has the same meaning. Try to pull replacement words from your mind, but don't wait too long before turning to the thesaurus. Double-check the dictionary definitions of words you pull from the thesaurus to ensure they have connotations that communicate your intent. When you're done, read the original and your revised poem. How do they differ?

Step Two: Adjectives and Adverbs

You'll need a fresh copy of the original poem. This time, go through and highlight all the adjectives and adverbs. Highlight entire phrases if necessary. When you're done, go through and replace each adjective and adverb with a word that has almost the same meaning but a slightly different connotation (for example, *green* becomes *mint*). Try to come up with replacement words on your own, but if you get stuck, use the thesaurus. When you're done, read the original and your revised poem. Did you succeed in creating a completely different poem by slightly changing the adjectives and adverbs? How are the two poems still alike?

Step Three: Double Up

Start over with two fresh copies of the original poem or two copies of another poem. First, highlight all the nouns, verbs, adjectives, and adverbs. Go through and replace all of these words with different words but try to keep the meaning, imagery, and general themes of the poem exactly the same.

Then go through the second copy of the same poem, but this time use words that have the same meaning but different connotations. Again, use the thesaurus, even if only to check your word choices. Did you successfully create one new poem that has the same sensibility of the original and one that is different?

Tips: After you've replaced words in a poem, use the new poem you've created as your next starter piece. You'll end up with a chain of poems, each one leading to the next.

Variations: Highlight adjective-noun and adverb-verb combinations (such as *home office* or *lightly sleeping*) and replace them with single words (such as *den* or *dozing*).

Lengthen a poem by replacing single words with longer phrases. *Green* becomes *the color of grass.* How does this change the overall impact of the poem? Is it weaker? Are its images clearer?

Applications: The most important benefit to this exercise is expanding your vocabulary and promoting variety in the word choices you make. However, if you modify your starter poem enough, it could become a new poem, which you can submit and publish.

8.2 Alliteration and Assonance

Developing a vocabulary of poetry terms and literary devices will help you better understand the writing techniques and tools that are at your disposal. It may not occur to you that you can build rhythm by repeating consonant sounds. When you know the meaning of *alliteration*, then this idea is more likely to influence your work.

Poetry terms, such as *alliteration* and *assonance*, show us how clever, creative word arrangements add musicality to any piece of writing, making it more compelling and memorable. These terms and the concepts they represent apply to all types of writing, not just poetry.

Alliteration is the repetition of the initial consonant sounds of words in close proximity to one another. Examples of alliteration include *black and blue*, *we walk*, and *time after time*.

In some cases, alliteration is used to refer to any repeated consonant sounds, even if they don't occur at the beginning of words. An example of this would be "blue notebook," where the *b* sound is repeated at the beginning of *blue* and in the middle of *notebook*.

Alliteration might also be used to describe the repetition of a consonant sound nestled in the middle or even at the end of words. *Blueberry*, for example, contains alliteration within a single word.

Assonance is similar to alliteration, except it deals exclusively with vowel sounds. Assonance occurs when accented vowel sounds are repeated in proximity:

Assonance allows literary writers to create fun phrases.

In the example phrase above, there are several runs of assonance. The opening *a* sounds in the words *assonance* and *allows* demonstrate one *run* of assonance. This run is marked with underlining. A second run is marked with bold lettering and occurs with the *a* sounds in *create* and *phrases*. Can you find a third run of assonance in the sentence?

Assonance often evokes a sense of rhyme without serving up a direct or technical rhyme. The phrase "fancy pants" is an example of this.

So, how are alliteration and assonance used for effect? Well, think about repetition in general. When you repeat something over and over, it becomes embedded in memory. Alliteration and assonance work the same way. If used correctly, these devices enhance the rhythm of a piece, making it more memorable.

The Exercise

Go through a piece of writing (your own or someone else's) and look for instances of assonance and alliteration.

The material you work with can be poetry, fiction, a journal entry, or a blog post. Any form of writing will do.

Mark the runs of assonance and alliteration with bold, underlining, italics, or highlighting. When you're done, read the piece aloud to get the full effect.

Tips: Double-check the runs you've identified for assonance to make sure they mark stressed (or accented) syllables. Watch out for sounds that are different but use the same letter (such as the *a* sounds in *cat* and *cape*).

Variations: As an alternative to identifying alliteration and assonance in a piece of writing, try writing a short piece with several runs in it. Or revise a page from an existing writing project to inject alliteration and assonance into it.

Applications: Musicality and repetition enrich any piece of writing. Too often, writers focus on content and not language. The study of poetry, poetry terms, and literary devices like alliteration and assonance reminds us to work on our language, word choice, and sentence structure.

8.3 Rock and Rhyme

Rhyming poetry goes in and out of vogue all the time, except when it comes to children's poetry, which is almost always packed with fun and clever rhymes.

Some poets take to rhyming rather easily, and soundalike words roll off their tongues like butter. Other poets struggle, dancing through the alphabet and flipping through rhyming dictionaries just to find a rhyme as simple as *bat* and *cat*.

Poems that rhyme are fun to write and a blast to read. They are especially fun to read out loud. Rhyming is good practice for exploring musicality in language and experimenting with wordplay.

The Exercise

All you need is a song—a rhythmic and rhyme-y song without a lot of fancy runs. You'll want a relatively simple tune. A short pop song will work well. Forget about classical music because most of it doesn't have lyrics, and what we're doing requires words. We're writers, right?

Rewrite the lyrics but keep the rhythm and rhyme scheme intact. You don't have to replace the rhyme *ring* and *sing* with a rhyme like *thing* and *bling*. But you do need to find another rhyming pair (like *dance* and *pants*). Your rhymes can be as strict or as loose as you want.

If you do just a few of these, rhyming will start to come more naturally to you, and your rhymes will flow with greater ease.

Try to rewrite the song on your own, but if you're really struggling, visit a rhyming dictionary or a thesaurus.

Tips: You might want to start with a short, three-chord pop song and then move on to longer and more complex tunes. If you know all the lyrics to your song, that will be immensely helpful. If not, do an online search to find the lyrics to the song you want to work with.

Variations: Here are a few variations that you can use for this exercise:

- Try it with nursery rhymes: "Hickory Dickory Dock."

- Try it with a famous poem. Shakespeare anyone?

- Try it using a song without lyrics. You're on your own!

Applications: Working with rhyme helps you think more carefully about word choice and points your focus to the sound and rhythm of a piece of writing. This is also an excellent exercise for anyone who has thought about writing song lyrics or children's poems and stories.

8.4 Show, Don't Tell: Imagery

Writers are often told *show, don't tell*. At first, it's a confusing piece of advice. Show what? Isn't writing all about telling readers something?

Yes and no.

When you tell readers that a couple walked hand in hand through the city streets, the image is bland. But when you say that a tall bearded man wearing a top hat and a trench coat and a small dark-haired woman in a red velvet gown walked hand in hand through deserted back alleys of a big city, a more vivid image enters the reader's mind. That's what we mean by *show, don't tell*. Imagery paints a picture.

Imagery is especially important in poetry because poetry often deals with the abstract: ideas, emotions, and themes. Wrangling these concepts into images isn't always easy, but the payoff is enormous.

Let's say you want to write a poem about injustice. You can tell readers some statistics about how many convicted criminals have been declared innocent thanks to DNA testing, or you could show them injustice by describing a man wrongfully convicted of murder and sentenced to death. Show this man as he eats his last meal, makes his last phone call, and faces his executioner. Finally, depict the real murderer, who is watching all of this on TV. This is how you show readers what you want to say instead of telling them.

The Exercise

To begin, think of a broad subject that you'd like to explore in a poem: love, hate, revenge, sacrifice, redemption, rebirth, time. Write a poem using imagery to depict what you want to say about this concept.

Tips: Imagery is part storytelling, part description, and part metaphor. Use images that are concrete and easy for readers to visualize. Try to avoid emotional language and instead focus on painting a picture through description.

Variations: As an alternative, go through some poems and identify the imagery that poets have used to convey a message or idea. Write your response to these images, and in your own words, explain why an image makes a poem's theme and concept more vivid.

Applications: Imagery strengthens every form of writing from storytelling and poetry to journal writing and journalism. It is one of the most powerful tools of the craft.

8.5 Cut-and-Paste Poetry

Most poetry-writing exercises are designed to help you focus on one particular area of poetry writing, such as rhyme, alliteration, or imagery. This one works on several levels.

First, this exercise provides a nice, Zenlike break from your daily routine, because it involves more than writing. You'll get to search through clippings and do a little cutting and pasting (the old-fashioned cutting and pasting with scissors and glue, not the computer-based cut and paste).

Second, this exercise provides an excellent alternative to recycling those growing stacks of old magazines, newspapers, and brochures that are sitting around collecting dust.

You can come back to this exercise again and again for future poetry writing sessions.

You'll need some supplies and some time. Try to set aside an hour or two (and note that you can break this exercise up over several days or even longer).

What You'll Need (Supplies)

- old printed material: magazines, newspapers, pamphlets, ads, photocopies, junk mail, etc.;

- a small box, basket, jar, or other container;

- a pair of scissors;

- a glue stick or a roll of clear tape;

- a piece of blank paper (construction paper works well; you can also use a piece of cardboard or a page in your notebook); and

- a highlighter (optional).

The Exercise

Step One: Go through old magazines, pamphlets, printouts, and photocopies. Any printed material will do. Scan through the text to find words and phrases that are interesting and capture your attention and imagination. You can highlight the text you like or move ahead to step two.

Step Two: Cut out the phrases you've chosen, and place them in your container.

Step Three: When you have a nice pile of clippings, pull some out and spread them across a flat work surface.

Sift through the words, pairing different clippings together to see how the phrasing sounds. Place the ones you like best on a piece of paper, arrange them into a poem, and use glue or tape to adhere them.

Tips: Look for words and images that pop. When you're all done, save the leftover clippings so you can repeat this exercise again later.

Variations: If you find it difficult to cobble together an entire poem from your clippings, then use a pen or pencil to add words and phrases to complete your poem. You can also clip images and incorporate them to create a multimedia poetry collage that is also a piece of art.

Applications: This exercise reminds you to focus on word choice and language. It encourages you to go outside yourself for inspiration by piecing elements from different sources together to make something new.

8.6 Metaphor and Simile

Metaphor is an excellent tool for breathing life into your writing by engaging readers' senses and firing up their imaginations.

Metaphors fall somewhere between symbols and similes. A symbol is something that represents something else. It can be a word, a sign, or an image. Close your fist and extend your forefinger and middle finger into a V-shape. That's the symbol for peace (or victory, depending on the context).

A simile is when one thing is *like* another: Her skin was like snow: white and cold.

A metaphor, however, is when we say that one thing *is* another thing. Her skin is not like snow: it *is* snow. However, metaphors are not meant to be taken literally.

The most effective metaphors engage readers by connecting an otherwise intangible subject to a clear, concrete image or by triggering one (or more) of the five senses: sight, sound, smell, touch, or taste.

The Exercise

Choose a topic to write about. Some subjects don't need the help of a metaphor: sex, food, music, and anything else that intrinsically affects the senses will not benefit from a metaphor the way abstract topics will.

Next, choose a metaphor to represent your subject. The best metaphors are things that affect all the senses. Food is often used as a metaphor because it is multisensory: you can see, smell, touch, and taste it, and you can also hear it—food and drinks pop, fizz, sizzle, and splash.

Now that you have a topic and a metaphor to go with it, it's time to write a poem. Think about how you can extend the metaphor and weave it throughout your piece.

For example, you could use the metaphor of a fish in a poem about dancing. Think about the qualities of fish. They wiggle when they swim. They leap. They're slippery. They might make bubbles. How can you use the qualities of a fish to represent dancing?

Incorporate simile by expanding on your metaphor to include related words and images: water, boats, bait (the dancer is a fish, and the music is like bait).

Tips: Be careful not to overwhelm your piece with too many different metaphors or too much of the same metaphor. An overused metaphor gets tired, and too many different metaphors can be confusing. Aim for fresh metaphors and avoid clichés.

Variations: As an alternative, make a list of topics and match them with metaphors that would represent them well.

Applications: Think about subjects you've explored recently in your writing. Were there any ideas that felt flat or dry? You can revise those pieces using metaphor to add dimension and make your writing more compelling.

8.7 Concise Writing

Many modern poets argue that poetry is most effective when the language is condensed. That means eliminating extraneous or unnecessary words.

We writers tend to rely heavily on verbiage, especially modifiers (adjectives and adverbs) and articles (*a, an, the*) to add balance and rhythm to our writing or simply to make it sound smarter.

Language is the heart and soul of poetry. In any kind of writing, we need to think beyond the subject matter and pay due diligence to language and word choice. Poets are especially encouraged to search for the perfect words and phrases and to eliminate redundancy.

This exercise helps you look at your writing from a minimalist perspective. Simplify, and remember that less is more.

The Exercise

Step One: Remove Modifiers
Choose a poem (or other piece of writing) that you've already completed. Go through your poem and cross out

all adjectives and adverbs. Take note of how many strikethroughs there are. Next, revisit your verbs and nouns, and see if you can replace them with alternative verbs and nouns that better reflect the image you were trying to convey when the modifiers were still in place.

Example: "The drooping tree" becomes "The ~~drooping~~ tree," which then becomes "The willow."

Step Two: Eliminate Articles

Continue with the poem you used in step one or start with a different piece. This time, go through and cross out all articles (*a*, *an*, *the*, etc.) Notice how many times these parts of speech appear in your piece. Now read it back without the articles. Does it sound better? Do you think you need to replace some of the articles for the poem to make sense?

Example: "~~The~~ old dresser sits in ~~the~~ corner" becomes "Old dresser sits in corner."

Step Three: No Excess

Now try the exercises again. This time, cross out the modifiers and the articles. Again, make note of how many strikethroughs you have. Read the poem aloud and see how it sounds. Better? Worse? Try replacing adjective-noun and adverb-verb combinations with nouns and verbs that are more descriptive (for example, *runs quickly* becomes *sprinted*). Do you need to put some of your modifiers and articles back into the piece? Were you able to find suitable and better replacements for the words you eliminated?

Example: "A bad dream haunts the young man" becomes "Nightmare haunts lad."

Tips: In working through this exercise, you will probably find that some modifiers and articles simply cannot be replaced. A chocolate chip cookie is not just any old cookie, and there is simply no other way to describe it clearly and effectively.

Variations: This exercise is ideal for groups or partners. Each person contributes a writing project, and then everyone swaps papers for the exercise.

Applications: This is an exercise in self-editing and learning how to cut extraneous and unnecessary words while replacing weak words with stronger, more compelling ones.

8.8 Freewriting Harvest

In the first chapter of this book, we explored freewriting. Freewriting has a number of useful applications. It can help you clear your mind so you can focus on a writing project, it works as a problem-solving tool, and it promotes creativity.

Freewriting is also an excellent way to generate raw material for your writing projects.

This exercise shows you how to use freewriting to create and harvest raw material for your poetry.

The Exercise

If you haven't read chapter 1 or completed any freewriting exercises yet, go back and read through the chapter. It's short and should only take a couple of minutes to read or review. You should also do a few freewrites (feel free to spread them out over several days).

In freewriting, you write whatever comes to mind, no matter how silly, outrageous, or nonsensical. If your mind goes blank, just write the word *blank* over and over until something else comes to mind. You can jot down ideas, words, and images. Write for about twenty minutes.

If you've already done some freewriting exercises, then you can use one of them for this exercise.

Go through your freewrite and highlight words, phrases, and images that pop or capture your attention. These might be excerpts that have a musical quality or passages that inspire a vivid scene or image in your mind. You might highlight a single word that you find interesting, or you might highlight an entire passage that is a few lines long.

When you've finished making your highlights, extract the highlighted portions of text. Either rewrite these sections on a fresh page in your notebook or copy and paste them into a new document. Now, you've harvested your freewrite for raw material and are ready to start building a poem.

Using the material you've harvested, add and remove words and phrases. Rethink the line breaks. Try to work it into a form (if you wish) or arrange the poem so that it flows rhythmically.

Tips: The more you freewrite, the more raw material you will generate. Try freewriting for twenty minutes a day for five days during the week, and then spend the weekend making poems out of your raw material.

Variations: You can go through several freewrites at a time. One freewrite might lead to three poems, or five freewrites might generate material that goes into a single poem. You can even harvest material from numerous freewrites into a new "freewrite remix" and then harvest that for your poetry material.

Applications: Many poets use freewriting to generate raw material. You will find that as you continue to freewrite on a regular basis, your freewriting sessions become more and more interesting (everything gets better with practice). Some freewrites might even translate directly into poems with very little revision necessary.

8.9 Twitter Poems

We're always changing and evolving. First we had the postal system, then the telegraph, followed by the telephone. Now, we're totally connected: cell phones, smart phones, video phones, and online chats.

Social media has changed the game in terms of how we write, where we write, and whom we engage with through written communications. The Internet demands that we become clearer and more concise.

Twitter has spawned a whole new generation of writing styles. Piggybacked on text-messaging shorthand (u no what i mean), Twitter insists that we communicate, share, and interact in 140 characters or fewer. That's a very small space to get any point across.

Yet it has proved to be a huge success. In the age of sound bites, Twitter fits nicely with all the blurbs, questions, and exclamations that we make in the public arena.

Writers have flocked to Twitter and found it tremendously useful in connecting with readers and other writers. Many have even developed new forms of writing around the 140-character limitation: Twitter stories and Twitter poems.

The Exercise

The exercise is short and simple: write a poem in 140 or fewer characters. If you can write exactly 140 characters, give yourself an extra pat on the back.

Tips: Haiku lends itself well to Twitter poetry. In fact, you can log onto Twitter and search for haiku (use hashtag #haiku).

Variations: Another popular trend online is the six-word story. You can invent your own forms (the eight-word poem, for example) and work them into the 140-character limitation.

Applications: The most obvious application is that you can post your poem (in its entirety) on Twitter. You can also write a series of short poems, or perhaps your 140-character poetry tweets can be strung together into a longer poem.

8.10 Word Prompts for Poetry

Sometimes poets run out of words. We get tired or busy. We get stressed out. We can't be inspired or full of ideas every day, but that's no excuse for not writing.

Writers often complain about writer's block, but it's quickly going out of fashion as an empty excuse for not writing. There are just too many sources of inspiration available to us, and we're living in a no-excuses age.

Writing prompts are one of the best ways to generate ideas when our muses are on strike. Some prompts present a quick premise, image, or scene. Others ask questions. Some are just simple lists of words that you can use to spark a writing session.

The Exercise

Below, you'll find several word lists. The first five lists are general and the other four lists are inspired by the seasons. Choose a list and write a poem using all the words in the list. Or choose a season list and write a poem about that season. Make sure you use every word from the list you choose.

One: bronze, forgotten, scratchy, dust, mount
Two: plastic, zealous, manipulate, charity, test
Three: velvet, opera, spin, collision, dance, slide
Four: pristine, highway, moth, skyline, curl, river
Five: terminal, check, wait, keys, silver, island, hatch
Spring: fresh, green, clean, shoot, seeds, hatchling
Summer: ball, bucket, ice, thunder, lemonade, tan
Fall: rake, squash, golden, harvest, feast, pumpkin, soup
Winter: blizzard, fire, skate, shiver, holiday, night

Tips: Look for words that have multiple meanings. For example, *rock* can mean a pebble or a boulder or it can indicate a genre of music. It can also be an action (rock the baby). Words with multiple meanings can add dimension to a poem.

Variations: The variations are limitless. You can mix and match words from different lists. You can put two or more lists together. You can also write a single poem with all the words from all the lists.

Applications: Writing prompts are lifesavers when you sit down to write and nothing happens. You can always use prompts for a writing session. Sometimes you'll get your best work this way. It may even be publishable!

Chapter 9: Philosophy, Critical Thinking, and Problem Solving

The importance of truth and reason

9.1 The Great Debate

Logic, order, and organization are essential in clear and coherent writing, whether you're telling a story or writing a poem. Critical thinking is a fundamental writing skill.

If a story doesn't stand up to logic, or if a poem has holes in its philosophy, readers will become disenchanted. If a character does something outrageous but doesn't have a reasonable motive, readers will become disengaged.

Writing requires foresight and analysis. We use what-if questions to create, and we use if-then arguments to substantiate everything we write.

We often think of arguments as conflicts, and most arguments are. A neighbor doesn't want to chip in for a fence that divides two properties, and an argument ensues. A spouse comes home late after forgetting to call. An argument ensues. A child comes home with a bad grade. Another argument.

Argument does not always stem from personal conflict. The greatest debates throughout history have dealt with philosophical issues—questions to which there are no absolute answers. While our characters will surely experience personal arguments, it is our mastery of the philosophical arguments that will make a narrative reasonable and believable.

The Exercise

First, you'll need to pick an issue or philosophical question (suggestions are provided below). Write a piece of dialogue between two speakers in which they engage in a debate, with each taking an opposing side in the argument. Write it as a simple script. Here are some topics to get you started:

- One speaker believes in a supreme being or higher power, and the other does not.

- Fate or free will? One believes in destiny, the other believes that life's outcome is strictly the result of choice and circumstance.

- Do good and evil exist? One believes good and evil are struggling to eradicate each other. Another argues that good and evil are relative, subjective, or mere human imaginings.

- Are morals and ethics circumstantial or static? One believes it's always wrong to kill another person, no matter the circumstance. The other believes in the death penalty or self-defense.

- One speaker believes in life after death, and the other believes it all just ends.

Another source of ideas for philosophical debates is political issues.

Tips: This exercise will work best if you pick an issue with which you're familiar but on the fence. For example, perhaps you know a lot about the death penalty but haven't taken a stance on it. Since you are not on either side, you will probably do a good job arguing for both sides. However, if you want to choose an issue that you feel strongly about, you should do your best to convey the opposing arguments in a convincing manner. You can also research any of these issues to get some ideas about positions on the matter.

Variations: As an alternative, you can write two short essays (one page each) for and against the issue you have chosen. You can also engage a friend to write an opposing viewpoint.

For an extra challenge, find a friend who truly disagrees with you on an issue, and write each other's arguments. See if you can present the other side's best positions and ideas, and then critique each other's papers.

Applications: You might have two characters in a story who have basic philosophical differences. Such opposition could split a tribe, end unity in a nation, or break up a relationship. Philosophical issues often arise as themes in storytelling, poetry, and journalism.

9.2 Facts in Fiction

We live in a world of sound bites. Everyone has an opinion, and "facts" are flung around carelessly without any consideration for their source or accuracy. There are entire websites dedicated to fact-checking major media outlets in an effort to quell the spread of misinformation.

In writing, when the facts don't jibe with what's happening on the page, readers get irritated and could be provoked to write a negative review. Writers end up looking foolish, because they failed to do a little research and fact checking, even within the context of their own story.

In chapter 1, you have a character who mentions that her mother will be angry if she chooses a particular college. Then, in chapter 10, we learn that character's mother has been in a coma since she was in junior high. So, it's not possible for her mother to have been angry about her choice of college, since she would have been unconscious at the time the college was chosen.

In a poem about war, you mention a battle but attach the wrong general or battalion to it.

Facts are even more important when you're writing nonfiction. If you fudge the facts or fail to do your research, your credibility suffers, and you could lose readers (and sales).

These kinds of mistakes make writers look bad. Readers have sharp memories. They are smart and educated. Do not underestimate them.

In this exercise, you'll learn to back up your claims with facts, even when you're writing fiction.

The Exercise

You'll need a piece of writing that you've already completed. The best pieces will be narrative (fiction or nonfiction) rather than poetry. If you've completed exercises earlier in this book, then you can use one of the stories you wrote. Go through the piece and do a fact check. Below are some examples of what to look for:

- Distances: If a family lives in California, and their child goes to college in New York but later embarks on a two-hour drive home for the holidays, you need to fix the facts.

- Time: If a character is twenty years old in 2010 and mentions seeing Saturday Night Fever at the theater when it first came out, you have a problem because the movie came out before he was born.

- Science and technology: Make sure your gadgets and devices exist in the time frame in which you're writing. Also, check facts that relate to science. For example, if your story is set on a planet with two moons, you should conduct research to find out how two moons will affect the tides and other natural phenomenon.

- History: Research is absolutely essential when you're writing historical fiction. However, even in contemporary fiction, there may be references to the past. If a character's aunt danced with Elvis, make sure the ages of the characters in the story align with Elvis's life, and make sure the dance didn't happen when Elvis was overseas.

- Props and costumes: Be aware of what characters are wearing and the settings they are in. If a character puts on tennis shoes before leaving the house, she can't lose a heel trying to climb into her car.

Tips: Checking facts in fiction can be difficult. As we read our own work, we might be more inclined to revise the language or look for typos than to question factual accuracy. One tool you can use is a timeline, which comes in handy when checking for accuracy in your timeline. Find friendly, knowledgeable readers who can review your work to check for fallacies and inaccuracies.

Variations: If you don't have a piece of writing that works with this exercise, do an observation exercise instead. The website moviemistakes.com lists mistakes that have been found in films. Some of these are continuity errors rather than factual errors (for example, in a single scene, an actor's hair is wet in one shot, dry in the next). Choose a movie, but don't look at the list of mistakes. Watch the movie, and look for the mistakes. Write a list of all the mistakes you observe. Then, check the list to see how many you found. Did you discover any new mistakes? How many did you miss?

Applications: Don't distract your readers by failing to align your facts, and don't damage your credibility as an author by forgetting to conduct proper research. The fact that a website called Movie Mistakes exists is a testament to the keen observational skills that fans, including moviegoers and readers, possess and the degrees to which they will go to publicize an artist's failure to get the facts right.

9.3 Everyone Has an Opinion

All good pieces of writing have a central conflict. The entire narrative builds up to the moment when the conflict reaches its final climax.

In addition to a central conflict, several smaller conflicts along the way build tension.

One way to create light conflict is through opposing opinions. After all, everybody has an opinion, and we constantly disagree with each other. That doesn't mean we're always fighting, but it does mean there is a bit of abrasion in our daily dealings.

Real people think differently from one another and so must characters. Think about your favorite books, movies,

TV shows, and music. Do your friends and family all agree with you on who should have won last year's award for best new artist? Of course not. It's unlikely that everyone you know belongs to the same political party, attends the same church, or even favors the same restaurants.

Opinions and personal beliefs often seem unimportant, but sometimes they affect the course of events. Here's a scenario:

> Someone breaks in to a chemical plant and is tinkering with the equipment. The two guards on duty apprehend the suspect, who turns out to be a former employee. He insists that there's a major chemical leak, which will cause a massive explosion, killing hundreds of nearby residents if they don't let him fix it. One guard thinks the suspect is telling the truth. But the other guard believes he is lying and is actually trying to set off the explosion rather than render it inert. Neither knows for sure, and the clock is ticking.

The entire scene balances on these two characters' opinions about the third character. Which guard will win the argument?

Characters might engage in debates over anything— from which superhero can run the fastest to whether or not there is an afterlife.

The Exercise

Nothing makes your characters seem real like giving them their own beliefs and opinions. From which fast-food restaurant has the best fries to who was the greatest leader in history, character opinions can run the gamut.

Write a scene in which characters reveal their opinions about a variety of things. Include three (or more) characters and at least six different opinions (two for each character) through the course of the scene. Try to reveal one insignificant opinion and one serious belief for each character.

Tips: Write a scene that flows smoothly. Don't make it obvious that the point of the scene is to reveal the characters' opinions and beliefs. To do this, you'll need to develop a context in which the scene takes place: a court hearing, a classroom, or a newsroom are all settings where debate might arise.

Variations: If you're already working on a narrative writing project, then feel free to engage in this exercise within that project. Work the characters' opinions into the conversation in an existing scene or in the next scene you write.

Applications: This exercise gets you thinking about your characters in new ways. What do they think or believe about insignificant and important matters? It also requires you to create smaller conflicts, instead of relying solely on a central conflict. This adds depth, complexity, and realism to your writing.

9.4 Moral Dilemmas

It's not enough for your characters to have simple opinions. Each of us also has deeper philosophical ideals and values. Our values come from our families, religions, and cultures. They shape our morals and the decisions we make.

People are complex. What we believe is right or wrong changes when we find ourselves in real situations. Consider an honorable character who believes that one's highest loyalty is to his or her family. When that character learns her brother is a serial killer, does she turn him in? Testify against him? Stories get interesting when characters' morals are put to the test.

The Exercise

For this exercise you will put a character's morals to the test. Below, you'll find a short list of moral dilemmas. Write a scene in which a character faces one of these moral dilemmas and has to make an agonizing decision.

- In the novel *Sophie's Choice*, a young Polish mother and her two children are taken to a concentration camp. Upon arrival, she is forced to choose one child to live and one to die. If she doesn't choose, they both die. Write a scene in which your character must choose between the lives of two loved ones.

- A single woman is close friends with the couple next door and has secret romantic feelings for the husband. She discovers his wife is having an affair. Normally, this woman minds her own business, but now she sees an opportunity to get closer to the man she wants.

- Some countries have strict laws regarding drug possession. A family has traveled to one such country for vacation. Upon arrival (or departure), one of the teenager's bags is sniffed out by a dog. The bag is opened, the drugs are identified, and the guard asks whose bag it is. Both parents are considering claiming ownership. Everyone in the family knows the sentence would be death.

- Travel through time and face this classic moral dilemma: The protagonist is holding a loaded gun, alone in a room with a two-year-old baby Hitler.

- A plane crashes into the sea. Most of the passengers escape with inflatable lifeboats but they do not board them correctly. Your character ends up on a lifeboat that holds eight people, but there are twelve people on it, and it's sinking. Your character can either throw four people overboard and eight will survive, or they will all die except your character, who will get rescued after the others drown.

During the scene, the character should agonize over the decision and reveal his or her reasons for the choice he or she makes.

Tips: Search online for "lists of moral dilemmas" to get more scenarios.

Variations: If you don't want to write a scene, challenge yourself to come up with a few moral dilemmas of your own.

Applications: These moral dilemmas also work as story prompts. They force you to put your characters in situations that are deeply distressing, thus creating conflict and tension.

9.5 Chain of Events

One could argue that every event in the universe, from the earth-shattering explosion of an A-bomb to a little leaf fluttering in the breeze, is part of a long chain of events.

For every action, there's a reaction. A chirping bird outside someone's window could keep him up all night, and he could get into a car accident the next day after falling asleep at the wheel. That car accident could be fatal to a passenger in another car. The death of that passenger brings on severe depression in one of his or her loved ones. That person seeks therapy. While in the waiting room, he or she meets an attractive stranger. They end up getting married, and it all started with a chirping bird.

If you think hard and long about how every little thing in the universe is connected, your mind might become overwhelmed, so let's keep it simple.

The Exercise

Start with an event. It could be something major, like a group of revolutionaries attacking a military command center, or it could be something minor, like a woman leaving her house and going to the store to buy milk late at night. Start with that event and then work backward, listing all the other little actions and events that led up to it. Try to go fifteen to twenty steps back. If you're working on a story or some other writing project, you can use an event or incident from your story. Working backward this way will help you see your narrative and plot in a new light.

When you're done, come back to the event you started with and work forward. Again, take fifteen to twenty steps in the timeline.

Your chains don't have to be too complicated. You're not writing a story, you're just exploring how events and actions are linked together in a chain.

Tips: In reality, events are not the result of a single-link chain of events. It's more like a chain-link fence. Multiple things might happen to cause a woman to run out and buy milk late at night: she had a full container of milk but left it out overnight, and it spoiled. Then she lost her shopping list when she went to the grocery store, so she forgot to buy more. It's late; her husband and kids are sleeping, but she knows the baby will wake up in the middle of the night and need a bottle. Multiple events conspired to cause her to go out at night for some milk.

Variations: If you really want to get creative and three-dimensional, elaborate on simultaneous events that led to your event or followed it.

Applications: This exercise is useful for checking the logic in a sequence of events. Often in storytelling, we don't show the reader every little thing that happens. The chain-of-events exercise works as a fast outline or timeline that helps you determine how minor actions in your story lead up to a major event, even if those actions aren't shown to the reader. This exercise can also prompt ideas for fiction writing.

9.6 A Sticky Situation

The stickiest situations are the ones without easy answers. Sometimes characters are forced to make decisions when they don't have enough information. If they cut one wire, the entire building will blow up, and everyone dies. Another wire will disarm the bomb. But they don't know which is which.

In other cases, misunderstandings and simple human mistakes lead to uncomfortable (though perhaps not life-threatening) dilemmas. Characters are put in uneasy positions. Friends ask them to lie. They have to choose between the opportunity of a lifetime and their own morals.

These are the scenes that make us squirm but keep us glued to the page. Readers become riveted, because there's no telling what the character will do or how they'll get out of the mess they're in. It's a big what-would-you-do moment, but nobody could possibly know what they would do until they are in that situation themselves.

The Exercise

Come up with three to five sticky situations for your characters. These situations should have no clear or easy answers, but they force a character to make a difficult decision that challenges his or her loyalties or morals. The character may also have to make a decision when he or she doesn't have all the necessary information.

Tips: Here are some examples of sticky situations:

- There's a job opening at the company where Kate works. Her two closest friends apply for the job. After interviewing both of them, Kate's boss asks her to recommend one or the other for the position.

- Jack's two best friends had a falling out a few years ago and no longer speak to each other. Now they're both getting married on the same day, and they both have asked Jack to be the best man.

- A single parent has worked hard to provide for and raise his or her twins, who are fast approaching high-school graduation. Both want to go to college, but there's only enough money to send one to school.

Variations: Instead of coming up with a list of sticky situations, write an entire scene in which your characters find themselves in a sticky situation (feel free to use one of the examples above). If you've ever found yourself in a sticky situation, write about it in a personal essay.

Applications: Sticky situations are great for generating comedy. They create tension and conflict, which are essential elements in writing, especially storytelling.

9.7 If-Then Logic Problems

In a murder mystery, the killer needs a believable motive. In a news story, the facts must be accurate. Everything needs to add up and make sense. Your writing needs to adhere to the rules of logic. If it doesn't, it loses its believability.

Even in nonsensical writing or in speculative fiction, the writer must create a world in which there are rules. If the rules are accidentally broken, readers will notice, and they'll cry foul.

If a character has a broken leg, he can't go dancing. If the driver has a sports car, she couldn't have transported eight people. If the glove doesn't fit, then the suspect couldn't have worn it. Right?

On the other hand, some writers can deftly explain why a character with a broken leg would go dancing, how a driver can fit eight people in a sports car, and why the suspect had an undersized glove.

The Exercise

Below are a series of unlikely scenarios. Each scenario seems impossible. Fix the logic by coming up with plausible explanations.

- A loving mother is convicted of killing her only child. Why was she convicted? Because she confessed. Friends, family, everyone in the community insists she's lying. There's no way she could have done such a thing, but she says she did.

- A young man has everything going for him: a cushy, high-paying job, a beautiful young wife, a child on the way, and a large, lovely home. Things couldn't be better. He's perfectly sane and happy, but for some reason, he gives up everything and runs away.

- There's a girl who can't see anything without her glasses. She's not a candidate for surgery, and her particular condition prevents her from being able to wear contact lenses. She has to wear her glasses at all times; otherwise she can't see. The only time she takes them off is when she's sleeping. Her mother comes into the girl's room and finds her reading a book—without her glasses.

These are the kinds of issues that arise in stories all the time. If you can't come up with a good explanation for the scenarios in your story, you need to find another scenario.

In some cases, these unbelievable situations turn out to be excellent plot twists, and the writer surprises us by explaining how something that seemed impossible actually did happen.

Tips: Whatever you do, don't take the easy way out. The girl who was reading without her glasses was not healed by the magic eye fairy. The young man who ran away from his life did not go insane. Work at finding plausible, reasonable explanations. Make the reader say, "Aha!"

Variations: Instead of coming up with plausible explanations for the scenarios above, develop a few impossible scenarios of your own. See if you can explain them.

Applications: This exercise reminds you that while your readers will suspend disbelief to enjoy your story, you still have a responsibility to make the details as believable as possible. Everything in your writing needs to make sense. Readers love it when strange things happen, as long as a logical explanation follows.

9.8 Solutions

The most effective pieces of writing present a problem and a solution. It doesn't matter if you're writing a story or sales copy. Problem solving is almost always the core element in writing, the hub around which everything else revolves.

In a story, the problem is the protagonist's primary concern, the issue he or she wants to resolve above all else. In a romance, the problem involves relationship issues: the main character is lonely, and she wants to find somebody to love. In a murder mystery, the problem is finding the culprit. Some stories have multiple problems; others focus on a single problem.

In advertising and marketing, good sales copy also focuses on a problem. It compels would-be customers by saying, "You have a problem and our products and services will solve it!" Tired of paying high rates? Want to feel better and look sexier? Need a new car? You've got problems. We've got solutions!

There are two ways to develop problems and solutions in a piece of writing. You can start with the solution, or you can start with the problem. In copywriting, we often start with a solution (a product or service). We have to work backward, figure out how this product or service solves customers' problems, and then explain to the customers how the products or services make their lives better (*you'll save tons of money, look fantastic, and feel great!*).

In fiction writing, we often come up with a problem first, just like in real life. The character is in danger—how does he save himself? The most intriguing problems in fiction seem unsolvable at first. And the cleverest storytellers can get their characters out of the most impossible situations.

Problems and solutions are also integral to nonfiction writing. In nonfiction, all the problems and solutions are provided for you, because everything already happened. However, the writer must explain what happened in a manner that is compelling and builds tension. In her memoir, *Eat, Pray, Love*, Elizabeth Gilbert shares the story of how she was emotionally and spiritually lost. She effectively built a narrative that takes readers on a one-year journey through which she finds herself again. In other words, the nonfiction memoir demonstrates how someone solved a real-life problem; it achieves this through narrative.

The Exercise

Choose one of the following problem-solution exercises:

- Choose a product on the market (it could be your own book or website) and write a short piece of copy explaining how this product solves a problem. Write a piece that is about 250 words and make it convincing. Focus on the customer's problem and make the solution (your product) enticing.

- Think of a fictional problem. Put an obstacle in front of your character (maybe the car breaks down in the middle of nowhere while your character is taking a passenger to the hospital for an emergency), and then come up with a believable solution. Write a short scene that presents the problem and the solution.

- Finally, think of a problem you've experienced or witnessed in real life. Maybe your computer crashed the night before a big essay was due. Perhaps you ran out of toilet paper at a bad time. A problem can be serious or funny, life-threatening or a minor inconvenience. Write a short personal essay (750–1000 words) telling the story of a problem you faced.

Tips: Avoid solving the problems too easily or without a lot of effort on the character's part. If a rich kid runs out of money, a trust fund is not the answer. If a car breaks down, a tow truck should not conveniently drive by right at that moment.

Variations: Instead of choosing one of the problem-solution exercises above, write short pieces about all three, or make a list of problems and solutions that you could use in a writing project.

Applications: If you have your own website, you might use this exercise to write a page pitching your work to the public. If you are working on a novel or a story, use it to create a problem-solution scene in your project.

9.9 Big Themes, Little Scenes

In writing, we often deal with the big things in life: good and evil, faith and science, redemption and sacrifice, birth and death.

Many writers and artists have a specific intent to address big philosophical and ethical issues in their work. Some want to make a statement about culture; others want to explore the question of what it means to be human.

Consider a piece of writing that is concerned with death and the big question: *What happens when we die?* Some people believe there is an afterlife, some believe there is nothing, and some just don't know. In our writing, we might explore the question by showing characters dying and then depicting our own ideas about the afterlife, or we might leave the question open. Instead of answering the question, we encourage readers to think about it and come up with their own answers.

Through the microcosm of a scene in a story or an image in a poem, a writer can grapple with issues and questions that philosophers spend hours, months, and even years contemplating.

The Exercise

Write a short scene dealing with a philosophical theme or issue. Your scene can be fictional, or it can come from real life (your own life, someone else's, or even from a news story or documentary). Start with a basic philosophical question (see exercise 9.1 for some ideas). Then figure out how to turn it into a scene in which the philosophical question is explored through dialogue and action.

Tips: This exercise may require some hard thinking. How do you create a scene in which you take a broad concept and demonstrate it through story? The best thematic material doesn't answer the philosophical questions that it raises (that would be preachy); instead, it makes the audience think and come up with their own answers.

Variations: Instead of writing a full scene, you can write a short outline for a scene, chapter, or story. You can also integrate this exercise into a project you are working on.

Applications: In storytelling, real or fictional, big themes tend to resonate well, especially with smart audiences who appreciate art that makes them think, question, and see the world in new ways. Thought-provoking literature is far more celebrated than literature that is preachy or dogmatic.

9.10 Politics and Religion

Today, politics and religion are so commercialized, sometimes it's difficult to sift through all the talking points and identify the core philosophical ideals upon which political and religious beliefs are based. Politics and religion concern themselves with some very, very big questions: Who should get what? What rights do we, as a people, have? How do we remove threats from our society, and what constitutes a threat? When do we help other people? How? What's fair?

You will inevitably run up against these issues in your writing. Even if you have no intention of bringing your political and religious beliefs into your work, it will probably happen eventually.

What happens when you're writing about someone whose religious or political beliefs differ from your own? Are you only going to write about people who are like you? Are all of your characters going to think exactly the same way you do?

That could get pretty boring. And it's not realistic. We're living in an increasingly diverse and interconnected world. It's getting harder and harder for people to cordon themselves off from other cultures and ideologies.

The Exercise

Invent a character who is your opposite in terms of spiritual beliefs and political convictions. However, (here's the catch), the character cannot be a villain. Write a scene in which the character demonstrates his or her beliefs through action.

Tips: Some writers struggle with the concept of making characters (especially "good" characters) behave in ways that the writer thinks are immoral. Vegetarians may not want to work with characters who hunt, eat meat, or work as butchers. If the story calls for a butcher, the worst thing a vegetarian can do is create a special storyline in which that butcher has some experience that causes him to become a vegetarian. He's a butcher! Leave him that way (unless the story's main theme is conversion to vegetarianism). Don't use this exercise or concept as a tool for preaching through fiction. Focus on telling a good story. The best fiction doesn't make moral commentary every step of the way.

Variations: Instead of developing a fictional character, write about a real person. Find someone whose beliefs are completely opposite your own. Create a list of philosophical questions about religion and politics, and conduct an interview with this person. Go for deep, probing questions, and do not load them with your own feelings or thoughts. Do not challenge the person you're interviewing or engage in debate or argument. Your job is to ask questions and record the answers. When the interview is complete, write a summary about what you learned.

Applications: As a fiction writer, you have to be able to put yourself in other people's shoes. Mystery writers aren't killers, but they have to write characters who are. You can model all your characters after yourself, but they will come across as generic. Push yourself to explore people who are different from you.

Chapter 10: Article Writing and Blogging

Addressing an audience and building a platform

10.1 Titles and Headlines

A title or headline is the first point of contact that a reader will have with your writing. It's your introduction, a chance to entice and intrigue readers so they want to buy your book or read your article. An effective title piques a reader's curiosity and provides some idea of what the piece is about.

Some authors use titles as part of their brand. Sue Grafton is working her way through the alphabet with her Kinsey Millhone series (*A is for Alibi, B is for Burglar*, etc.). Many romance novelists use words like *kiss, love,* or *dance* in their titles. In the sci-fi realm, anything associated with space is fair game: *galaxy, universe, Mars,* and *stars.* And a well placed mythological term, such as *dragon* or *wizard*, clearly marks a fantasy novel.

In addition to book titles, many authors have a separate title for a series. This allows the author to use two different titles on a single piece of work. New readers will be drawn in by the book title, and existing fans will gravitate toward the series title.

In poetry, titles can be more abstract. A poem's title may seem irrelevant to the poem. Many poets take a word or phrase from the poem and use it as a title. Others will use a title that functions as part of the poem. The best poem titles evoke an image and give the reader an indication of what the poem will feel like.

Magazines use headlines prominently displayed on the front cover to entice customers. Newspapers use them to draw readers into a story, and bloggers, as many of you know, use headlines to generate buzz, links, and tweets.

The Exercise

Choose one of your writing projects or ideas and make a list of possible titles. Don't run off a quick list. Take some time to contemplate each title. Consider how it will resonate with readers and the impact it will have your project's success. Make sure the titles and headlines you write represent the piece accurately. Avoid words and phrases that are misleading.

Tips: Look to some successful works by authors you admire to get ideas for titles. Peruse magazines, newspapers, and blogs for headline ideas.

Variations: If you don't have any writing projects that need titles, then make a list of titles from some of your favorite books, magazines, movies, TV shows, articles, and poems. Develop alternative titles for these pieces.

Applications: Every piece of writing has to be titled, and a title or headline is essential in selling the piece to its audience. Developing catchy, intriguing titles is an essential writing skill.

10.2 How-to Articles

In the old days, if you wanted to learn how to do something, you had to go through a lot of effort. You went to the library and checked out a book. You became an apprentice or took an entry-level job so you could learn the basics. You took classes. You started from scratch.

These days, instructions for everything imaginable are available on the Internet, and most of them are free. You can learn how to ride a bike, build a house, and start a business with a few quick clicks.

It's pretty cool that we now have free and open access to so much knowledge. What's even cooler is that someone has to write all those how-to articles.

How-to pieces and step-by-step instruction guides are among the most popular articles found in magazines and on the web. Readers gravitate toward these types of articles, because there's a promise that they will learn something new and obtain something they want: "How to Get a Rockin' Body," "How to Save Thousands of Dollars with Tax Write-Offs," "How to Find the Love of Your Life."

People are on a perpetual quest for sex, love, health, money, and good looks. How-to articles promise to show them the path to fulfilling their desires.

Tutorials, on the other hand, show readers how to do a specific task. These step-by-step instructional articles take the reader through a process: "How to Change a Furnace Filter," "How to Self-Publish a Novel," "How to Organize Your Closet."

The Exercise

Write a how-to article or step-by-step tutorial. Start by picking something you know how to do. You can write a general how-to article or a detailed step-by-step piece. Choose something you know a lot about, and write a clear, polished piece.

Tips: We tend to assume all the things we know how to do are common knowledge. Yet there are things you know how to do that your coworkers, friends, and family don't know how to do.

If you have a blog or website, then write something that relates to your site's topic so you can publish it when it's done.

Variations: Write a list of potential how-to articles about things you know how to do, then go online and search for publications that might accept your article as a submission.

Applications: How-to articles are popular in magazines and on blogs. If you have a fresh idea that will entice readers, you might be able to get it published (you might even get paid for it). You can also use your how-to article on your own blog or as a guest blog post.

10.3 List Articles

List articles are just as popular as how-to articles. They are appealing because they tend to be clear and well organized. Expectations are set as soon as the reader sees the title. For example, in a book titled *101 Creative Writing Exercises*, you expect that inside that book, you'll find 101 creative writing exercises. You know what you're going to get, and you know how much of it you're going to get. These articles and books seem like a smart investment, so readers embrace them.

Lists can be instructional in nature. You might write a list article on "Ten Ways to Improve Your Writing." They can also be inspirational: "Twelve Habits of Happy People." Lists can be trivial: "The Twenty Best Movies of the Twentieth Century." They can be promotional: "The Fifteen Best Websites for Storytellers."

There are plenty of opportunities for writing list articles about any subjects that interest you.

The Exercise

Write a list article. Choose a topic that you're passionate about or that you are knowledgeable about.

Tips: Start your article with an introduction. It should be one to three paragraphs. Format your list using numbers or bullets. Write one sentence or a short paragraph for each list item explaining why its inclusion on the list is warranted. Conclude your article with a one-paragraph summary.

Variations: You can combine a how-to article and a list article: "Ten Steps to Writing a Novel." These articles include lists but are also instructional in nature.

Applications: List articles are extremely popular in magazines and on blogs. If you write a good piece, you can probably get it published.

10.4 Everyone's a Critic (Book Review)

We've all read books we've loved, seen movies we hated, and then spread the word: *You've got to see this show! Wait till it's out on DVD. You want to know? Buy the book.*

There's a big difference between saying something is good or bad and explaining why it's good or bad. There are reasons you love one book and can't get past the first chapter in another. Maybe you didn't like one story because the writing was too obscure, or the characters had no personality. In another story, the plot is packed with puzzles, and the characters feel like friends. What keeps you interested in a piece of writing, and what turns you off?

A well-written review is thoughtful. It looks for the good and the bad and does more than spout the author's opinion. It analyzes the work and determines what's working and what's not working.

Writing book reviews forces you to evaluate a work carefully. Too often, we close a book or walk away from a movie with our thumbs up or down without trying to understand why.

The Exercise

Choose a book you've read and write a detailed review of it. Your piece should start with what you liked about the book and should also list areas where the work was flawed. Address the piece to potential readers.

Tips: Do not write a synopsis or retell the story; your job is to explain to the audience why they should (or shouldn't) read the book, without including spoilers. Finally, if you didn't like the book, add a statement about who might like it. If you loved it, add a comment about what type of audience might not enjoy or appreciate it.

Variations: You can also do this exercise for a movie, play, or TV show.

Applications: If you become a published author, your work will inevitably get critiqued and reviewed. Being on the other side of a review is good practice. Also, by critiquing and reviewing other artists' work, you'll see your own work from a fresh perspective. Many writers make a living (or some income) writing reviews. And many readers (and writers) post reviews on the web to help others make better decisions about what to read and watch.

10.5 Critiques

Critiques are similar to reviews except they are for writers rather than potential readers; a critique explains what's working and not working to the author in an effort to help a fellow writer improve his or her work.

In a critique, you start by listing the strengths of the piece. Then, you list the areas that could be improved. Don't try to change the piece into what you would have done as a writer; take it for what it is.

Finally, a proper critique discusses the work, not the person who created it. Your objective is to use positive, supportive language framed in the context of how the piece could be improved.

The Exercise

Choose a piece of writing and compose a critique. You can use a book, short story, poem, article, or blog post. You will address the critique to the author, but you will not send it to the author. Also, your critique will discuss the work, not the person who created it.

The length of your critique will depend on how long the piece of writing is and how deeply you evaluate it.

Tips: You should also look for spelling, grammar, and punctuation mistakes, as well as typographical errors.

Variations: You can also do this exercise using a movie, a TV show, or any kind of story or art medium.

Applications: This exercise teaches you to look at a piece of writing objectively and assess it thoughtfully in an effort to consider how it might be improved. Writing critiques will help you build skills that will benefit your own writing projects.

10.6 The Weekly Column

There was a time when a writer could dream about landing a weekly column with a newspaper. If you got a spot at a big paper, money was good. You could make a living writing one column per week.

These days, weekly columns are on the endangered species list. More and more magazines and newspapers are going digital. Some of them easily find writers who are willing to work for free. As we all know, working for free might be good experience, and it never hurts to get a byline, but it sure doesn't put food on the table.

Highly skilled writers tend to demand some kind of compensation for their work, so the quality of columns has suffered considerably. There are still good ones out there, but we have to look harder to find them.

Blogs swept in and gave writers their own publishing platforms. However, blogs don't come with a readership (or a paycheck). If you want to make money or build an audience with your blog, you have to do more than write a post every week. You have to promote and market your site. It's a lot of work, but many writers find that there's a nice payoff, eventually.

There are many types of blogs. For the purpose of this exercise, we'll look at blogs that are similar to newspaper columns. Here's how it works: Every week, the writer shares a story along with his or her thoughts or opinions about it. In some cases, columns are personal. The show *Sex and the City* featured a columnist who wrote weekly pieces about her romantic escapades in New York City. Each week, she shared her personal story and waxed philosophical on love, romance, and friendship. Other topical columns might address politics, religion, food, or entertainment. Columns are written from a personal perspective; over time, the audience comes to know the columnist.

The Exercise

Start by choosing a theme or topic for your column, and then, write your first column. Make sure you tell a story, address an issue, and weave your personal thoughts and experiences through the piece.

Tips: Columns are a bit like reflective journaling or personal essays in that they're very much about the columnist's own ideas, attitudes, and experiences regarding the subject matter. They are written in first person.

Variations: Instead of writing a column, write a proposal for a column. Include the focal subject matter, explain why you're qualified to write about this issue, and list some personal experiences you've had related to the topic. Make sure you identify an audience for your column.

Applications: This is a great exercise if you're thinking about launching a blog (or if you already have one). Many of today's bloggers write column-style posts. While columnist jobs are on the decline, they are still out there; there's also a good chance that as the web matures, this style of writing (and paid gigs) will become more commonplace.

10.7 Wanna Be a Blogger?

Blogs are here, and they're here to stay. In early 2012, Blogpulse identified over 182,397,015 blogs on the web with over eighty thousand new blogs launching every day.

If you're planning on being a writer, either professionally or as a hobby, then you are living in the right era. Blogs have freed writers in numerous ways. They provide a relatively easy-to-use platform for self-publishing and building a readership. They also make it easy to find, connect, and network with other writers.

The blogging community is enormous. In fact, it's more like a universe. In the greater blog universe, there are tons of galaxies—groups of blogs that revolve around specific topics and ideas. There are hobby blogs, fan blogs, professional blogs, news and information blogs. You can find blogs about movies, TV shows, careers, art, philosophy, science, pets, sports, and literature—if people are interested in it, then there's a blog about it.

Some blogs don't have a topic at all; bloggers simply write and publish their personal journals.

While many technophiles have leveraged blogging as a route to professional success, few professionals have benefitted from blogs as much as writers. Fifty years ago, a writer had to rely on literary agents, professional marketers, PR firms, publishing houses, and bookstores. Today, with a little enterprise, a writer can use a blog to connect with other writers, build a readership, and promote and sell their work.

The Exercise

Write a short business plan for your author's blog. Begin by choosing the niche or subject you'll write about. Include the following details:

- Write a short description of your blog (try to keep it to fewer than one hundred words).

- State the blog's purpose or mission.

- Identify the audience for your blog.

- Make a list of ten titles for future blog posts.

- Give your blog a name.

- Write a paragraph explaining why you're qualified to write on this subject.

Tips: If you're unfamiliar with blogs, then do a little research before tackling this exercise. Peruse at least ten blogs. Try to explore a mix of topics. Look for a few different author blogs, a few blogs about writing, and a few that are not writing-related. Think about your other hobbies and interests, and then look for blogs in those niches.

Variations: If you already have a blog, use this exercise as an opportunity to improve it. Make sure your blog has an "About" page or a "Bio." Identify your blog's core purpose and readership. Create an editorial calendar or stockpile a few extra posts.

Applications: If you plan on being a professional writer, you will most definitely need a blog. Start planning now!

10.8 The Op-Ed

In traditional journalism, an editorial is an opinion piece written by a magazine or newspaper's editor or some other member of the editorial staff. An op-ed (which is an abbreviation of *opposite the editorial page*) is an opinion piece by a named writer who is not a staff member.

Some op-eds are written by regular contributors. These are writers who have established a relationship with the publication. Others are written by well-known experts or professionals in a particular field, which is usually related to the subject of the piece. The op-ed provides a platform where people (ordinary people, experts, or celebrities) can share their opinions on a given subject or issue.

An op-ed can function as a career booster. Politicians, for example, often write op-eds. This gives them a platform to state their positions on various issues and an opportunity to win voters. It's also a platform where people can review or critique art, events, and cultural movements. Some publications publish op-eds in which a writer responds to an article or editorial that appeared in an earlier issue.

Op-eds can deal with world issues and controversies, or they can deal with subjects of a more personal nature. For example, op-eds often remark on the state of the nation, wars, politics, scandals, and high-profile court cases. However, they can also examine issues surrounding child rearing, healthy (or unhealthy) living, and a host of other community and personal issues.

The Exercise

Write an op-ed about an issue or problem that concerns you. Before you begin, identify a target publication and audience.

Tips: In an op-ed, you'll make a personal argument for or against something that is of current interest to the readership of the target publication.

Variations: Read three to five op-ed pieces. Note your observations about the writers' voices, tones, and positions, as well as the arguments they use to back up their claims. Are the pieces emotional, rational, or a balance of both?

Applications: One way to start getting published is to write and submit op-eds to your local paper. You can also write letters to the editor.

10.9 You're the Expert

You know a little bit about a lot of things, but there are a few things you know a lot about. And knowledge is power.

One of the traditional duties of a writer is to collect and redistribute knowledge and information. After all, writers are responsible for textbooks, instruction manuals, and reference collections, like encyclopedias.

The Internet has made this type of material more accessible than ever before. People no longer have to trudge down to the library or buy expensive sets of encyclopedias, which quickly become outdated, to research and learn. They just log in and look it up.

The Exercise

Choose something you know a lot about. In fact, choose the one thing you know the most about. It could be a subject you studied in school. It could be a video game you've played for countless hours. It could be something simple, like the parts of speech in the English language, or it could be something complicated, like how photosynthesis works. Write an informational article explaining this thing to a layperson—someone with zero experience or knowledge about the topic.

Tips: Assume your reader is ignorant about the subject. If you're doing a piece on photosynthesis, assume your reader doesn't know what carbon dioxide is. If you're doing a complex piece, break it down into simple steps and definitions.

Variations: If you'd rather not get into the nitty-gritty about your subject matter, write a statement explaining your own expertise. Why are you qualified to write about photosynthesis?

Applications: Many writers have built careers around writing about what they know best or what they can research and explain to readers.

10.10 Conducting Research

All good writers know the value and importance of conducting proper research. Research is necessary in every form and genre of writing, so it's essential for all writers to learn how to conduct credible research.

Even journal writers and memoirists find that they have to conduct research occasionally. Let's say you're writing in your journal about a concert you attended, but you can't remember the name of the opening band. You'll have to do a little research to find out who it was. In a memoir, research might involve conducting interviews with people who can help you remember the details of your own past.

Poets may need to research their subject matter, especially when they're writing a highly focused poem. If you're doing a sonnet on tigers, you might read up on the species so you have plenty of material to work with.

The Exercise

Pick a subject that you know a bit about but in which you are not thoroughly knowledgeable. Spend an hour or two conducting research about your subject, and then write a short piece about it. You can write a story, poem, or article.

Tips: If you decide to write a nonfiction piece, make sure you cite the sources from which you gathered information. You don't have to spend weeks poring over books and journals, but try to learn a few facts that you can use. Take notes and make sure you write down the names (titles and authors) of the works you referenced.

Variations: You can also apply this exercise to one of your current writing projects. If you're working on a novel in which one of your characters is an astronaut, and you know nothing about astronauts, you can interview one, watch a documentary about astronauts and space travel, or read a book or article on the lifestyle of astronauts. Then write a character sketch based on your research.

Applications: Research is integral to good writing. Readers have sharp eyes and will catch you if the facts aren't correct. As a writer, you should always be aware of what you know and what you don't know. You should also learn how to gather the information you need for any given project.

Chapter 11: Creativity

Gathering ideas and looking for inspiration

11.1 Maps and Legends

In fiction, setting is one of the four key elements (along with character, plot, and theme). It is essential for readers to have a sense of place, and in order for that to happen, the writer must have a deep understanding of a story's setting.

In a complex piece of writing that covers a lot of geographic ground, maps can help a writer maintain a story's geography. With modern technology, rendering a map for a piece of writing is easier than ever.

Exploring maps and making your own maps are excellent exercises in creative thinking. Maps exist for a wide variety of physical places: worlds, nations, neighborhoods, underground tunnel systems, weather systems, and the stars. Maps show you new ways to look at the world of your writing, allowing you to imagine how place might influence events.

What if you're writing about a place that doesn't exist? The answer is simple: you make your own map.

The Exercise

Choose a piece of writing that you're working on, and render a map that shows where events unfold. You might need a map of the world, or you may need a simple blueprint of a house. You can search for maps online, print them out, and then add symbols (dots, stars, and lines) representing significant locations and movements from your piece of writing. Make sure you include a legend that explains the symbols and what they mean. If you have made up your own place for a story, then create a map from scratch.

Tips: You can print a map, trace it, and then fill it with various elements from your story. Be creative. Use color coding for different characters. Use symbols for the most significant events. Use lines to show travel routes. Remember, a map is merely a drawn representation of a place. You can map anything from a room or a garden to an ocean or a galaxy.

Variations: If you don't have an adequate piece of writing to use for this exercise, then map a story from a favorite book.

Applications: Some books include maps to help readers visualize setting. Articles and essays often include maps. This exercise encourages you to think in spatial terms, and it inspires deeper creativity in your writing by engaging in a nonwriting activity that informs your written work.

11.2 The Name Game

> What's in a name? That which we call a rose
> By any other name would smell as sweet;

—from *Romeo and Juliet* by William Shakespeare

This famous quote from Shakespeare suggests that a name is meaningless, that meaning exists only in the thing the name represents. The word *rose* is unimportant. The scent of the rose is what matters.

Names are words used to represent people, places, and things. They are words. And words, by definition, have meaning.

What if Luke Skywalker's name had been Joe Smith? Would we fall in love with a wizard named Harry Johnson instead of Harry Potter? Does Suellen O'Hara's name have the same resonance as her sister's (Scarlett O'Hara)? How would we feel about an adventuring archeologist named Lenny Jones rather than Indiana Jones?

And names are not limited to characters. What if Neverland was just some crazy island without a name? What if New York was called Aberdine? What if a computer was called a robrain? What if our planet was called Dearth?

Names matter.

The Exercise

Take a break from your writing projects and create a repository of names. For this exercise, come up with a minimum of twenty-five names. You can name characters, places, gadgets and devices, companies, planets, species, and anything else that you can think of.

Tips: Start a name file or name notebook where you can jot down your ideas for names along with a few notes. Use baby-name dictionaries to look up the meanings of names, and use names that lend deeper meaning to your writing. You can also search online for name generators, which are especially useful in the science fiction and fantasy genres.

Variations: Write a list of your twenty-five favorite names from literature and pop culture. Try to come up with a mix of names, real and imagined. Include names for people, places, and things.

Applications: In your creative work, you will undoubtedly need to name various entities. This is good practice.

11.3 The Taste Test

Food. It is essential for survival. We need it for nourishment, but we've also come to enjoy our food. We appreciate its taste and celebrate chefs who prepare delightful dishes. Food is art that melts on the tongue.

As writers, we appreciate that food is uniquely capable of triggering all five senses simultaneously. We smell chocolate chip cookies baking in the oven. We savor the rich, sweet taste as they crumble and melt in our mouths. Then we gulp a cold splash of milk to wash it all down.

Food can function as many things in a piece of writing. It can be the object of a quest in a story where characters are trying to survive. It can provide sensory cues in a poem about a grandmother's kitchen. Food can be a metaphor or a symbol, or it can be the subject matter in pieces of nonfiction: restaurant reviews, recipes, cookbooks, and cooking-show scripts.

The Exercise

For this exercise, you will dine and write about it in succulent detail. Your task is to set out in search of food. Hot and spicy, sweet and sour, rich, light, healthy, or artery clogging, sit down and enjoy a delightful meal. Make your own meal or visit your favorite restaurant. After your dining experience, figure out a way to work the meal into a piece of writing. You can create a scene in which your characters enjoy a similar meal, or you can write a personal essay about your dining experience.

Tips: Take notes while you're eating. Use all five senses to describe your experience.

Variations: Make a list of words and phrases to describe your dining experience. Write out your favorite recipe, or write a review of your favorite restaurant or food product.

Applications: Food writing finds its way into every form and genre. If you are a foodie—or just someone who appreciates good old-fashioned home cooking—you'll find that writing about food makes your work more visceral. If you've ever read about food and found that it made your mouth water, you have experienced this firsthand. And if you're really into it, you can always become a food writer.

More importantly, this exercise shows you how to experience life first and write about it later.

11.4 It's Your Holiday

Most of us take holidays for granted. Some holidays have been reduced to massive spending, reckless gifting, and obnoxious amounts of eating. Others are a day off, time to catch up on errands, clean the house, or spend a day luxuriating at the beach.

Holidays are steeped in meaning. Each one is based on something deemed important enough to warrant a day of recognition and celebration. While holidays vary across cultures, they are present everywhere and throughout history.

A holiday starts out as a significant event, one that has an impact on a culture's history. Some holidays celebrate the life, birth, or death of groups or individuals who have changed the world for the better. Customs that reflect the meaning of a holiday evolve: decorations, food, attire, rituals, and art come together to mark the day.

Considering all the great people who have lived and died and all the significant events that have shaped our world, it's actually surprising that we have so few holidays.

The Exercise

Create a brand new holiday. Start with something or someone you believe warrants annual recognition on a national or global scale. You can also build holidays around natural events like solstices and equinoxes.

Tips: Before you start this exercise, choose one holiday and do a little research to learn about its origin and how it has evolved.

Consider the following as you develop your holiday:

- What does this holiday celebrate or honor?

- When is the holiday, and how long does it last?

- How do people gather? In public spaces? In homes?

- Do people dress formally or casually? In costume?

- What foods are traditionally served? Do people fast?

- What rituals are observed?

- How is art incorporated? Music, dance, stories, poems, and performances are integral to most holidays.

Variations: Change one of the holidays we already celebrate. Can you improve upon it? Can you bring it back to its roots or make it more meaningful?

Applications: Writers benefit from having a broad understanding of culture, and holidays are a key component of any culture. Holidays have inspired poetry, songs, and stories. If you write speculative fiction, you might even find a home for your newly invented holiday.

11.5 What's Your Superpower?

What if you could fly or make yourself invisible? What if you could heal with a touch or read minds? Superpowers like these are the stuff of science fiction.

Savants and prodigies are superheroes in their own rights, and they exist in the real world.

A prodigy is someone (often a young child) with an extraordinary talent or ability: a twelve-year-old college graduate or a fifteen-year-old Nobel Prize contender.

A savant is someone who is an expert, whereas someone with savant syndrome (savantism) is a person with a developmental disability who also has superhuman expertise, ability, or brilliance in a particular area.

The Exercise

Create a new superpower. Write a clear description of it, and make sure you include the following:

- Explain how the superpower is obtained.

- Invent a weakness (like Superman's kryptonite) that can counteract that superpower.

- Describe how someone might use this superpower for good or evil.

If you're so inclined, create a character who possesses this power and write a story about it.

Tips: Stay away from overdone powers like flight, invisibility, and super strength. Avoid psychic powers like telepathy and telekinesis. Think up something fresh: for example, someone who can breathe in outer space.

Variations: If science fiction isn't your thing or if you're tired of superheroes, then come up with a character who is a prodigy or who has savantism.

Applications: Many stories, both real and fictional, feature ordinary people in extraordinary circumstances. In this exercise, you flip convention on its head and create a character who is extraordinary. How does an extraordinary person fit into the ordinary world?

11.6 Observation Station

You might think that your creative ideas spontaneously erupt from your mind. In a sense, that's true, but these ideas also manifest from all of the observations you've made and experiences you've had.

Every moment is an opportunity to bear witness. Each experience you have is a chance to examine the human condition. Every second of life is a seed from which creative ideas can grow.

As creative people, it's essential for us to understand inspiration and to avoid blaming pseudoconditions like writer's block when we don't feel like doing our work. Writer's block is easily cured once you understand how to cultivate ideas from everyday life.

The Exercise

This exercise asks you to put your writing aside and explore the world in search of inspiration. Your task is to get up and get out, visit a public space, and note your observations. Monitor the people at a mall. Could they become characters in your story? Examine the environment in a national park. Could it become the subject of your next poem? When you've finished recording your observations, return to your writing space and look for ways you can use your observations in your writing.

Tips: Be on the lookout for the unusual: someone wearing odd clothing, a misshapen tree, and unique buildings. Engage all of your senses. Make it a point to note the sights, sounds, smells, and textures. If edibles are present, make notes about the tastes. Use vivid, sensuous language to describe your observations in your notebook.

Variations: If you can't get out of the house or the office, then try to take a new angle on your own familiar habitats. What would your home or workplace look like to an outside observer? Write a descriptive essay about it.

Applications: The better we understand the creative process and the steps involved in generating ideas, the better we can maintain our creativity and cultivate creative thinking.

11.7 *The Story of Music*

We writers often look to the obvious for inspiration. We pore over news articles and reflect on our own experiences. We ponder our favorite stories and think about how they can inform our work. We can also look to other art forms to inspire and guide our creativity.

Song lyrics often tell a story. What about the music itself? The crescendo of a string section fills a listener with tension. The loud boom of a base drum evokes a sense of impending doom, while the sharp tap of a snare renders a sense of purpose.

Each movement, instrument, melody, and rhythm has the potential to take you deep inside your own imagination where stories are waiting to be discovered.

The Exercise

Listen to a piece of instrumental music. Try to find or use a piece that resonates with you, a piece you love. Sit or lie still as you listen to it once, letting yourself become one with the music. Then listen to it a second time, and as you listen, write down the images that fill your head. Can you turn these into stories or poems? Think about how this music and the way it affects you can be used to inspire your next writing project.

Tips: For your first listen, turn the lights low, and sit back or lie down in a comfortable position. Use headphones for an optimal auditory experience. If you can't use headphones, set the volume comfortably loud. Get lost in the music. The second time you listen, as you write down your notes, feel free to use doodles and drawings to render what the music inspired you to imagine. Some musical genres you might explore include classical, world, and jazz, as well as movie soundtracks and TV scores.

Variations: You can, of course, cull inspiration from lyrical pieces of music. Choose a song with lyrics and let the words and music inspire writing ideas, or spend some time creating playlists that you can listen to during your writing sessions.

Applications: Learning how the arts inform one another is extremely helpful in creative work. This exercise shows you how to look beyond the obvious for sources of inspiration.

11.8 Angles

There is a parable, which originated in India and has crossed over to many other cultures, about six blind men and an elephant, which originated in India and has crossed over to many other cultures.

The short story is that six blind men are asked to explain what an elephant looks like. Each man touches one part of the elephant, and then they all offer different descriptions of the same animal. They are all correct, although their descriptions vary. However, they are also incorrect, since their limited experiences of the elephant only allowed each of them to describe one small part of the greater whole.

This story has been used to illustrate a range of truths and fallacies in philosophy. For our purposes, it serves to remind us that our perception of the world is highly dependent upon our particular perspective.

The Exercise

Write a description of something, looking at it from a new angle. You will write a clear, concise description from an unfamiliar perspective.

Tips: Below are some ideas to help you get started:

- You usually view your home from the inside or from your backyard or driveway. Go outside and view your house from a new angle. What do you see?

- In your daily activities, you follow many of the same routes to work, stores, and restaurants. Take a different route. How does it change the experience?

- Look around at the many objects that surround you. We generally view dishes, cups, and bowls right side up. We look at things from the front. Choose an object and turn it around or upside down. What do you see?

- What if you were from another country? What if you spoke another language? How does your culture look to someone from the outside? How would our world look to an alien?

Variations: As an alternative, pretend you are either an alien from a faraway planet or a member of a tribe that is technologically primitive. Choose an object, gadget, or device, and come up with ideas for what it might be used for. Here's an example: a tribesman finds a glass soda bottle, blows into it, and determines that it is a musical instrument.

Applications: Creativity is at its peak when you are looking at the world from a fresh perspective. You can find new ways of looking at ordinary things by simply moving to a new position or regarding an object as an unknown entity.

11.9 A World of Color

The best writing is full of life and color. Although text is usually printed or displayed in black and white, we have to make our writing descriptive enough to fill readers' heads with vivid, colorful images.

Working with color is a great way to promote creative thinking. Normally, writers work with words and concepts. Stepping away from our grayscale documents and into a world of color triggers creative ideas and serves as a reminder to infuse our work with imagery.

With print technology becoming cheaper, and with the many options available on word processing software, it's easier than ever for writers to literally bring color to their words. But making text purple or green often backfires. It tells readers that the writing is not colorful enough and needs some design help. In fact, colored text often comes across as gimmicky. Try to avoid it.

The Exercise

For this exercise, you will put all your writing aside and work strictly with color. You can use crayons, markers, or paints. You can cut out pieces of colored paper. Do not try to render a scene or specific image. Instead, use chunks of color in abstract shapes to create a color composition.

Tips: Vary your colors and shapes. Try mixing and layering your colors. Use simple but varied shapes: squares, circles, ovals, triangles, and odd or unusual abstract shapes.

Variations: If you have a hard time working in the abstract, feel free to use basic images as a basis for your composition: trees, houses, stars, boxes, etc. Try to create a scene.

Applications: Creativity sometimes needs to come from outside our craft. Writers can get so caught up in words that our ideas becomes stale or stagnant. This exercise forces us out of the world of black-and-white words and into a more colorful universe.

11.10 The Incubator

Many creative professionals and hobbyists have found that creative ideas need time to incubate. In other words, you don't start working on an idea as soon as it occurs to you. You mull it over, give it some time to take root, and wait for it to mature a little before you start executing it.

Some of us are full of ideas, and some of us spend a lot of time waiting or searching for ideas. In either case, the trick is to figure out which ideas are worth pursuing. Sometimes, an idea that seems brilliant at first turns out to be a big flop, whereas a mediocre idea evolves into a masterpiece.

How do you know which ideas are worth your time and energy? Let them marinate for a while. Experiment with the ones that seem most interesting. The ideas and concepts that haunt you are the ones to pursue. Those are the ones you should commit to.

The Exercise

For this exercise, you will create an incubator for your creative ideas. This is a special place where you store ideas and items that inspire you. Once you've created your incubator, you should rifle through it every week or every month, so your ideas stay fresh in your head. When you feel an idea is ready for production, pull it out and start developing it.

Your incubator can be a box, a jar, a folder on your computer, or a special notebook.

To get started, go through your notes and journals and try to find five to ten ideas you've had but never developed. These will be the first ideas you put in your incubator.

Tips: You may find that you need to organize your ideas. For a single novel idea, you might have several related ideas: characters, plots, and scenes. You might want to keep your poetry ideas separate from your fiction ideas. You can organize your incubator in any way that's comfortable for you. If you're using a box, you might want to use file folders or envelopes to organize things. If you're using a jar or basket, you might use colored papers for different projects or categories. In a special notebook, you can use page markers or divide the notebook into sections. In a computer folder, you can organize ideas with subfolders. Your incubator can hold notes, photos, and other images—anything that is related to your idea.

Variations: As you surf the web, you might come across items of interest or sites that contain information or images that you want to use for inspiration. Create a special bookmarks folder for these items.

Applications: Nothing's worse than losing a good idea. Make sure you put your ideas in the incubator as soon as they occur to you. That might mean wrenching yourself out of bed or pausing in the middle of dinner to jot down a note. But once you start storing your ideas and reviewing them regularly, you'll find that more and more ideas keep coming. Pretty soon, you'll have plenty of fodder for writing.

Chapter 12: Moving Forward with Your Writing

As your adventures in writing continue, there will be times when the sentences come effortlessly and times when you strain to squeeze out a word or two. You'll get frustrated as you work through draft after draft in an effort to polish your work for a reading audience.

If you submit your work to agents or editors, you can count on getting plenty of rejections before seeing your name in print. If you self-publish, you'll struggle to find your first readers, and you'll have to become an entrepreneur, managing everything from the editing to the cover art.

Writing requires a tremendous amount of patience and dedication. Just as athletes train and performers rehearse, writers must practice their craft. Each rejection slip brings you one step closer to getting published. And every crumpled-up draft that gets tossed in the recycle bin is a step toward reaching your full potential as a writer.

The writers who succeed are not the ones with the most talent or best mastery of the craft. They are the ones who refuse to give up.

Here are a few final tips to help you as you move forward with your creative writing:

1. Read. Curl up with a good novel, brush up on your nonfiction reading, flip through some poetry collections. Reading is the single best way to naturally acquire writing skills and inspiration. Read as much and as often as you can, and your writing will improve dramatically.

2. Write. In order to be a writer, you must write. Try to write every single day. Some days, you'll write several pages. Other days, you might squeeze out a paragraph. But you're writing, and that's all that matters. Even if you can only dedicate a few minutes to writing each day, it will become an ingrained habit.

3. Revise: proofread, edit, and polish. It's blatantly obvious when a piece of writing has not been properly polished. Typos, grammatical mistakes, and poorly written sentences will offend anyone who attempts to read your work. In other words, you'll turn readers off. Put your best work forward.

4. Brush up on grammar. It's rare for a piece of writing to be so amazing that readers are willing to ignore bad grammar. Many writers are lazy in this area, because learning grammar is a lot of work, and it's academic work rather than creative work. The good news is that once you learn the rules, they will be with you forever. Pick up a stylebook or grammar guide, and take time to look up anything you don't know.

5. Develop your skills. You will learn that some aspects of writing come easily to you (maybe you're great at dialogue), but other aspects are a challenge (your plots are full of holes). Once you accept your weaknesses, you can work on eliminating them through practice and study.

6. Find your process. Your process is the series of steps you take to complete a project. Experiment with different techniques and strategies from discovery writing to outlining, and find what works best for you.

7. Share your work and invite feedback. One of the quickest ways to improve your writing is through feedback. Get a well-read person to review your work and give it a critique. Embrace the feedback, even if it hurts, and then put it to work for you by ironing out all the wrinkles that your friendly reader found.

8. Collect tools and resources. Writers don't need much. For centuries, a pen and paper were the only tools required. Nowadays, we have computers, programs and apps, and a host of resources from books to blogs that help us become more productive, professional, and skilled.

9. Cultivate creativity. Have fun with your writing. Fill it with color or scale it back to a minimalist style. Try new words and off-the-wall images. Take breaks from writing to experiment with other art forms. Do creativity exercises. This will keep your creative juices flowing and help you see your own creative problems from new angles, so you can solve them and produce the best work possible.

9. Engage with the writing community. These days, there is no excuse for failing to connect with other writers. There are plenty of blogs, forums, and social networking sites that make it easy for writers to connect and forge relationships. Be supportive of other writers, and they will support you in return.

Make a conscious commitment to strive for better writing every day. And most importantly, keep writing.

Book Two
10 Core Practices for Better Writing

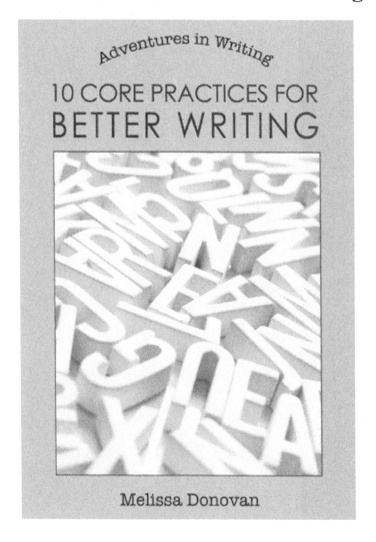

Introduction

"When I'm writing, I know I'm doing the thing I was born to do." - Anne Sexton

Words. They have the power to captivate the imagination, impart knowledge, express feelings, and share ideas. They are magical, and they are powerful.

A writer makes things out of words: sentences and paragraphs, essays and articles, books, poems, stories, and scripts. We use writing to create, communicate, share, and express ourselves. We use it to connect with people.

Writing is one of the most useful skills a person can possess. Think about how stories, speeches, films, and books have impacted society and culture, how they have shaped people's thoughts and beliefs, and you'll get an inkling of just how influential writing can be.

Everybody learns how to write. We go to school, learn our letters, practice reading, and eventually, we can put words on the page.

We aren't born writers; we become writers.

We all have to work at building and growing our writing abilities. Whether writing is a hobby or a career, if you want to be good at it, you have to make a commitment to it.

Good writing requires an extensive set of skills. We have to organize our thoughts and ideas, express them clearly, and compose sentences that are correct and make sense.

Great writing requires a whole lot more. An expert writer understands language, syntax, and context. A firm grasp on grammar and orthography is essential. A vast vocabulary, a talent for puns, and a knack for storytelling are all skills that benefit any writer.

There's a lot to learn, and in order to establish the skills that every successful writer needs, we must develop lifelong writing habits. We must live the writing life.

It won't happen overnight, and you might have to make some sacrifices, but by managing your time wisely and investing in yourself and your writing, you'll develop good habits and core practices that lead to better writing.

What This Book Does and Does Not Do

This book is for people who are ready to commit to producing better writing.

This is not a learn-how-to-write-overnight or write-a-best-selling-novel-in-thirty-days book. It won't fill your head with story ideas. It won't drill down into the nitty-gritty of grammar, spelling, and punctuation. This book won't tell you how to land an agent or get a publishing deal, nor will it walk you through the steps of self-publishing or marketing your writing. It's not a book about getting rich or famous.

This is the book you read before doing all that. It's for becoming the best writer you can be.

It's also not an all-encompassing book on better writing. There are thousands of things you can do to improve your writing—methods, practices, techniques, and styles that you can adopt. As you progress with your writing, you'll find some techniques and methods that work for you and some that don't.

The concepts covered in this book are beneficial for all writers. These are the core practices upon which you can build to make your writing good, then great. Think of the practices contained in this book as seeds; if you plant them, water them, and nourish them, they will flourish and you will continually grow as a writer. If you make the time and put in the effort to adopt these practices, your writing will blossom.

The core practices described in this book are habits that any serious writer who becomes adept at the craft develops over time. They're not exercises you can do once and be done with. These are habits that will be with you for as long as you write, which will hopefully be for the rest of your life.

How to Use This Book

It would be an impossible challenge to try and work all of these habits into your daily life immediately. You would become overwhelmed within a few days. Instead, work each practice into your schedule slowly.

I recommend reading through the entire book once. It's not a long book; you can probably get through it in a few days. Then go back and revisit chapter one. Each month, revisit another chapter. Focus that month on adopting the chapter's practice and making it a regular habit. Within a year, you'll have adopted a writer's lifestyle.

And that's exactly what this book is meant to do: help you live a writing life. It includes a comprehensive supply of information, tools, and resources that will allow you to continually and consistently develop your skills and talent.

Before you know it, your writing habits will be ingrained and you will be on a steady path to better writing.

Why I Wrote This Book

When I started my blog, *Writing Forward,* in 2007, I chose writing as the topic because I was passionate about writing and it's the thing I'm best at doing. I had no idea that the site would help so many writers, that teachers would use it in their classrooms, or that I'd end up coaching other writers. Other than writing something I'm personally proud of, helping other writers has been the most rewarding aspect of my career.

I wrote this book because I love working with other writers and helping them be the best writers they can be. I especially love helping young, new, and beginning writers. To see writers develop, to see their work improve with time and effort, and to contribute to their development is incredibly fulfilling.

What separates the great writers from the mediocre ones is not luck or talent. It's grit and determination and a lot of hard work. If you want to write well, put in the time, and eventually you'll become a master.

If you love to write, then the work will oftentimes be enjoyable. But there will also be times when the work is hard or frustrating. Sometimes it might even seem impossible.

I encourage you to push through those times when writing doesn't come easily, when ideas aren't readily available, and when words and sentences refuse to flow and the whole process becomes maddening.

Always remember that the ends make the means worthwhile.

I hope this book will inspire you to make a conscious commitment to strive for better writing every day.

Keep writing!

Sincerely,

Melissa Donovan
Founder and Editor of *Writing Forward*

Chapter 1:
Reading

"If you don't have time to read, you don't have the time (or the tools) to write. Simple as that."
- Stephen King

To write well, there are only two things you absolutely must do: read and write. Everything else will flow from these two activities, which are essentially yin and yang. Without each other, reading and writing cannot exist. They rely on one another. They are two parts of a greater whole.

Writing is a complex and complicated skill. While basic writing skills can be taught, it's impossible to teach the art of fine writing. It is possible to learn, but this learning is only fully achieved through reading.

The human brain is like a sponge. We soak up everything we observe and experience throughout our lives, and each thing we are exposed to becomes part of the very fiber of our beings. What we read is no exception.

You may not be able to recite all the Mother Goose nursery rhymes you read as a child, but they're still somewhere in that head of yours. When a little voice whispers *Jack be nimble, Jack be quick*, there's a good chance you'll recall *Jack jumped over a candlestick*. You absorbed that nursery rhyme many years ago, and it remains with you always.

If you want to write well, you must read well, and you must read widely. Through reading you will gain knowledge and you will find inspiration. As you read more, you will learn to read with a writer's eye. Even grammar sinks in when you read. If you're worried about memorizing all the rules of grammar, then just read books written by adept writers. Eventually, it all will become part of your mental makeup.

A well-read writer has a better handle on vocabulary, understands the nuances of language, and recognizes the difference between poor and quality writing.

A writer who doesn't read is like a musician who doesn't listen to music or a filmmaker who doesn't watch movies. It is impossible to do good work without experiencing the good work that has been done.

All the grammar guides, writing tips, and books on writing will not make you a better writer if you never read. Reading is just as crucial as writing, if not more so, and the work you produce will only be as good as the work you read.

What is the Difference Between Good Writing and Bad Writing?

Strengths and weaknesses in a written work can be wide and varied. The ideas can be groundbreaking while the prose is dull. The work can be technically adept, demonstrating mastery of the language (grammar, spelling, and punctuation), but the story uninteresting.

Good writing is subjective. One person's favorite novel is another person's least favorite, and that same novel could be considered one of the greatest classics in the literary canon. Meanwhile, a current bestseller might be mocked by critics despite the fact that millions of readers have fallen in love with it.

Some readers prefer stories that say something about the human condition. Others like a story packed with adventure or romance. Some won't bother with works that aren't written in a literary style, while others don't care about the language as long as the information is solid or the story is entertaining.

Ultimately, you get to decide what types of writing speak to you and which types of writing you will read and write yourself.

However, if you want to produce quality work, it's essential to read material that is mechanically sound. It's also necessary to explore variety in the work you read.

Looking for Good Books

It's impossible to read everything. We have to pick and choose, but how do we do so when there are so many books to choose from? Do we look at the market and read what's selling? Do we turn to the reviewers and award winners? Consumer ratings online?

There are no rules. You'll find that your friend's list of favorite books includes your favorite book but also includes your least favorite book. A reviewer might applaud a book you couldn't finish because it was so boring. You might love a book that has hardly any reviews online. It's all a matter of taste.

To discover your personal taste in writing, you should test all the waters—read a few bestsellers, check out some of the classics, and pick up a couple of prizewinners. Explore different forms (essays, poetry, short stories, novels) and various genres (science fiction, mysteries, historical fiction).

And listen to the fans.

It's easy to go online and look through reviews to find out what others think of a piece of writing. Sites like Amazon and Goodreads allow users and consumers to rate and review books. The consumer reviews often reveal just how differently one piece of writing can affect different people. A single book will have a range of ratings from one star to five stars and reviews that range from utter distaste to complete satisfaction.

I have found that consumer reviews are reliable if you cast a wide net. I like to see a lot of five-star ratings on a book, but I also check the lower ratings to see what people are griping about. If they don't like a character or think the plot was too fantastical, I might decide to find out for myself. If they complain that the text was full of typos and poorly structured sentences, with a plot that had no clear conclusion, I might find something else to read.

Many online bookstores offer also-bought lists. When you visit a page for a book that you enjoyed, you can see which titles other people who read that book also bought. That's a good way to get a lead on similar types of stories.

Another option for finding good reading material is to rely on reviews from critics. The Internet has given rise to critics who have not studied literature, which is something to keep in mind. If critics have read books only from their favorite genres or from the bestseller list, they are not widely read. That doesn't invalidate their opinions, but it limits their experience.

On the other hand, some critics are a little too well read. Their expectations are so high that only a scant few books earn their approval. There's nothing wrong with high standards, but often these critics forget that a book's strengths can more than make up for its weaknesses.

When looking at reviews, try to find critics who have similar tastes to your own. You should be able to peruse their past reviews to see what other books they did or didn't like and determine whether their preferences match yours.

Magazines have always published "best" lists: "The Best Way to Lose Weight," "The Ten Best Films of All Time," "The Best Way to Save Money," etc. With the Internet, these lists have exploded and now appear on almost every website. If you're looking for a good book or other reading material, be wary when you shop from these kinds of lists. Always check the source. Is it some unknown blogger who has posted his or her favorite books and labeled them as the best of the best? Is it a list of most profitable books? For what year? All time? Is it a list of books that have withstood the test of time or books that are popular in classrooms? Award winners? The word *best* is used for a variety of purposes, although another word would often be far more accurate. Still, these lists can be hugely helpful in finding books that will appeal to you.

If you are already a fan of a particular author, read other books by that author, and if you can find out which authors your favorite authors enjoy reading, then you will probably hit the jackpot and find a treasure trove of reading material that you'll like. This is true for films and music as well. Find out what books, movies, and music your favorite artists love and then check them out. A fun part of this is seeing the source of inspiration for artists you admire.

Quick Tips for Identifying Good Writing

While many qualities of writing are subjective, there are some standard characteristics that universally constitute good writing:

- Professional writing is not peppered with typos, poor grammar, and frequent misspellings

- Good writing doesn't confuse the reader. If concepts that should be straightforward barely make sense, there's a clarity problem.

- A well-organized piece of writing flows smoothly from one scene or idea to the next.

- The narrative has a clear, consistent, and distinct voice, which matches the tone and subject matter.

- Sentences are properly structured, words are used correctly, and the vocabulary is robust.

- In nonfiction, the work and its author should have established credibility, and in fiction, even if the story is fantastical, it must be believable.

Reading Widely

"Read, read, read. Read everything—trash, classics, good and bad, and see how they do it. Just like a carpenter who works as an apprentice and studies the master. Read! You'll absorb it."
- William Faulkner

We are like mirrors. We reflect back into the world all that we have taken in. If you mostly read textbooks, your writing will be dry and informative. If you read torrid romance novels, your prose will tend toward lusty descriptions. Read the classics and your work will sound mature. Read poetry and your work will be fluid and musical.

It's important to read technically adept writing so you don't pick up bad grammar habits, but what about voice and style, word choice and sentence structure? What about story and organization? How does what we read influence the more subtle aspects of our writing?

If you know exactly what kind of writer you want to be, you're in luck. Your best bet is to read a lot within your favorite genre. Find authors that resonate with your sensibility and read all their books.

At the same time, you don't want to rope yourself off from experiencing a wide range of styles. You might like high literature and want to pen the next Pulitzer-Prize-winning work of fiction. You should read the classics, of course, but don't completely avoid the bestsellers. There's a mentality among some writers that you should read only that which you want to write. It's hogwash. Reading outside your chosen area of specialty will diversify and expand your skills, and you'll be equipped to bring new techniques and methods into your craft. If you so choose, you'll even be able to cross genre lines.

Everybody should read the classics, but why? The most obvious reason is that these works have withstood the test of time. Jane Austen, for example, has a huge and active fan base even though she wrote in the late eighteenth and early nineteenth centuries. Why are people so passionate about her work a hundred years later?

Another reason to read the classics is to engage in thoughtful discussions. When writers discuss their craft, they rarely use contemporary examples as a basis unless they're in a book club. That's because it's likely whoever they're talking to hasn't read the same contemporary books that they have. It's a vast market, and while some tight-knit reading and writing groups have a shared literary collection to draw from, when we discuss works in a broader setting, such as on a panel, in an interview, or to a blog audience, we cannot assume that everyone (or anyone) in the group has read the same modern books we have. It's more likely that we've all read a few of the classics; they provide us with common ground because many of us read the same books as school assignments and many of these classics are so often referenced, mentioned, and discussed that we read them out of sheer curiosity, to see what all the fuss is about.

Lots of young and new writers complain about the classics. They don't want to waste time reading anything they don't love because there are so many appealing books to read. The stuff they like to read never wins awards and they don't want to be members of the literati. They want to wind their way through a good mystery novel or let their imaginations take flight on a space adventure. Or maybe they want to get intimate with a bit of romance. These genres rarely end up as classics. You'll find them on bestseller lists, but not on critics' must-read lists. In a hundred years, it's unlikely anyone will still be reading them.

And many writers insist they should not have to suffer through the complex and dated language of Shakespeare or endure a book just because a bunch of academics has declared it brilliant. They know what they like to read, and classics don't qualify.

It's good for a writer to know where he or she stands in the sea of literary categories. While I appreciate fine craftsmanship and have greatly enjoyed many classics and literary works, I also have great admiration for writers who want to write for regular people. You know, people who just like to read and be entertained by a good story. I think this is a grounded and down-to-earth approach, and some of my favorite books have never won awards or been taught in a classroom.

But we should not dismiss such works just because they don't encompass what we ourselves want to write.

The literary elites and critics may turn their noses up at some really fun stories, but they have made it their life's work to analyze and dissect written work and to pass judgment on it. Their word isn't law, but it is reliable and there is a lot of work in the literary canon that will teach you about what constitutes good writing. Does that mean you should spend the next two years reading your way through Shakespeare's entire repertoire? No. But you should try to work in a few classics and literary works each year, so you can gain an intuitive understanding of what types of stories and styles of writing enter the cultural canon for the long haul.

And it's true—the literary elites can be overbearing with their harsh judgments, highbrow tastes, and disdain for the common fare that is usually found on the bestseller lists and in the genre sections of any bookstore. But they know their stuff. They can identify a good turn of phrase and can pontificate on why another phrase is just lame. They are especially attuned to the richness of language and to stories that address the human condition. If you don't know why they gush at Austen but laugh at *Twilight*, then go read their arguments. You'll find that they have sound reasoning, even if you don't agree with it.

If you want to be a science-fiction writer, then by all means, stock your shelves with loads of sci-fi. Buy out the science-fiction section in your local bookstore. But don't seal yourself in a box, otherwise your work will become trite. If you're too immersed in a particular genre, your writing will feel formulaic and not in a good way. You'll end up playing by all the genre rules (and this is a key reason why much genre work is ignored by academics and the literary elite—it's too focused on catering to its genre and not focused enough on good storytelling). For example, do we need another epic fantasy with names that nobody can pronounce and that are oddly strewn with apostrophes? No, I don't think we do.

So yes, you should concentrate on your genre, but don't cut yourself off from the rest of literature. You should read a few books outside your genre each year and make sure you toss in some of those classics for good measure.

Just for Writers

Every time I hear someone say that books about writing are useless, I cringe, and not because I myself write about writing. I think it's fantastic that some writers can sit down and compose a masterpiece having learned the craft solely through reading novels or poetry.

But some of us like to approach our craft more methodically. Most of what I learn in books about writing are things I already know, but not consciously. And I've picked up tons of tips and techniques about the writing process that I otherwise never would have discovered.

For example, I tried writing several novels over the course of a few years. I researched, outlined, and promptly abandoned each project in search of a more exciting idea. What was killing my enthusiasm was the absence of mystery. Once I had a detailed outline and knew what was going to happen, the magic was gone and I lost interest in writing the rest of the book.

It was through reading a book on writing (*No Plot? No Problem!* by Chris Baty) that I learned about discovery writing (which is often called *pantsing*, as in *writing by the seat of your pants*). It seemed incredible to me that a writer could sit down and draft a novel with no notes, no outline, just a couple of characters. But nothing else had worked, so I gave it a try. And finally, I finished the first draft of an entire novel.

I don't think it's healthy to bury your nose in books and articles about writing and never come up for air. If you get too immersed in studying the craft and the industry, you'll get locked into the dream cycle: you'll talk and fantasize about becoming a writer and, in fact, you'll know everything there is to know about being a writer, but you won't actually be writing.

However, a few key resources on the craft are essential for any writer's development. Be sure to acquire and read books on the craft for your own personal library.

The Eye of the Writer

One of the most important skills a writer can develop is the ability to read critically. Writers must learn to view what we read through writers' goggles.

It's easy to kick back and read an entertaining novel. If we're reading a good story, we'll be intrigued and captivated. Often, we relax so much when we're reading that we enter a state of leisure. But to read with a writer's eye means to read with special awareness, to read actively.

There are various things that a writer should be able to notice in a written work, things that the average, non-writing reader might overlook. A writer should be able to catch typos, obviously. But he or she should also be able to pick up on the subtler elements of a work.

I'm always intrigued, for example, by character names. I don't always pay close attention to them, but I often wonder how the author managed to choose such perfect monikers for the characters. Names fascinate me so deeply that I once wrote an entire essay analyzing the names of characters in the book *Tuck Everlasting*. My essay explained the deeper meanings that the names implied. My instructor said she'd never realized character names had deeper meanings. She was a professor of literature at the college I attended. I was a creative-writing major.

This highlights the fact that writers simply start to look at writing differently than readers do, even the most intelligent or well-read readers.

As a writer, you should be able to follow the flow of a story. A story has a beginning, a middle, and an end. Can you pinpoint the transitions between these three phases?

There's something about a good book that evokes an emotional response from readers. They become attached to the characters. Throughout history, people have referred to books and their characters as friends. Just think of how much people love Harry Potter. It's almost as if he were a real person. That's superb writing—getting the audience to feel so deeply for a character. When a writer reads, he or she should look for techniques that other authors have used to engage the reader's emotions.

One of the most important things you can read for is voice. This is one element of great writing that is impossible to teach or even learn. It happens with practice and experience. As you read, you'll notice that each writer has a distinct voice, one that makes his or her work recognizable. If you read enough of an author's work, you'll probably be able to pick that author out of a quotation lineup (I had to take that test in college).

As we read, we look for these details in well-crafted texts. How did the author make such astute word choices? What made the story emotionally compelling? How were the sentences and paragraphs structured to flow smoothly? As you read, you'll learn lots of tricks and techniques for great writing.

But the most important aspect you read for is the one that's troubling you.

Let's say you write creative nonfiction, but you have a hard time organizing your material into digestible chunks. This is not uncommon. Often, when people become experts (which hopefully has occurred prior to writing a book about any subject), they see the subject matter so holistically that it doesn't seem possible to separate the various elements. For some writers, the writing process is a free flow. Going through and organizing a manuscript that contains tens of thousands of words of freely written prose is a daunting task indeed.

But if you've read a lot of nonfiction books, you can see how other writers have broken down massive amounts of information for easier reading. You will also discover some who have found clever ways of tying everything together, even though it's all been separated.

There are many other things you can look for when you're reading as a writer. Search for story elements that excite you or intrigue you and examine them closely. Always be on the lookout for those aspects of writing that give you difficulty. Studying how other writers address these issues will give you great insight.

Reading for Knowledge and Inspiration

There is an added benefit to reading that cannot be overlooked. By reading, you will accumulate vast amounts of knowledge and inspiration.

For centuries, books have been hailed as dispensers of knowledge. Written works have also been credited with providing writers and other artists with a wellspring of inspiration. The greatest writers throughout history have proudly declared that they do not borrow ideas from other writers: they steal.

In many ways, writers are the keepers of knowledge and information. More accurately, they are the distributors of knowledge and information.

Whatever we write, knowledge is the foundation upon which we shape our ideas. Whether we're telling a made-up story or giving an account of a real event, the facts we gather and the experiences we accumulate constitute our knowledge and make their way into our written work.

In nonfiction, the need for research is obvious. One must have the facts if one is to write about the facts. Yet in fiction, and poetry too, the knowledge we gain from reading rears its head and swims through our prose and verse.

For example, if you write a story, it is set in a particular place. The characters won't have the same life experience or career that you have. Questions will arise and you will need to conduct research in order to answer them. Much of this knowledge you will intuitively possess from being well read. Let's say you're writing a scene that's set on a beach but you've never been to the seaside. If you've perused articles about the beach, read novels set in beach towns, and soaked up poetry that describes the ocean and sandy shores, you'll be fairly knowledgeable about your setting.

Which is why so many passionate readers declare that through books they've made friends (characters), had adventures, and traveled to distant shores. Books (and art in general) give us knowledge that is as close to real experience as we can get. So until virtual reality evolves and is available for mass consumption, reading is where we turn for knowledge and experience by proxy.

Finally, one of the greatest benefits that comes from avid reading is inspiration. Of course, there is plenty of real-life inspiration all around us. Inspiration often comes from our personal thoughts and experiences: our first kiss or our first heartbreak, our first experience with death, our world view and belief system.

Sometimes inspiration comes spontaneously, seemingly out of nowhere, which is why artists find it so curious and assign it all sorts of mythological origins, such as the muses.

One of the most overlooked sources of inspiration is art itself—paintings, photos, sculptures, films, music, and dance.

But books offer a special kind of inspiration. Books, stories, articles, and essays will spark ideas and inspire you to write. In fact, many writers make it a point to read for a bit before their scheduled writing sessions because reading ignites their passion, filling them with ideas and making them want to write.

The Aversion to Reading

**"There are worse crimes than burning books.
One of them is not reading them."
- Joseph Brodsky**

So, why are some would-be writers so averse to reading?

Writers are famous mostly among readers and other writers. They rarely attain vast wealth, and though a lucky few receive honors and awards, they almost never reach the levels of success that we see music and film celebrities achieve. It's not as though being a writer is glamorous. Why anyone who doesn't read or doesn't enjoy reading would want to become a writer is curious indeed.

Perhaps non-readers want to write because they have stories to tell. Maybe they have ideas to share or knowledge to impart. They don't care about writing or reading; they just want to transfer the contents of their own minds to other people.

How can such persons assume their ideas are interesting or publishable if they are not reading? If a person wants to write a book about baseball, he should read books about baseball lest he discover his book has already been written by someone else. If another person wants to write a novel but refuses to read novels, she runs the risk of telling a poorly constructed story, never mind one that has already been told. Storytelling is a craft, and few people are born with the gift. Most of us learn it by reading.

There's no good argument against reading, and there is a book for everyone. I've long held the philosophy that people who don't like to read just haven't found the right book yet. And a writer who doesn't read is an oxymoron.

Books have been cherished by the greatest thinkers and leaders throughout history. They are gateways to the imagination, fountains of knowledge, and a way for people to connect emotionally and intellectually.

A writer who doesn't read is disconnected from his or her audience. Such a writer cannot possibly understand the experience that he or she is creating.

Questions

- Who are your favorite authors? What is it about their work that you admire?

- Do you have a preference for certain genres? What are your favorite books? Why do they appeal to you more than others?

- Have you ever put down a book without finishing it? Do you finish books even when you're not enjoying them? What was it about them that you didn't like?

- Activities

- Keep a reading journal: Include the title and author, dates you started and finished the book, and a few words about what you liked or didn't like about it.

- Sign up for Goodreads: Goodreads is a social networking site for bookworms. You can use it to keep a reading journal (it tracks book titles, authors, start and finish dates of books you read, and more). You can also use Goodreads to connect with other readers and find books that you're likely to enjoy.

- Rate and review books you read: This is a great way to help authors who you want to support. Leaving a five-star (or high) rating and a positive review helps authors sell more books, and more sales enable those authors to write and publish more books. The act of writing reviews also helps you articulate what you liked about a book.

Chapter 2:
Writing

"If you wish to be a writer, write." - Epictetus

It goes without saying: if you want to be a writer, you must write. Thinking about writing is not enough. Talking about writing is not enough. You have to sit down and get words on the page. That's what writers do.

You certainly can't improve your writing without practice. The more you write, the better your writing becomes. Experience breeds expertise, so if you write a lot, you'll become an expert writer.

According to Malcolm Gladwell, author of *Outliers*, it takes 10,000 hours of practice to become an expert in any field. Does that mean you have to spend 10,000 hours writing to get good at it? I don't think so. I think some of those hours can be spent reading and studying the craft. However, the majority of those hours must be dedicated to practicing the craft.

Practice is what turns an amateur into a professional. Lots and lots of practice.

Yet many people who say they want to be writers avoid writing altogether. They plan on writing, think about writing, and talk about writing. They probably write a little here and there but not enough to complete a project, not enough to become great at it, and never enough to make a career of it.

There are lots of reasons people want to write. Some are naturally talented, so they feel they should write. Others love to read, so they'd like to write a book someday. Some think writing is a quick way to become rich and famous (they're wrong), others are genuinely passionate about writing, but they don't have time to write, are uninspired, only write when they are inspired, or simply don't think they have what it takes to be a writer.

Permission to Write

"A professional writer is an amateur who didn't quit." - Richard Bach

I admire people who are fearless. When they want to do something, they do it. They don't worry, plan, wonder, analyze, or seek permission. They simply do what they want to do.

But most of us are more cautious. We've experienced failure. We don't like taking risks. We've seen amateurs trying to pass themselves off as professionals. We've had our writing critiqued and the feedback wasn't good. We set the bar high—nothing short of a potential bestseller is worth writing.

When the mind is clouded with these thoughts, it's hard to try new things. We don't want to make fools of ourselves. And who are we to take up writing anyway?

Some people are intimidated by the blank page. Others are intimidated by grammar. Many think they are simply not qualified. There are plenty of reasons to refuse to write even if writing is what you want to do:

- I didn't go to college.

- I went to college, but I didn't take a writing class.

- I have a story to tell, but I'm not a writer.

- I was never good at English.

- I could never be as good as my favorite author.

- It's too hard to get published.

- I don't know anything about publishing or marketing.

- Writing is too hard.

- There's no money in it.

The first thing you need to do is stop making excuses, and then you need to give yourself permission to write.

Almost every excuse for not writing is fear based. You're afraid you're not qualified. You're afraid it will be too difficult for you. You're afraid of failure.

We all experience fear. It's not unusual for people to want to write, but to feel as though they shouldn't. I'm here to tell you that the fear may never completely go away. Most of the time, I crack open a new notebook or document and dive right in. But when I'm working on a big, meaningful, or important project, I get a little nervous. I procrastinate. I question whether I'm cut out for it.

But that doesn't stop me. I force myself to write that first sentence, even if it sucks. Then I write the next sentence and the next one. Who cares if it's no good? Nobody can see it but me, and I get to go back and clean it up before I show it to anyone else. I've got nothing to lose, so why would I let all those irrational fears stop me?

One day, one of my relatives approached me, sat me down, and said in all seriousness, "I'm thinking about writing," and then looked at me expectantly, while I sat there thinking, *Okay. So go write.*

Suddenly, I realized that this person was asking me for permission to write. I somehow became part of the equation of whether or not someone would pursue writing. Which is ridiculous.

Look, nobody needs to give you permission to write. If you want to write, then write. Stop making excuses, stop looking for a magic talisman that will turn you into Shakespeare. Just write.

Am I a Writer?

Lots of people fret over this question. There are discussions all over the Internet about who qualifies as a writer. Do you need a degree? Do you have to have published something? Earned income from writing? At what point do you go from being a normal person to being a writer?

For me, the answer is simple: if you write, then you're a writer. Now, that doesn't mean you should jot *writer* down as your profession on a form or application. It's only your occupation if you make a living at it (or any income whatsoever). But in a general sense, people who write are writers. If you want to split hairs and talk about writers who write professionally or who make a living writing, then we call those people *authors*.

The real question is not whether you're a writer. It's what kind of writer are you? Are you a writer who writes when the mood strikes? Do you wait for inspiration and then write only a few times a year? Is writing a hobby or do you want to make writing your career? Is your goal to get published? Do you want to improve your writing?

If so, then you need to make a commitment to writing.

Making a Commitment to Writing

What separates professional writers from would-be writers and what separates writers who produce quality work from those who produce amateur work is not talent—this is a common misconception—it's commitment.

Every New Year's Day, people make resolutions, setting goals they plan on accomplishing throughout the year. They're going to lose weight, get a new job, save money, start exercising, or write a book.

By spring, most of those resolutions have been abandoned and people fall back into their old routines.

Some people make these same resolutions year after year and never reach the goals they keep setting for themselves.

But some people fulfill their resolutions. Personally, I find that most people who accomplish these kinds of goals don't set them at the start of a new year. They set their goals when they're good and ready to make a real commitment.

And commitment is what differentiates those who reach their goals from those who don't. They don't set a goal because they'd like to be thinner or richer, or because they've always wanted to write a book. They set a goal because they are prepared to make a commitment to it.

Sure, everyone who sets goals and resolutions intends to achieve them, but there's a difference between a good intention and true commitment. When you're deeply committed to something, you feel it in your bones. You're prepared to make it a priority in your life, even if it means making sacrifices for it.

If you're ready to make that kind of commitment and make your writing practice a priority, then you'll be able to improve your writing in leaps and bounds. The equation is pretty simple: the more time you put in, the more your work will improve, and the sooner you'll become a pro.

It all starts with making time to write and establishing a routine.

Making Time to Write

Everyone wants to write a book, even people who don't consider themselves writers and who don't want to be writers. But who has the time? Aspiring writers often complain that they'd love to take their writing hobby to the next level, but they are too busy.

It's not easy to find time to write. Even professional writers get caught up in paperwork and marketing and have to scramble to get the actual work of writing done.

But with careful planning and better time management, we can all learn how to carve out a little more time for writing.

Finding time to practice writing might seem impossible, but if you know where to look, you'll find precious pockets of minutes and hours that you can use to your advantage.

Here are some ways you can make or find more time to write, even if you have a packed schedule. Experiment with these productivity methods and see which ones work for you:

- Write first thing every morning. Most people feel refreshed after a good night's rest (and a cup of hot coffee!) so there's no better time to get creative than in the a.m. If you can get some writing done before you hop in the shower, you'll already have made a great start for the day.

- Schedule writing sessions. If you have an overpacked schedule and your life is dictated by your calendar, then pen in your writing time! Even if you can only squeeze in twenty minutes per day, you'll see a dramatic increase in your output and improvement in your work.

- Give yourself a break. Squeezing writing time into breaks and lunches at work is a great way to get writing done on a tight schedule. Even a ten-minute writing binge could mean a huge breakthrough in your plot or that perfect bit of dialogue you've been looking for. Because some of our best writing ideas come when we're enmeshed in other activities, mini writing breaks scattered throughout the day can move your project along in small but significant steps.

- Do it in the car. Don't use pen and paper here, folks. Many cell phones are equipped with recording capabilities, and there are freestanding recording devices as well as apps for your smart phone or other mobile device. Use driving time to record your thoughts and transcribe them later. Bonus tip: Don't have a recording device? Call yourself and leave a voice mail!

- Sacrifice. Sometimes in life we have to make choices. Give up one of your TV shows and use that time for a weekly writing session. Reconsider accepting every single party invitation, and ask yourself if extra-curricular activities like playing on a community softball league are more important than getting your writing done.

- Ask for help. If you have too much on your plate and simply cannot find time to write, try delegating, sharing, and swapping tasks with friends, co-workers, and family members. This will free up time in your schedule that you can devote to writing.

- Turn off the Internet. Need I say more?

Establishing a Routine

"I only write when I am inspired. Fortunately I am inspired at 9 o'clock every morning."
- William Faulkner

Ideally, you'll write every day.

Writers who come to the craft out of passion never have a problem with this. They write every day because they need to write every day. Writing is not a habit, an effort, or an obligation; it's a necessity.

Other writers struggle with developing a daily writing routine. They start manuscripts, launch blogs, purchase pretty diaries, and swear they're going to make daily entries. Months later, frustrated and fed up, they give up.

Routines don't work for everyone, but they do work for most people. Almost all the writers I know say they have to write every day. If they miss a day, they end up missing two days, then three, four, and pretty soon they haven't written in several weeks.

A scant few writers can produce good work by binge writing. They don't write at all for a few months, and then they crank out a novel in a few weeks. But this is the exception rather than the rule.

So, are you the exception or are you the rule? The only way to find out is to experiment. I'm a huge advocate for writers trying different things. Go ahead and try writing only when you're inspired. Over the course of a month, how much did you write? How about in the span of a year? Did you write a whole novel? A page? Nothing? If you're productive working this way, stick with it.

When weeks have passed and you haven't written a single word, when unfinished projects are littering your desk and clogging up your computer's hard drive, you can give up entirely and take out a lifetime lease on a cubicle in a drab, gray office. Or you can step back, admit that you have a problem, and make some changes.

These days, we're all crunched for time. You'd think technology would give us more time for leisure and personal pursuits, but it seems to have the opposite effect. The world just keeps getting busier and busier.

What you'll find is that if you write only when you feel like it, you won't write very often. The world is full of distractions—phone calls, emails, television, video games, social media...The list goes on and on.

We've already established that the best way to improve your writing is to practice. You can improve your writing by writing occasionally, but the improvements won't be significant and it will take decades for you to become an expert. What you need to do, even if you just try it for a month to prove to yourself there's a better way, is to make writing part of your daily routine.

The single best way to develop a routine, to make something a habit, is to do it every day. Okay, you don't have to write every day, but you should get in a good twenty-minute writing session at least five or six days a week—I would say that's the absolute minimum. If you can write for a full hour, all the better. Remember, this is time spent writing—not reading, editing, or brainstorming. It's your writing time.

I once had a music teacher who said it's better to practice for fifteen minutes every day than to practice for two hours three times a week. I think the same is true for writing. Even if you dedicate only a few minutes to writing every day, it will become an ingrained habit. Writing will become an integral part of your life.

Think of it this way: if you exercise for five hours every Saturday, you end up sore. By the following Saturday, your muscles have weakened again, so you have to start all over. On the other hand, if you exercise for forty-five minutes a day, five days a week, you'll build up your muscles. The soreness will subside and you will get stronger and leaner. And overall, you've actually put less time in.

Your writing practices are not unlike your diet and exercise habits. You'll get the best results if you start slow and develop a regular routine.

This doesn't mean you have to do the same thing every day. Sure, you may be working on a novel, but you can take breaks to write poetry or essays. If you don't have a project in the works, then do some writing exercises. I have found blogging to be an excellent way to ensure that I write consistently, especially between projects.

On Journaling

One of the easiest, most natural, and creative ways to commit to writing and produce better writing over time is to keep a writing journal or notebook.

Writers who are not working at the professional level are juggling their writing projects with full-time jobs, families, school, and a host of other obligations. Writers also get stuck. You're working on a manuscript and then one day, the ideas just stop flowing. You decide to step away for a day or two, and three months later, you've practically forgotten all about that book you were writing. In fact, you can't remember the last time you sat down and actually wrote something.

Journal writing is many things, but first and foremost, it's a solution. Journaling is best known for its artistry and is highly recognized for its self-help (vent-and-rant) benefits. But few young or new writers realize that a journal is a writer's most sacred space. It's a place where you can jot down or flesh out ideas, where you can freewrite or work on writing exercises when you're blocked, and where you can scribble notes when you're short on time. It's a space where you can develop better writing skills and learn new techniques through trial and error.

The truth is, you don't have to write every single day to be a professional or published writer. Daily writing is the best practice, but many writers keep a regular, five-day work week. A few writers get their work done by writing heavily for a few months, then not writing at all for a while. But this truth is self-evident: those who succeed treat their writing as a job and they commit to it.

Journal writing is an ideal way for writers to fulfill that commitment. When you keep a journal, you rid yourself of excuses. You can no longer say that you're stuck on a plot twist because you can write in your journal until the plot becomes untwisted. In fact, writing in your journal may help you do just that. When you're short on time, you can always turn to your journal for a quick, ten-minute writing session, even while larger projects are sitting on the back burner. And your journal is distraction free, so you can stay focused during your writing sessions.

Do you have to keep a journal in order to succeed and become a professional or published writer? No, of course not. There are many paths to professional writing, and there are many ways to improve your writing. Journal writing is just one trail on the mountain, but it's a trail that is entrenched with the footprints of successful writers throughout history who have benefited from journaling.

Here are some tips for journaling:

- Stock up on journals, notebooks, and pens.

- Try different products and find what you like best.

- Try using different notebooks for different projects, and try using a single notebook for all your writing projects.

- Keep a notebook and pen or some other writing tool with you at all times.

You can keep a journal on your computer, or you can use an old typewriter if that appeals to you. But most writers use a good, old-fashioned notebook: pen and paper. While we can certainly crank out more words when we type, we are also at risk for the many distractions of the computer and the Internet. When your journal writing sessions are offline, your productivity may increase tenfold because you spend the entire session writing. After all, your journal doesn't have Twitter or solitaire on it.

Procrastination and Productivity

"Planning to write is not writing. Outlining, researching, talking to people about what you're doing, none of that is writing. Writing is writing."
- E. L. Doctorow

Procrastination and lack of productivity are huge problems for most writers. After all, you don't have a boss hovering over your shoulder, and there's no paycheck coming in from your writing.

You alone are responsible for being disciplined enough to get the work done. That's quite a burden to bear, especially if you're not an eager or enthusiastic writer who is obsessed to the point of writing prolifically without outside motivation.

Most of us wrestle with procrastination and distractions. Writing time comes and suddenly there are dishes to do, lawns to mow, errands to run, people to call, games to play, and websites to surf. All of these things are so much easier than facing the blank page.

That's because writing is work. It requires tremendous focus. It's also intimidating for a lot of people. The fear of writing something awful often inhibits would-be writers to the point of freezing them up entirely.

Here are a few tips to help you overcome distractions and procrastination:

- **Overcome procrastination:** One of the best ways to overcome procrastination is to allow yourself the freedom to write poorly. Don't worry about how good or bad it's going to be. You can clean it up later.

- **Eliminate distractions:** The best way to prevent distractions is to eliminate them. Turn off your ringer, disconnect the Internet, lock yourself in your room, and don't come out until you finish your writing session.

- **Track productivity:** A great way to stay motivated and avoid procrastination is to track your progress. Keep a log of how many pages or words completed during each day's writing session. Once you get a sense for your writing rhythm, set goals to write more each day.

- **Time and space:** Schedule your writing time and set up a dedicated space without distractions, where you won't be bothered or interrupted. It could be as simple as taking your notebook out to the garage for twenty minutes at the same time every evening.

- **Accountability:** Holding yourself accountable to others is the best way to be accountable. Find a writing buddy, join a writing group, hire a writing coach, or post your daily word count online.

Activities for Writing Practice

What matters is that you spend time writing, but you'll also need something to write.

If you love to write and have tons of ideas, you'll have plenty of fodder for your writing practice. By practice, I mean regular writing sessions. You might be writing a novel that you fully intend to publish. In this case, you're not writing just for the sake of practicing, but you're getting practice by working on a serious writing project.

You might be writing blog posts. Or you could be experimenting with characters, scenes, story ideas, poetry, and personal essays with no clear plan other than you need to write something in order to get better at writing.

If you don't have much experience yet, and if you haven't established a clear sense of direction for your writing, my advice is to try a little bit of everything. Experiment with different forms and genres, see what feels right. Here are some ideas:

- **Keep a journal for thirty days:** I encourage people to approach journaling with an open mind. Allow yourself to doodle and sketch in your journal. Write about what happened today, what you want to happen tomorrow, or reflect on something that happened years ago.

- **Write a series of personal essays:** Personal essays are structured pieces that look at a topic through the writer's personal experience. They often include storytelling that is woven with thoughts and insights about the subject matter.

- **Write a series of topical essays:** Topical essays are formal and often require research. They can be factual or informative, persuasive or analytical.

- **Write a short story:** Some say the short story is a lost art, commercially speaking. But the short story is making a comeback with the rise of e-books. Many writers can finish a short story in a day to a week.

- **Write outlines, synopses, or character sketches for a novel:** You could skip the preliminaries and write the novel itself, but if you're looking for something to practice writing, story outlines, character sketches, and world building are great ways to warm up your writing and experiment with ideas before starting a manuscript.

- **Write fictional scenes:** We all have fantasies. Maybe you've thought it would be funny if everyone in a restaurant got up and started singing and dancing like they do in musicals. Maybe you've fantasized about revenge or a romantic encounter. Stop daydreaming and write these scenes down!

- **Write a script or screenplay:** Script writing is not traditional prose, but it's an excellent way to practice writing dialogue and to practice writing in a tight, concise manner.

- **Write a poem a day for a week:** Some people find it easier to write song lyrics than poetry. Just remember that poetry doesn't have to rhyme.

- **Start a blog:** Blogging did wonders for my writing routine. When you write in the public space and acquire a readership, you are also holding yourself accountable to other people.

Make sure that when you write, you give it your best. Don't scrawl a personal essay in your notebook and then forget about it. Write it to the best of your ability, including editing, proofreading, and polishing. There's no point in practicing your writing if you are halfhearted about it.

And while perfection is an impossible dream, we can certainly do our best to make our writing as close to perfect as possible, each in our own time and in the way that best suits us. You know the saying: practice makes perfect.

So what are you waiting for? Go practice writing!

Questions

- How often do you write?

- How often would you like to write?

- If you don't write as often as you'd like, what's stopping you?

- Is there space in your schedule for a twenty-minute writing session at least five days a week? Can you do an hour a day?

Chapter 3:
Revision

"The best writing is rewriting." - E.B. White

We use the terms *first draft* or *rough draft* when we are initially writing a piece because almost every single project is going to go through multiple drafts. But how is the drafting process tackled? And what are the benefits of multiple revisions?

Some writers love the revision process; others think it's a drag. Regardless of how you feel about revising your work, one thing is certain: if you want to produce better writing (and become a better writer), then revisions are absolutely essential.

To revise means *to change* or *to alter*. In the world of writing, to revise means "to alter something already written or printed, in order to make corrections, improve, or update: to revise a manuscript." (dictionary.com)

Revision involves making substantial changes to improve the writing. In fiction, this could mean changing characters' names, realigning the plot, or resequencing the scenes. In other forms of writing, revision might entail major structural changes (moving chapters around) or a content overhaul (adding, removing, or changing information). Sometimes, revision involves rewriting a project entirely.

When I first started writing poetry, I believed that each poem was sacred in its original state. It seemed blasphemous to change a poem once I'd captured it and scrawled it in my notebook. Then one day I was flipping through my poems and it became clear to me that they could be a lot better if I made a few minor changes.

I'm not sure why, but it felt wrong at the time. I remember keeping the originals as well as every revision I made. It seems ridiculous now to shy away from improving something that I created. Luckily, my desire to produce better writing was stronger than my silly, emotional attachment to my rough drafts.

I found that as I rewrote my poems, I noticed lots of little things that I could change and improve. I tightened the rhyme scheme, sharpened the images, and chose more colorful language. I wasn't always happy with the end result, but I did consistently improve each and every poem. And I learned something else—my first drafts were getting better too.

As you revise, you catch things in your writing that don't work. We all have bad habits, and as you go through multiple revisions, you'll start to notice negative patterns in your own writing. Maybe you have a tendency to leave words out. Perhaps you use too many words (or too few). Maybe you repeat words too often or use obscure language that readers won't comprehend. You could have grammar weaknesses, holes in the syntax, gaps in continuity, and a host of other problems that occur in writing.

Over time, revision teaches you what your weaknesses are. Early on, I realized that I had a problem with word repetition. I would notice a word used several times in a single poem. It didn't sound right, so I fixed it by finding replacement words. Then I saw the same problem in another poem, then another, and another. Eventually, I started catching myself, not during the revision process, but during the initial writing.

And I realized that revising what I'd already written improved what I had yet to write.

We all want to achieve better writing, and there are many ways to do that. You can study the craft of writing, learn grammar, collect writing tips, and practice writing every single day. All of these things (and many more) will make your writing better. But revision is where you truly turn your writing into a dazzling piece of work.

Writing Methods and Revision Techniques

There's more than one way to approach revisions.

Some writers use their initial draft to get ideas out of their heads and onto the page (or the screen, as the case may be) as quickly as possible, without worrying about the details. The goal is to get that first draft completed and then you can clean it up later. This often means more revisions when the drafting is done.

Other writers prefer to labor over each sentence while composing a first draft, which means fewer revisions later but more work during the initial writing.

Revising as You Go

If you have already developed your project, then revising as you go might be a good approach. For example, if you're working from a detailed outline and have a good sense of what you want to communicate, you can focus on wording, grammar, and punctuation as you work through your first draft.

Some writers are compelled to edit as they write because poorly written sentences and typos weigh on them and make it difficult to move forward, or it might seem as if trying to get it right on the first draft will save time later, which is unlikely. Going over each sentence and paragraph several times before moving on to the next could very well be just as time consuming as going over an entire draft multiple times.

I often revise as I go when writing blog posts and other short projects. I've found that there are some benefits to it. I start by outlining so I know what I want to say, then I draft paragraphs, revising each one before moving on to the next. Then I do a final proof or two. I find fewer errors during proofreading by using this method.

The writing happens fairly quickly, but since I'm working on short pieces, I can easily keep all the ideas for each piece in my head as I'm writing. When I'm working on a more elaborate project, like a book, there's a lot more going on, so I prefer to draft first and revise later.

Draft First, Revise Later

A book is an enormous undertaking. Some writers spend several years on the first draft alone. For example, in a novel there's a lot to think about: characters, plot, setting, scenes, action, dialogue, description, themes, and story arcs. Even if you have a basic sense of your story, once you start drafting, you'll encounter all kinds of problems.

If you're revising as you write, these problems get compounded and can seriously hold up your progress. If you're simultaneously working on grammar, spelling, and punctuation or fine tuning the most minute details of every scene as you write the first draft, you'll find yourself stopping every few words to make changes and fix mistakes, and you're likely to lose your train of thought. When you're deep in a scene, you could lose the entire flow because you're worrying over minutia that could be dealt with later.

Most writers seem to get the best results by plowing through the initial draft and then revising several times. This allows ideas to stream without interruption. Then, through a series of revisions, the work is slowly improved until it's polished. Some writers revise chapter by chapter, others revise scene by scene. I've heard writers say they do revisions for particular elements: one revision to fine-tune the plot and characters, one to strengthen the scenes, one for dialogue, and so on. This allows you to focus your attention on specific elements with each revision. Some writers work through the entire manuscript from beginning to end several times.

With the draft-first-revise-later method, every revision makes the manuscript better, resulting in a clean, polished project.

Steps for Writing and Revising

If you're going to write by drafting first and revising later, you should plan on going over the project multiple times. Here's one revision process you can use:

- **Raw draft:** As you write the first draft, focus on getting your ideas on the page. Don't stop to do any editing and don't reread what you've written unless you absolutely have to in order to get your bearings. If you come across something you don't know, whether it's a fact or a character's name, just leave a note for yourself. The goal is sort of a brain dump.

- **Rough draft:** Go through the raw draft and give it form and shape. This is when you'll address any notes you made and resolve open-ended issues. Since you've already gotten to the end of your project, you'll have a good idea of which portions need work and which details you need to figure out.

- **Rewrite:** Read through the rough draft, taking notes as you go. Then, go back through and rewrite it. This is when you tighten up sentences and paragraphs, smooth out the scenes, fine-tune the descriptions, and check for sentence flow and word choice. Note: A lot of writers do several focused rewrites during this stage; for example, one for dialogue, one for fact checking, and one for descriptions.

- **Edit:** You'll probably clean up a lot of technical errors as you rewrite and revise, but when you edit, you should be focused on grammar, spelling, punctuation, and sentence structure. If you're not sure about the rules of grammar, this is when you should look them up.

- **Proof:** Finally! Now you just check for those last remaining pesky typos.

You might have to repeat some of these steps. For example, I usually proofread a piece until I can't find any more mistakes or typos. That doesn't mean I've gotten them all, but it does mean I'm ready for a second set of eyes. Ideally, once you're done, you'll bring in a professional editor. Remember, no matter how many times you go over your manuscript, a few mistakes and inconsistencies will slip through. An editor or proofreader will catch things you missed.

Editing Your Work

Almost without exception, even after several drafts, there will be room for improvement in your writing. Many professionally published works, some of which have gone through numerous edits and proofs by a team of professionals, are printed with a typo here and there. I've seen typos in novels, magazine articles, and even in an encyclopedia.

At some point, it's likely that you will find a typo in one of your published pieces. Don't beat yourself up about it. If you can fix the typo, do so and move on. If not, then just accept that typos occur and move on. Typos happen to everyone and it's not the end of the world, even if it is a little embarrassing.

There are some writers out there who are neither bothered nor embarrassed by typos. They'll publish work that is full of typos and packed with poorly structured sentences. They don't bother to edit or proofread and if they do, they just give it a cursory glance. Writers will submit these pieces to agents and publishers (they are not likely to get accepted for publication) and they will self-publish these pieces (resulting in lots of negative reviews that complain about how the work is full of errors). This approach is unprofessional, and it sends a message that the writers don't care about their work or their readers.

Typos, mistakes, and bad sentences happen, but we want them to occur as infrequently as possible. We want our writing to be smooth, strong, and error-free. Editing and proofreading are essential steps in the writing process, because this is where the writing is massaged and perfected and where typos are eradicated.

I believe writers should try different approaches to writing and find what works for them. But there's no alternative to proofreading and editing. It's something we all have to do. Ideally, after we've edited and proofread our own work, we'll get someone else (hopefully a professional) to go over it again—multiple times if necessary.

Readers are the most important reason every writer should revise, edit, and proofread. By readers, I don't simply mean the folks who buy books and magazines. Readers are also your teachers, members of your workshop or writing group, and even your friends and family. It's almost a matter of etiquette—it's disrespectful to ask someone to read your sloppy rough draft or a project you've reviewed only once or twice. If you don't take time to polish your writing, why should anyone make time to read it?

For all of these reasons (and I'm sure, many more), proofreading and editing are essential to producing writing that is polished, professional, and publishable.

Types of Edits

There are various types of edits that are done to a manuscript before it is published. In the publishing world, there are probably upward of a dozen different kinds of editing. Some aren't related to writing at all (like acquisitions editing). Some projects have an editor strictly for fact checking. Others have an editor who performs indexing.

For our purposes, we'll look at three main types of editing that all writers should be familiar with. You'll perform these edits on your own work and, hopefully, you'll get someone else to do these edits on your work too.

Developmental Editing

Some developmental editing happens before you start writing or while you're working on a rough draft. If someone is helping you plan the project, that would be considered developmental editing.

Developmental editing can include any of the following:

- Help with planning the project's structure, organization, and format (plotting a novel, for example).

- Making deep changes or suggestions for the project (major changes to plot or characters).

- Rewriting or restructuring portions of the draft, including moving and changing entire sentences, paragraphs, scenes, and chapters.

- Checking for and fixing consistency in formatting and structure (for example, giving chapters unique names or numbering them).

- Identifying major gaps and flaws (like plot holes).

- Removing material that is unnecessary or superfluous.

- Establishing style guidelines and early layouts (especially if images are included).

Many writers use alpha readers, who perform similar functions as developmental editors. They might review a manuscript chapter by chapter, as the author is writing the first draft, and provide feedback on how the project is developing. Alpha readers and developmental editors are the only people who should see a work in its raw, unedited state or as it's being written. Some writers may not work with developmental editors or alpha readers at all.

Copyediting

There are various levels of copyediting, so if you're getting a piece of your writing copyedited, you should ask for a detailed description of what, exactly, it entails. Here's what you can expect from a copyeditor:

- Fix grammar, spelling, and punctuation.

- Ensure words are used correctly and vocabulary is consistent, and identify poor, vague, or incorrect wording and statements.

- Double-check cross-references.

- Check for consistency in grammar and orthography (adhering to a style guideline) as well as style and tone.

- Check sequencing (make sure chapters or tables of contents are in the right order).

- Ensure story continuity and consistency through tracking (plot and characters).

- Fix transitions and strengthen overall readability.

- Ensure logical, consistent structure with headings and titles.

- Suggest and/or apply changes, including deletions and additions to the text.

- Ensure sentence and paragraph structure is clear, concise, and appropriate.

Proofreading

Proofreaders check for grammar, spelling, punctuation, and any errors involving typos and misuse of words. Some proofreaders check lists, labels, and cross-references. If the manuscript is being typeset, proofreaders might review typesetting and check for proper word, sentence, and paragraph breaks. They might ensure that the manuscript adheres to style and formatting guidelines.

Actual duties may vary between editors, but these descriptions give you a general idea of what various editors do and what you can expect when you work with them. You can also use these guidelines to help you figure out how to edit your own work, keeping in mind that no matter how much editing you do, ideally, a complete manuscript would get a full copyedit (which is also called substantive editing) from a professional editor.

Editing Tips for Writers

"Almost all good writing begins with terrible first efforts. You need to start somewhere."
- Anne Lamott

The human mind is a funny thing; it likes to play tricks on us.

For example, when we edit our own writing, we tend to read it as we think it should be, which means we misread our own typos and other spelling, grammar, and punctuation mistakes, and we overlook problems with word choice, sentence structure, context, and overall readability.

If you have friends or family members who have good grammar skills, maybe they can help you out by editing and proofreading your work before you submit it for publication. If you're self-publishing, your best bet is to work with a professional editor; at the very least, get a professional proofreader.

For most of us, it's not likely that anyone is going to proofread and edit every single piece of writing that we create. That's especially true for writers who put out a lot of material—like bloggers, copywriters, and freelancers. Proofreading and editing services can get expensive, and friends and family probably don't want to spend all their evenings checking your work.

Sometimes, the only option available is to do it yourself.

Here are some proofreading and editing tips that you can put into practice for polishing your own writing:

- Proofread and edit every single piece of writing before it is seen by another set of eyes. Even if you hire a professional editor or proofreader, check your work first.

- Understand the difference between proofreading and editing. Edit first to make deep or structural changes, then proofread to check for proper grammar, spelling, and punctuation.

- Use the track-changes feature in Microsoft Word when you edit. This feature saves your edits and marks up your document so you can revert to previous versions.

- Step away from a piece of writing before you proofread it. The longer the piece, the longer you should wait to proofread it. Let a novel sit for a few weeks. Let a blog post sit overnight.

- Before proofreading and editing, run spelling-and-grammar check. Then, run it again after you're done polishing to check for any lingering typos. However, don't count on software for spelling and grammar. Use it as a fail-safe.

- Read your work aloud. Pronounce each word slowly and clearly as you read and check for mistakes.

- Proofreading should never be a rush job. Do it s l o w l y.

- Don't review your work once and then send it out into the world. I recommend editing until the piece reads smoothly and proofreading until you can't find a single mistake.

- Read the piece backward so you can see each word separately and out of context.

- Look up the spelling of proper names and scientific or technical terms that you're not familiar with, to make sure you're spelling them correctly.

- Don't make any assumptions. If you're not sure about something, then look it up so you can fix a mistake (if there is one) and learn the correct way.

- Don't forget to proofread titles, headlines, and footnotes.

- Pay attention to the mistakes you've made in your writing. You'll find that you tend to make the same ones repeatedly. Keep track of these and work on avoiding them during the initial writing process in the future.

- Choose one of the many style guides and stick with it. This will make your work more consistent, and you'll have a reliable resource to use when you have questions about style and formatting.

- Start building a collection of grammar books and writing resources, so when you do run into questions (and you will), you have access to credible answers.

- If you intentionally let grammatical mistakes slip through, do so by choice and make sure you have a good reason. It's okay to break the rules if you know why you're breaking them.

- Pay attention to formatting. Use the same formatting on all paragraphs, headings, and other typographical styling. Learn how to use these features in your word-processing software.

- Proofread when you're fresh and wide awake. Proofreading doesn't go over well when you're tired or distracted.

- Proofreading and editing can be tedious, so break up your revision sessions by doing other tasks that help you clear your mind: exercise, play with the pets or kids, go for a short walk, or listen to some music. Try to avoid reading or writing during these breaks. Lots of short breaks make tedious tasks easier.

Some people love the proofreading and editing process. Others despise it. If you're into grammar, the mechanics of writing, and polishing your work, then proofreading and editing will be easier and more enjoyable for you. If not, just look at it as part of your job—something that goes along with being a writer.

Editing and proofreading have become habitual steps in my writing process, and I've come to enjoy these steps since I now know they lead to better writing.

Every time you fix a mistake, you'll feel good about it, knowing you just improved your writing and made it more readable. That's another thing—editing your work is considerate to readers. Poorly written, incorrect texts that are full of typos and other mistakes throw readers off and distract them from the flow of a piece. So don't skip the revision process: proof, edit, and repeat. Then, if necessary, do it again!

Activities

- Find an old piece of writing that you haven't worked on or looked at in a while. Save a copy of the original, and then open it in a word-processing program. Read through the entire piece once, then go back through a second time and make major changes to the structure and content. Move sentences and paragraphs around, make better word choices, fix issues with plot and character or concept. Then go through a third time and check strictly for grammar, spelling, punctuation, and typos. Use highlighting to mark sections you're not sure about (such as whether you're using a word properly or whether a sentence is technically correct). Wait a day, then review the original and the revised copies side by side. How much improvement were you able to make? Could you go over it a couple more times?

- Find a writer friend and exchange projects for editing and proofreading. You can swap short pieces like blog posts or entire chapters from novels you're working on. Before you hand your pieces to each other, do your best to edit and proofread your own work. Make sure you use the track-changes feature in Microsoft Word so you can see what changes you make to each other's writing (you can also do this activity with printed copy and a red pen). Did you friend catch anything you missed? Were there suggestions for improvements that you hadn't considered?

Chapter 4:
Grammar

"The greater part of the world's troubles are due to questions of grammar." - Michel de Montaigne

It's helpful to know the rules of grammar, spelling, and punctuation when you're writing. Your writing process will flow more smoothly and you won't get hung up on questions about whether your sentences are correct. You can write freely and focus on your scenes and ideas.

During revisions, grammar isn't merely helpful; it's essential—non-negotiable. Good writing adheres to good grammar. That doesn't mean you can't break the rules, and you don't have to write in a way that sounds outdated, formal, or old-fashioned (many strict or traditional grammar rules lead to writing that sounds stiff). It does mean that you should know the rules before you break them, and you should know why you're breaking them when you do.

There are a host of resources you can use to learn grammar, but first, you should know what grammar is and why it's important for writers to learn it.

Grammar vs. Orthography

Let's get technical for a minute. What, exactly, is grammar?

According to Wikipedia,

> ...in linguistics, grammar is the set of structural rules that govern the composition of sentences, phrases, and words in any given natural language. The term refers also to the study of such rules...Linguists do not normally use the term to refer to orthographical rules, although usage books and style guides that call themselves grammars may also refer to spelling and punctuation.

Technically speaking, spelling and punctuation are not components of grammar; they belong to the field of orthography.

There are two common ways that language manifests. It is either spoken or written. Grammar deals with how we structure the language, and it is applied to both speech and writing.

Orthography, on the other hand, addresses the rules of a language's writing system or script. Orthography deals with spelling and punctuation because these elements are relevant only when the language is written.

When you say a sentence aloud, you don't say *period, question mark,* or *exclamation point* at the end. If you're reading a sentence, you need these punctuation marks to help you navigate the text; they also provide cues that inform the way we stress words or inflect the reading.

Grammar addresses how we structure our language and includes concepts such as tense agreement, modifiers, sentence diagramming, word order in a sentence, and sentence order in a paragraph.

But when we're dealing with written language, proper spelling and punctuation are just as essential as tense agreement. It would be quite difficult to get through a written text that was not punctuated or where the majority of the words were spelled incorrectly.

I've found that spelling and punctuation are incorrect or misused far more than structural (or grammatical) elements in writing. Most people know how to put their words in order, and a writer of average skill is usually good at verb and tense agreements and other grammatical aspects of writing.

Conversely, plenty of folks struggle with orthography (punctuation and spelling) even if their grammar is in good order. This makes sense because we are exposed to language primarily through speaking and listening. We absorb the rules of grammar simply by engaging in conversation (and this how we also adopt bad grammar habits, depending on who we converse with). We absorb spelling and punctuation through reading. Since we tend to talk and listen more than we read and write, it's logical that most of us are better at grammar than orthography.

Technically speaking, grammar may not include spelling and punctuation, but without all of these elements in our writing—without grammar and orthography together—we cannot produce clear, coherent, and correct texts.

Why Grammar, Spelling, and Punctuation Matter

Grammar, spelling, and punctuation are the most basic components of good writing. Grammatically correct texts are easier to read, easier to get published, and easier to sell to readers; in many cases, a firm understanding of grammar also makes the writing process easier.

Grammar is unpleasant for some writers. We're in it for creative expression—we want to tell a story, make a statement, or share ideas. Why do we have to fret over parts of speech and punctuation marks?

But grammar is necessary. You can get by as a professional writer without totally mastering grammar, but you will fall flat on your face if you don't know the basics.

Too many writers avoid studying grammar because they prefer to focus on the creative side of writing. Some work under the assumption that grammar is unimportant (they are wrong!), while others rely on editors and proofreaders to do the dirty work.

But developing good grammar habits, while painstaking, enriches the experience for everyone involved—from the writer to the editor to the reader.

If you've ever read a piece of writing that was peppered with typos and grammatical mistakes, you know how frustrating these oversights can be for a reader. They're like bumps in the road, jarring you out of the text. When you're deeply immersed in a story or article and encounter one of these errors, you're pulled out of the reading experience.

Writers gain great benefits from developing skills in grammar. Have you ever been writing and gotten stuck on some technicality? *Should I put a comma here? Am I using this word correctly? Are these words in the right order?* If you've learned grammar and studied a style guide, eventually these kinds of questions won't interrupt the flow of your writing.

I've found grammatical mistakes in novels, magazine articles, even in textbooks, and (especially) on blogs. Now, a lot of these errors are typos. It's not that the writers or editors didn't know their way around the English language—they just let one (or two) mistakes slip past. If people who are experts at editing can't catch every mistake, can you imagine the number of errors in a piece produced by someone who doesn't have a good handle on grammar? Those works are riddled with mistakes!

And when mistakes appear to be more than mere typos and instead seem to reflect a deficiency in good grammar and basic writing skills, then I find myself questioning the quality of the work. If writers can't be bothered to learn the tools of their trade, why should I bother reading their work?

There are many things that lead to better writing, and there are a few things that raise a flag to signal poor writing. Bad grammar is one of them.

Learning the rules of grammar might be a drag (I happen to find grammar fun and interesting), but it's a worthwhile pursuit if you want to get your work published and find an audience for your writing. Study a little bit of grammar each week, and you'll be writing better in no time.

Once you master grammar, you won't have to worry about it anymore. It becomes a natural part of your writing process. Proofreading and editing become less of a chore, and your writing sessions flow more smoothly.

Why Should You Study and Master Grammar?

Learning proper grammar has its advantages:

- **Readability:** If your work is peppered with grammatical mistakes and typos, your readers are going to have a hard time trudging through it. Nothing is more distracting than being yanked out of a good story because a word is misspelled or a punctuation mark is misplaced. You should always respect your readers enough to deliver a product that is enjoyable and easy to understand.

- **Communication:** Some musicians learn to play by ear and never bother to learn how to read music. Many of them don't even know which notes or chords they're playing, even though they can play a full repertoire of recognizable songs and probably a few of their own. But get them in a room with other musicians and they may have difficulty communicating because they don't know the vocabulary of their trade. They can play a C chord but they don't know it's called a C chord. You can't engage with others in your profession if you don't speak the language of your industry. Good luck talking shop with writers and editors if you don't know the parts of speech, the names of punctuation marks, and all the other components of language and writing that are related to good grammar.

- **Working with an editor:** Some writers say they don't need to learn grammar because they can hire an editor. If you can't talk shop with other writers, you certainly won't be able to converse intelligently about your work and its flaws with a professional editor. How will you respond to feedback and revision suggestions when you don't know what the heck the editor is talking about? Remember, it's your work. Ultimately, the final version is your call and you won't be able to approve it if you're clueless about what's wrong with it.

- **Saving money:** Speaking of hiring an editor, quality professional editing services are quite costly. And editors will only go so deep into correcting a manuscript. It's unseemly to return work to a writer that is solid red with markups. Most freelance editors and proofreaders have a limit to how much they will mark up any given text, so the more grammatical mistakes there are, the more surface work the editor will have to do. That means she won't be able to get into the nitty-gritty and make significant changes that take your work from average to superior, because she's breaking a sweat just trying to make it readable.

- **Investing in yourself:** Learning grammar is a way to invest in yourself. You don't need anything more than a couple of good grammar resources and a willingness to take the time necessary to hone your skills. In the beginning, it might be a drag, but eventually, all those grammar rules will become second nature and you will have become a first-rate writer.

- **Respectability, credibility, and authority:** As a first-rate writer who has mastered good grammar, you will gain respect, credibility, and authority among your peers and readers. People will take you seriously and regard you as an artist or a professional who is committed to the craft of writing, not just some hack trying to string words together in a haphazard manner.

- **Better writing all around:** When you've taken the time to learn grammar, it becomes second nature. As you write, the words and punctuation marks come naturally because you know what you're doing; you've studied the rules and put in plenty of practice. That means you can focus more of your attention on other aspects of your work, like structure, context, and imagery. This leads to better writing all around.

- **Self-awareness:** Some people don't have it. They charge through life completely unaware of themselves or the people around them. But most of us possess some sense of self. What sense of self can you have as a writer who doesn't know proper grammar? That's like being a carpenter who doesn't know what a hammer and nails are. It's almost indecent.

- **There is really only one reason to avoid learning grammar:** plain laziness. Anything else is a silly excuse. As I said, I'm all for breaking the rules when doing so makes the work better, but how can you break the rules effectively if you don't know what they are?

No matter what trade, craft, or career you're pursuing, it all starts with learning the basics and understanding your tools. Actors learn how to read scripts. Scientists learn how to apply the scientific method. We are writers. We must learn to write well, and writing well requires comprehensive knowledge of grammar, spelling, and punctuation.

So commit yourself to making grammar and orthography integral to your writing, and soon you'll feel comfortable and confident about your work.

How to Strengthen Your Grammar Skills

There are only three things you have to do to learn the rules of grammar:

- Get a good grammar and style guide.

- When you're not sure about something, look it up and learn it.

- Apply what you've learned by incorporating it into future drafts and compositions.

To improve your grammar, you have to know where to look for answers to all your nagging questions. Sometimes you'll find answers to questions you didn't even know you had. Even the most experienced and knowledgeable writers and editors have to look up answers to grammatical questions that arise from time to time.

There is no grammar authority, no supreme court of grammar where judges strike down the gavel at offenders. Grammar is not an exact science, and even among the most educated and experienced linguists, some of the rules are heavily debated.

Of course, there are some basic rules we can all agree on, and these can be found in any good grammar resource. There are gray areas, too, which are deftly handled by style guides.

As writers, we need these resources. They help us navigate written language so we can use it effectively, and they show us how to produce work that is readable and publishable, work that people will pay to read.

Every time you look up the answer to a grammar question, you expand your knowledge about language and your writing skills grow. For example, if you're polishing a short story and are not sure if you've formatted the dialogue properly, you can look it up to verify how formatting should be handled. A few weeks later, when you run into the same issue in another writing project, you'll know the correct way to format the dialogue, and you'll get it right the first time.

Do not rely on spell-check or grammar software to clean up messy, incorrect sentences. Most of these automated tools will fix only the most basic mistakes. Often, there are plenty of errors programmed right into the software. I've seen the most trusted, industry-standard writing software make grammatical recommendations that are downright abysmal.

Grammar and Style Guides

A grammar guide addresses the formal rules of language, rules that are applicable across any style, form, or format. As comprehensive as the English language may be, there are plenty of instances where the rules of grammar are unclear or don't exist at all. While a grammar guide is useful, most style guides include the rules of grammar, spelling, and punctuation, plus guidelines for many situations that aren't included in the established rules.

There is a host of style guides available and the one you choose will depend on what you write. *The Chicago Manual of Style* is my preferred style guide; it's intended for authors and general usage. There are other guides that are geared specifically toward journalism or academic writing, and many large companies and organizations have their own style guides.

A wide range of people use style guides—authors, journalists, and reporters being the most obvious. But style guides are also used in academia (students, scholars, and teachers), science (doctors, engineers, and scientists), law (lawyers and legislators), and in any profession where writing or editing is part of the job.

What is a Style Guide?

A style guide is a manual that establishes rules for language, spelling, formatting, and punctuation. Within academia, these guides also provide standards for citations, references, and bibliographies. Many disciplines have their very own style guide, such as the *Publication Manual of the American Psychological Association,* which is commonly called the *APA Style Guide.*

These manuals promote good grammar and ensure consistency in areas where grammar conventions may be unclear. Style guides answer those thorny writing questions that are absent from the rules of grammar. Yet at the same time, the average style guide also answers questions that deal specifically with the rules of grammar. Basically, it's an all-purpose writing resource.

A style guide is appropriate for any form or genre of writing. Since a style guide's primary function is to help the author render a work consistent and ensure correct grammar and orthography, any written work will benefit from its application. That includes creative writing, freelance writing, and blogging.

In many cases, a style guide is not only appropriate, it's mandatory. If you're writing for submission, it's a good idea to check a publication's submission guidelines to see if they require adherence to a particular style guide.

A style guide will make your work more consistent. Did you use a serial comma in the first paragraph but leave it out in the third? For that matter, do you know what a serial comma is? Have you used italics on one page to indicate a book title, but on another page used quotation marks?

By establishing standards that you can follow, a style guide helps you streamline your work and ensure that it is clear and consistent. After you've used a particular set of guidelines for a while, the writing process will flow more smoothly since you won't have to stop and deliberate on issues you're not sure about.

Rules Are Made to Be Broken

"And all dared to brave unknown terrors, to do mighty deeds, to boldly split infinitives that no man had split before—and thus was the Empire forged." - Douglas Adams

If you do break the rules of grammar, it helps to know them first. Otherwise, your writing will come off as amateurish.

Everyone knows the old saying: rules were made to be broken. But some people love rules, live by them, and wouldn't dream of breaking them. For these folks, good grammar means strict adherence to every rule, no matter how archaic or minute.

That's too bad.

Don't get me wrong. Rules are good. They keep us organized, consistent, and civilized. If there were no rules, we'd all be living in a perpetual state of anarchy.

In the world of language, rules help us understand each other. After all, language is merely a series of sounds that are organized according to a set of rules. Without rules, language would just be a bunch of noise.

The rules of grammar are designed to help us communicate clearly, both in our speech and in our writing. When proper grammar is absent, writing is sloppy, inconsistent, and difficult to read. To put it bluntly, we need grammar in order to make sense.

When a writer hasn't bothered to learn the rules of grammar, it shows. The prose doesn't flow smoothly or naturally, punctuation marks are strewn about haphazardly, and there's no tense agreement. Sentences are jumbled, words are misused, and paragraphs are disorganized. It's a mess. The work is lazy and sloppy. Nobody wants to read it.

Failing to learn the rules of grammar leads to bad writing.

But some writers stubbornly refuse to bother with grammar, and they're full of excuses: writing should be an art, the rules don't make sense, and who made up these rules anyway? But these are all just excuses, poor rationale for avoiding the work that is involved in learning grammar and applying it.

Grammar is not easy to learn, let alone master. Writers, editors, and proofreaders must make a lifelong commitment to learning the rules and determining when the rules should be broken.

Writers who are dedicated to their craft will invest the energy required to master their most basic tools, grammar being foremost among them. But there are situations in which it's best to break the rules—as long as you know which ones you're breaking and why.

There's a difference between breaking the rules to make the writing more effective and breaking the rules because you don't know what they are.

When we break the rules of grammar, one of two things happens. Either the writing improves or it suffers. Writers who break the rules because they don't know them are more likely to produce shoddy work. But when writers take the time to truly learn the rules, breaking them becomes an option, a technique that a writer can use to add flair, color, and meaning to the text.

Sometimes sticking to the rules doesn't make sense. This is especially true when we're writing dialogue. People don't speak in a manner that translates easily into proper grammar. So if our dialogue is written according to the rules of grammar, it can sound unnatural.

Additionally, many grammar rules were established a long time ago. Language is constantly evolving. If a particular rule makes the writing sound old-fashioned or outdated, then discarding the rule is probably the best option.

Learn the rules as thoroughly as you can and then decide how to apply them on a case-by-case basis, depending on the audience and context.

Recommended Grammar and Style Resources

"Grammar, he saw, was agreement, community, consensus." - D.T. Max

Here are some grammar and style resources to help get you started on your path toward mastering grammar, orthography, and style. These are a mix of websites and books. Some are free, others require an investment, but keep in mind that when you invest in resources like these, you're investing in yourself and your writing.

- *Grammar Girl's Quick and Dirty Tips for Better Writing* by Mignon Fogerty is a fun and accessible book packed with grammar tips for writers. It's a grammar book, but it doesn't read like a textbook.

- Before the book, Grammar Girl's podcast made her an online sensation. Her website (http://grammar.quickanddirtytips.com) features full written transcripts of her audio podcast for folks who prefer to learn via reading.

- *The Chicago Manual of Style* is the most widely used style guide in publishing, and it includes grammar and orthography. It's perfect for general writing, including fiction and creative nonfiction.

- *The Gregg Reference Manual* is widely used in professional and business writing. It is considered the most authoritative source on grammar, usage, and style.

- *The Elements of Style* is easily the most popular book on writing, style, and basic grammar. It's a slim volume that practically fits in your pocket and it's a fast, easy read. A must-have for every writer.

Chapter 5:
Skills

"It's none of their business that you have to learn to write. Let them think you were born that way."
- Ernest Hemingway

Nobody's born knowing how to read or write.

The lucky ones have talent, but we all start out learning the letters of the alphabet. We memorize the sounds that letters make, and we learn how they come together to form words. Pretty soon, we're reading. Someone puts a pencil in our hand and then we're scribbling letters on paper. We learn how to group the letters into words and then we learn how to group words into sentences. At last, we can write.

It takes years of study and practice before we can write a simple sentence. So what does it take to become a professional writer?

It takes skill, and skill is acquired by practicing and working hard at the craft.

When we talk about writing skills, we usually think of the basics: the ability to write sentences and paragraphs correctly with proper grammar, spelling, and punctuation. But a lot more than that goes into writing well.

Ambitious writers strive to consistently produce better writing. We study the rules of grammar, spelling, and punctuation and we work at expanding our vocabularies.

We memorize literary devices and storytelling techniques. We develop a distinct voice.

There's a lot to learn, but over time, we learn to write prose and verse that captivates readers.

From learning how to comprehensively use tools, like writing software, to mastering concepts that are specific to form and genre, a professional writer needs to build skills that go far beyond the basics.

But the basics are where we begin.

Basic Writing Skills

Ideally, every high school graduate would possess basic writing skills. Unfortunately, a lot of people enter college or the workforce without knowing the difference between *they're*, *their*, and *there*. An astonishing number of smart or educated people don't know the difference between an adverb and an adjective and can't identify a subject or an object in a sentence. Plenty of people go through life never mastering these basics and that's okay—because they're not writers.

It's not that writers have to acquire knowledge of language and orthography that rivals that of lexicographers. But language is our primary tool and we should have a fundamental grasp of how it works and how to use it.

Yet that basic understanding of language—a comprehensive working knowledge of grammar, spelling, and punctuation—coupled with the ability to write decent sentences and paragraphs are only the first skills that a writer acquires. Those skills are sufficient for beginner writing. When we want to move past the ability to write sufficiently and strive to write professionally and with excellence, we must acquire a broader set of writing skills.

Nothing ruins a great story like weak words and poorly structured sentences that don't make sense. Nothing derails a poem like poor word choices and clumsy rhymes. And nothing destroys a piece of creative nonfiction like a disorganized narrative.

There are some elements of writing that must be developed over time and with practice. It's difficult to know why one grammatically correct sentence simply sounds better than another or why one word works better than another word that has the same meaning. The ability to write the better sentence or choose the better word does not come from a book, the way grammar can come from a book. It comes with experience.

With grammar, you can study the rules, memorize them, and then apply them to your writing almost immediately. The subtler aspects of writing can be learned, but they are usually learned over time through a combination of reading, studying the craft of writing, and practicing.

But we can still develop these skills by training ourselves to watch for opportunities to experiment with them. We can look for them in the works we read and the projects we're writing.

Comprehensive Writing Skills

Below is a list of comprehensive writing skills and best practices that you should consider when assessing a piece of writing and in developing your own writing abilities. While this is not an exhaustive list (there are infinite ways to improve and strengthen your writing), it will give you a good start:

- **Word choice:** Choosing the right words to describe what's happening in a piece of writing can be challenging. The best words accurately capture the sentiment that the author is trying to convey. If something doesn't sound right, if a word isn't accurate or precise enough, then it needs to be replaced with a better word. Why refer to a "loud noise" when you can call it a *roar, din,* or *commotion*? The more specific the words are, the more easily readers will understand what you're trying to communicate. Choose words that are as concise, precise, and vivid as possible.

- **Vocabulary:** Nothing makes a sentence sing like words that are clear, specific, and concrete. Expand your arsenal by building your vocabulary. Read a lot and look up words you don't know. Peruse the dictionary. Sign up for a word-of-the-day newsletter. Keep a log of vocabulary words and spend a minute or two each day adding to it and studying your new words.

- **Sentence structure:** Sentence structure is even more critical than word choice. A weak word is like a missed beat, but a weak sentence is total discord. It breaks the flow, confuses readers, and pulls them out of the narrative. Read sentences aloud to see how they flow.

- **Rhythm:** Make sure to vary sentence length; when all your sentences are the same length, the writing drones on.

- **Paragraph structure:** Each paragraph contains a single idea. In fiction, each paragraph contains one character's action and dialogue. Extremely long paragraphs tend to bore readers. If you write long paragraphs, try to alternate them with shorter paragraphs to give balance and rhythm to your structure.

- **Transition:** Sentences and paragraphs should flow seamlessly. If you must jump from one topic to another, use headings or transitional phrases to separate them. Place transitional phrases and sentences within chapters to move smoothly between scenes.

- **Word repetition:** Nothing deflates a piece of writing like the same descriptive word unnecessarily used over and over. *She had a pretty smile. She wore a pretty dress. She lived in a pretty house.* This kind of repetition robs a story of its imagery, making it two-dimensional. There are many ways to say that something or someone is *pretty.*

- **Thesaurus:** A thesaurus helps you build your vocabulary and provides a workaround for repetition. Some writers avoid using the thesaurus, believing that reliance on it constitutes some writerly weakness. But your job is not to be a dictionary or word bank; it's knowing how to find the perfect words for your sentences.

- **Concept repetition:** Repetitive words are one problem; repetitive information is another—or it can be a good thing. Repeat concepts when you're teaching because it promotes retention. But don't tell the reader what day of the week it is three times in a single scene.

- **Simplification:** Run-on sentences and short sentences strung together with commas and conjunctions create a lot of dust and noise in a piece of writing. In most cases, simple, straightforward language helps bring the action or ideas to center stage.

- **Concise writing:** Concise writing is a matter of style, but it is overwhelmingly preferable for contemporary readers who don't appreciate long passages of description or long-winded sentences and paragraphs that drone on and on. With concise writing, we say what absolutely needs to be said and we say it in as few words as possible, using the simplest and most direct language available. That does not mean the writing can't have flair or be colorful. It certainly can! Shave off any excess and focus on the juicy bits.

- **Organization:** A poorly organized manuscript is a nightmare to read. Thoughts, ideas, and action need to flow logically. Similar ideas should be grouped together. Outlines are ideal for planning and organizing a complex piece of writing.

- **Consistency:** If you use italics for thought dialogue, always use italics for thought dialogue; don't alternate between italics and quotation marks. If you use a serial comma in one sentence, use it in all sentences that could take a serial comma. Make sure your headings and titles have the same formatting. Be consistent!

- **Literary devices:** Some literary devices are particular to form and genre, but most can be used across all forms and genres. Literary devices range from techniques for making word choices (like alliteration or assonance) to methods for infusing prose with vivid imagery. Studying these devices and using them in your work will be a huge asset to your writing skills.

- **Filler words:** Filler words are vague, meaningless, and unnecessary. Consider the following examples: *very skinny, really tired, just going to the store.* Words like *very, really,* and *just* usually do nothing more than emphasize the words they modify. Remove filler words or replace them and the words they modify with single words that are more vivid: *bony, exhausted, going to the store.*

- **Passive vs. active voice:** Passive voice comes off sounding formal and old-fashioned. When used in contemporary dialogue, it can sound unnatural. In passive voice, we say *The car was driven by her.* Active voice is more natural and direct: *She drove the car.* When in doubt, go with active voice and use passive voice only if you have a good reason to do so.

- **Filter words:** A common bad habit in narrative writing is framing one action within another: *He started walking* or *I thought the car was too fast.* Characters don't start walking: they walk. In first-person narrative, everything represents the narrator's thoughts, so it's sufficient to say *the car was too fast*; readers understand that this is the narrator's thought.

- **Redundancy:** Redundancy is unnecessary repetition or stating the obvious. I suspect it occurs when we're writing and trying to sort through our own thoughts, so we say the same thing in various ways. Here's an example: *I am taking my car to the shop tomorrow, so I won't be able to go anywhere because my car will be in the shop.* The sentence is redundant. Here's a replacement sentence: *I won't be able to go anywhere tomorrow because my car will be in the shop*.

- **Formatting:** A writer should know how to format a piece of writing—not just properly, but well. For example, we don't use italics or quotation marks to tell readers where to place emphasis on words in a sentence.

- **Pronouns:** Make sure every pronoun is clear, so the reader knows what it represents. Don't refer to *this* or *that* if they are abstract concepts. Don't use *he, she, him,* or *her* three times in a sentence if two or more people or characters are in play.

Skills of Substance

"To produce a mighty book, you must choose a mighty theme." - Herman Melville

Great writing is not just about how we string words together. Saying something well is not enough; we also must have something worth saying. A piece of writing, no matter how well written, must have substance. A story needs a theme; a poem needs an experience; an essay needs a solid idea with information to back it up.

The substance of our writing lies in its content. Let's look at some best practices for writing with substance:

- **Logic:** A piece of writing must stand up to logic. If a character is a high-profile CEO, she probably doesn't live in a low-rent studio apartment. Everything in a piece of writing has to line up and make sense. Beta readers (readers who review edited drafts before you polish and submit or publish) are excellent for finding flawed logic.

- **Chronology:** While many works of fiction experiment with time, either directly through time travel or indirectly by telling a story out of chronological order, the general rule of thumb is to make sure things happen on a timeline that makes sense. For example, a character does not wake up, get dressed, and take a shower—the shower comes before getting dressed.

- **Literary techniques:** Use literary techniques to strengthen areas of your writing that are weak or to add depth and meaning to a piece of writing. Literary techniques range from storytelling structures and formulas (three-act structure, hero's journey, etc.) to methods for developing characters.

- **Details:** Knowing when to be specific and when to be vague can be tricky. When we're writing, sometimes we visualize irrelevant details while more significant elements escape us. When we revise, we should look for areas where there's too much detail or not enough.

- **Information dumps:** If your story requires explanation and background information, try to avoid giving it to readers through information dumps—long, descriptive passages providing information that is necessary to understand the rest of the text. One example would be pausing in the narrative to relay several pages of the character's backstory. Instead, find ways to reveal the most important information through dialogue and action.

- **Imagery:** Use imagery and action to show readers what is happening rather than telling them. For example, *she was tired* tells readers the character was tired. *She yawned and blinked, and then she checked her wallet to see if she had enough change for a coffee* shows readers that the character is tired.

- **Clichés:** Clichés are words, phrases, and sentences that are overused. They suck the life from a piece of writing. Most clichés are metaphors: *you're too blind to see the writing on the wall.* Instead of using overused phrases like these, look for fresh ways to express the same sentiment.

- **Sensory details:** Engaging the senses is a great way to show readers what's happening or relay your ideas. Look for opportunities to explain how things look, sound, smell, feel, and taste.

This list only scratches the surface. Beyond these basic best practices for writing with substance, there is a host of other skills that you'll need, depending on whether you write novels, short stories, poems, or essays. There is yet more to learn within various genres of writing. Form and genre are beyond the scope of this book, since each form and genre warrants a book of its own. Make sure you study form and genre as you develop your writing skills.

As you read other works, whether they are novels, blog posts, poems, articles, or essays, look for these elements and examine them to see what works and what doesn't. Do the same when you're writing and especially revising your own work.

Also, know that there's always a time and a place to break the rules, and there are exceptions to every best practice. There will be times when you don't stick to a chronological timeline, when you need to use an information dump or repeat a word over and over.

On the other hand, don't assume that you or your writing are the exception. Don't break rules or disregard proven writing techniques and practices simply because you're lazy or trying too hard to be original. Most readers want to be engaged and entertained more than they want to read some new kind of experimental story that's never been told before.

Software Skills

Learning how to use writing tools and resources properly is often overlooked in favor of focusing on the act of writing. While crafting compelling sentences and paragraphs that are substantive is certainly more important than mastering writing software, it's worthwhile to learn how to use your tools. Doing so will make your writing process easier.

Many writers complain about difficult software, but the software isn't difficult at all. You can fire up a word-processing program and start typing and that's easy enough, but when you get into formatting and structuring a document, there's a learning curve. Once you learn how to use a piece of software, it becomes quite easy, even if it still presents annoying quirks at times. And once you master one word-processing program, it will be easier to master another, although there will be a new learning curve.

- Microsoft Word is the industry standard for all types of writing. Many secondary writing applications (in publishing, for example) are built to import text from MS Word.

- Another program, called Scrivener, is giving MS Word a run for its money, and authors are migrating to it in droves. Ideally, you'll have both of these programs on your computer. Scrivener is especially useful if you're writing longer works, like books.

- Pages is Apple's answer to MS Word and it can import and export to Word, but some formatting might get lost. Pages is fine if you're using it for personal purposes, but if you're writing professionally and passing documents back and forth, it would behoove you to get Word and install it on your computer.

Software ownership or lack thereof should never prohibit you from writing. Don't hold off on starting your novel because all you have is a text program. If you're saving up for a professional piece of software, that's fine, but don't postpone your projects. You can import from text applications to any other word-processing software and deal with the formatting later.

Whichever program you use, you should be able to use it proficiently. I receive a lot of different MS Word documents from writers and clients. Each one seems to use the program in a unique way. Very few people I've encountered have bothered to really learn how to format MS Word documents, and this makes working with those documents tedious, frustrating, and time consuming.

There are tons of books, articles, and tutorials that will teach you how to use your writing software of choice. Some software has comprehensive help files or built-in tutorials that walk you through the most important functions and features, and you can easily find out how to accomplish just about anything on any kind of software by simply doing an online search.

Here are a few basic things you should know how to do with your word-processing software:

- Create new documents, open and save existing documents, and make copies of documents.

- Set margins and send to printer.

- Choose fonts and font sizes and apply formatting, such as bold, italics, underlines, and highlighting.

- Format paragraphs: indents, line height, and spacing between paragraphs.

- Align text: left, center, right, and full justified.

- Insert and align images and other objects.

- Use the find function (and find-and-replace).

- Track changes (keeps track of revisions) and view markups (shows revisions).

- Set up styles and create templates.

One of the most useful features you can master in MS Word is called Styles. Styles allow you to create a style that is formatted in a particular way. For example, you can create a style called "paragraph text" and set it to Times New Roman 12 point double spaced with the first line indented. That way, whenever you want to use that format, you can simply apply the "paragraph text" style.

Styles are also immensely helpful in ensuring consistency in a document. You can create styles for chapter titles and subheadings so that your titles and headings are all formatted the same way throughout a long document.

Finally, with styles, you don't have to go through and format every document manually, adjusting each paragraph or line. You set up your styles once, then quickly apply them as you write. It's the hugest time saver for writers, and I highly recommend learning how to use styles in whatever word-processing software you use.

Skills for Published Authors

There are additional skills that professional writers must use shortly before or right after their work is published. Many of these skills don't involve writing at all and are focused mostly in the marketing arena.

Frankly, the more you know about marketing, the more of your work you'll be able to sell.

All published authors, whether self-published or traditionally published, must do some level of marketing to promote their work. Some publishers will handle a little bit of the marketing, and there are certainly celebrity authors who get large marketing budgets from their publishers—or earn enough from their advances and royalties to hire out most of the marketing. However, the vast majority of authors must do a lot of their own PR (public relations).

An author's marketing activities can range from managing a website and blog to using social media. Book tours, speaking events, and interviews are also activities that writers use to promote their books. Most writers will focus on certain marketing tactics, either because those tactics are more suited to their skills or comfort level, or because they seem to have the best results.

While marketing isn't something you have to do until your work is published, it's not a bad idea to study a little marketing in advance so you can plan ahead. At the very least, you should start formulating a marketing plan before your work is published. For example, if you're publishing a novel, you'll want to have a marketing plan in place many months before the novel comes out.

However, the best marketing strategy is to write a great book, then write another one and another and another. Nothing beats a loyal fan base and word of mouth. That said, it's never too early to learn about building an author's platform.

Form and Genre

Beyond basic writing skills are those that relate to form and genre. There are certain skills that fiction writers must possess, which may be different from those that poets must develop. Science-fiction writers will need a slightly different set of skills than romance writers. For example, if you write fiction, you should know about the three acts, character arcs, and themes. If you write poetry, you should know the difference between a couplet and a stanza.

Form is essentially the medium of the writing: fiction, poetry, essay, novel. *Genre* provides categories within forms: western, romance, horror.

Form provides the basic structure to our writing. We approach a project differently depending on whether we're writing a memoir or a short story.

Genre is more for marketing and readers. People tend to prefer certain types of stories over others—they know when they go to the bookstore, they're likely to find what they want in the literary-fiction section or the children's section. Genre is a way of sorting and organizing books and other pieces of writing, and it's immensely helpful in marketing because genre makes it easier for most writers to find their audiences.

Some writers are frustrated by genre, especially since the list of genres continues to grow. It can be difficult to categorize your writing when all you're trying to do is tell a good story. On the other hand, if, as an author, you're a fan of a particular genre, you can study it and learn the tropes within it.

As part of your development, it's useful to familiarize yourself with form and genre. A great place to start is to peruse an online bookstore and check out all the categories for their books. Where in those categories do you see your own work?

Chapter 6:
Process

"I always worked until I had something done and I always stopped when I knew what was going to happen next. That way I could be sure of going on the next day." - Ernest Hemingway

A process is a system or series of steps that we take to complete something. When you write, you use a process, even if you're not aware of it.

There may be a few writers who can sit down and write without any planning or preparation. They go through a different process for each project and don't really think about it. They just dig in and do the work. While they may not be conscious of their process, these writers will be able to look back and explain the process they went through to finish the work.

But most of us do use a process and we become increasingly aware of it over time. It may vary from project to project, but we know what steps we have to take to get to the finish line.

For most writers, this process develops organically. We start a project, tackle it in whatever way makes sense at the time, and eventually complete it. As we successfully finish more and more projects, we eventually find ourselves using a consistent series of steps to complete our projects. We refine the process a little bit with each project until we have perfected it.

When we start with a plan and move through various phases of a project, we can measure our progress. Starting with a plan is also a time saver. We don't necessarily have to plan the details of the project itself; for example, we might not outline a novel, but we know we're going to do a draft, then revise it, edit, and so on.

We tend to use the same process over and over because it's proven. It works. And it gets results.

There's no right or wrong writing process. If whatever you do works for you and the result is a completed project, then you're doing something right, whether you're aware of your process or not.

On the other hand, developing a process is an excellent way to refine your writing and get the most out of your writing sessions. With a process, you may be able to write more or write better. You'll probably finish your projects faster.

Think of it this way: if you decide to take a road trip from California to New York, you can just get in your car and go, stopping to ask for directions along the way, or you can map your route ahead of time. Your route can be as detailed as you want. Maybe you'll plan your trip down to the minutes and miles and adhere to a rigid travel schedule. Or maybe you'll flag a few major pit stops and see what happens along the way.

We each have our own writing process. Some of us use note cards and outlines. Others use mind maps and storyboards. Some need a detailed plan, while others prefer discovery writing. Some edit as they go; others polish after they've unscrambled all their ideas.

One thing does seem to be consistent: successful, experienced writers are acutely aware of their writing processes.

By listening to other writers and from my own experiences, I've learned that understanding and honing your own process is instrumental to developing better writing.

Think about a writing project you have completed. What steps did you take to complete it? Did you attack it without any foresight or did you work your way through a detailed plan? Did you take steps to complete the project that were unnecessary? Were there any steps you didn't take that would have improved the project?

As you work on future projects, be conscious of the steps you take. Do you start by outlining or do you jump right in and start writing without a plan? Is there some point in the process where you ask others for feedback? Do you ask for feedback on some projects but not others? Why? How much time do you spend on major rewrites? How many times do you edit?

Understanding your writing process begins with recognizing what you're already doing. Then you can ask yourself whether you can do it better, more effectively, and more efficiently.

Sample Writing Process for Short Projects

Much has been written about various writing processes and steps that writers can use to finish their projects efficiently and effectively. Here's a simple five-step process that I often use for shorter projects:

- **Brainstorm and outline:** With short projects, my outline might be a simple list of a few words or phrases that represent the main ideas I want to cover. I might spend just a minute or two brainstorming to capture my ideas before writing them out in sentences and paragraphs.

- **Raw draft:** This is where I get my thoughts and ideas out of my head and onto the page. The raw draft can be messy and might include a lot of notes and shorthand. It often resembles an elaborate outline, and it functions as a frame or skeleton. If my writing project were a drawing, this would be a sketch.

- **Rough draft:** Once I have the basic framework for my project in place, I fill it in, fleshing out ideas or getting my topics in order. Now I have a real draft, something that resembles a piece of writing, but it still needs a lot of work.

- **Rewrite:** During the rewrite, I get extremely focused. This is where I iron out the details, make sure everything is covered, and eliminate any excess or unnecessary blocks of text. Research should be done by the time the rewrite is completed and the formatting should also be established.

- **Edit:** Editing is where I fine-tune, making sure I've made the best possible word choices and tweaking sentences and paragraphs so they flow smoothly. I check for grammar, spelling, and punctuation, but my attention is more focused on tone and structure. I might edit two or three times depending on how messy the rough draft turned out.

- **Proof:** The last step is proofreading, and this is where I'm consciously seeking out typos and other grammatical and orthographic mistakes. I usually proofread a piece over and over until I can't find any more errors. Ideally, after my final proof, I'll pass it to someone else, but with blogging and other short projects, that's not always possible.

There's a lot more you can do in a writing process, especially if you're working on a longer or more complex project.

Sample Steps in the Writing Process for Big Projects

"When something can be read without effort, great effort has gone into its writing."
- E.J. Poncela

For larger projects, we can take many more steps to get to the finish line. There's definitely an order to these steps; obviously, we would start with brainstorming and finish with proofreading. But many of these steps overlap, and often we revisit various steps as the project unfolds. For example, we may do our best to conduct all necessary research before we start writing, but we may need to take a break during a draft to go back and do more research.

Planning and Preparing

Setup: Gather your tools and resources. These may include notebooks, pens, writing resources like grammar and style guides, and research materials that you'll need. You might prepare documents and file folders on your computer or set up a backup system for this project. Useful tools also include file folders, note cards, sticky notes, binders, paper clips, staples, and highlighters.

Brainstorming: By the time you start brainstorming on paper, you may have a lot of ideas gathering in your mind. Brainstorming helps you get all those ideas out of your head and onto the page. Brainstorms are messy and disordered; one way to clean them up is to use mind mapping. A brainstorm for a novel might include short descriptions of key characters, a few notes about plot twists, and details about the setting. When you brainstorm, you can approach it freely, letting random ideas flow, or you can brainstorm to generate specific ideas (character names, for example).

Outlining and plotting: Some writers swear by outlines, and others absolutely refuse to use them. An outline can provide a roadmap for a complicated project. On the other hand, if you know everything that's going to happen, that might take the fun out of writing it. Your outline can be as sparse or as detailed as you want or need it to be, or you can forgo outlining altogether. You can also outline as you draft, if you want to create an outline that you can use for reference later.

Research: I find that research may be necessary throughout the entire writing process, even through the final polishing stages. If you know you have to do some research, it might be a good idea to get it out of the way before you start drafting so looking up facts won't interrupt the flow of your writing sessions. I try to keep my research materials well organized so I can easily find information I need when I need it.

Character sketches: Character sketches are used only by fiction writers, but nonfiction writers might create short biographies for the real people they're writing about. Character sketches are useful for establishing the details about a character and then sticking with those details consistently throughout the manuscript. You can also develop character sketches as you draft a story. Often, through drafting, you'll discover things about characters that are worth noting in a separate file. You also may find that certain traits and details change as the story evolves; be flexible with character sketches and change them as needed.

World building: World building isn't necessary for contemporary projects that are set in the present-day real world or stories set in a time and place with which you're familiar. But science fiction, fantasy, and historical stories are set in faraway or non-existent worlds. Historical fiction usually requires tons of research to get the setting and culture right. With science fiction and fantasy, you might create an entirely new world. It's a good idea to keep a record about the rules and details of the world, since that will help you ensure that the world remains consistent and realistic throughout the narrative.

Drafting

Raw draft: With a raw draft, you work your way through the project quickly and get all of your ideas onto the page. Turn off your inner editor; don't worry about grammar, spelling, and punctuation. Don't worry about the details. Use broad strokes to create the foundation for your project. Use notes and highlights as you write to mark areas that need more attention later.

Rough draft: Now that you've got a foundation to work from, go through and fill in the details. Get a solid structure in place.

Rewrite: Before doing a rewrite, you might want to do a read-through and take notes. This is also the time to bring in alpha readers (alpha readers read the rough draft to give general feedback on the direction of the piece and highlight issues that should be resolved before editing begins). The foundation and structure are in place; when you rewrite, you're fine-tuning the piece. Many writers do multiple rewrites, going over a piece until everything is smoothed out.

Polishing

Formatting: Formatting is a critical step in the writing process that is often overlooked. Setting margins, choosing fonts, and creating an attractive, navigable layout are all steps you can take to make sure your project presents well.

Editing: This is where you dig into the language. Get out the magnifying glass and examine your work at the word, sentence, and paragraph levels. Have you made the best possible word choices? Do the sentences have rhythm? Do the paragraphs flow smoothly? Fix any grammar, spelling, and punctuation problems and be willing to do more than one edit if necessary.

Proofreading: Put away the magnifying glass and get out the microscope. Clean up all those pesky typos and other lingering grammatical and orthographic errors and make your work as perfect as possible.

Feedback: It's time to show your work. You might want to show it before proofreading, depending on how much feedback and help you need. Some projects, especially shorter ones, won't require any feedback at all. Feedback can come from a writing partner, critique group, professional editor, instructor or peers (if you're taking a class or workshop), or writing coach. Once you receive the feedback, determine which suggestions you'll take and apply them to your manuscript. Feedback may very well send you into a loop where you go back and revisit the rewriting and editing steps.

Final polish: Before sending your work to agents or editors and before publishing it, give it a final read to make sure it's flawless.

I also use deadlines and scheduled writing sessions as part of my process. For example, before I wrote this book, I made a list of steps I'd need to take to complete it. When I'd finished the outline and research (the research mostly involved collecting quotes) and I started the raw draft, I scheduled writing sessions for every day of the week. I also set deadlines for different phases of the project.

As you develop your own writing process, you might find that some of these steps work for you while others don't. There might be steps you bring into the process that aren't mentioned here.

Tips for Developing a Writing Process

"You have to play a long time to play like yourself." - Miles Davis

Your writing process can be as simple or as elaborate as you need it to be. I often make a list of everything I need to do for a project. I put the steps in order, but there's a good chance they will overlap. I might be brainstorming and world building simultaneously. I might pause during a rough draft to go back and rework the character sketches I created during an earlier step.

Be flexible as you develop your writing process, and be willing to try new things, even things that seem counterintuitive. If you like to follow a strict series of steps, then just for one project, try diving in without a plan. If you tend to write freely and without a plan, then try outlining for one project.

- Start by identifying your current writing process. Make a list of steps you take to get a project done. If you use different processes for different projects, make several lists.

- Review your current process and determine whether you're wasting time on unnecessary steps. Are there steps missing that would help improve your process? Look for opportunities to group similar activities together (like conducting research, interviews, etc.).

- If you're not sure about your process, think of a project you have planned or recently started and map out a process that you think would work for that project.

- Consider building deadlines into your process. If you schedule your writing sessions, establish goals using timers or word counts.

- To determine the effectiveness of the process you've developed, try it. Start with shorter projects, like essays, blog posts, or short stories.

We tend to look at certain approaches and think they would never work for us. When I first heard about discovery writing (or *pantsing*), which is a method where you write without any plan whatsoever, I thought it was interesting but way outside of my personal working style. Then I tried it when I participated in National Novel Writing Month (NaNoWriMo) and was thrilled with the results. In fact, that was the first time I managed to complete a novel that I had started.

Don't assume that a particular method or process would never work for you; you won't know for sure until you give it a try.

I work on a wide variety of projects—web pages, blog posts, poems, essays, and fiction. I can't tackle these projects without some kind of plan or system.

My writing process varies from project to project and depends on the level of difficulty, the length and scope of the project, and even my state of mind. If I'm feeling super creative, a blog post or a short article will come flying out of my head. If I'm tired, hungry, or unmotivated, or if the project is complicated, then it's a struggle and I have to work a little harder. Brainstorming and outlining can help. A lot.

We don't have to rely on one writing process. We can have several, and we can adjust the process to accommodate each project's specific needs so that we're always going through a series of steps that are best suited to that particular project.

For example, when I am involved in a copywriting or nonfiction project, I find that brainstorming and outlining are essential. I need to organize my thoughts and make sure that I cover the subject matter thoroughly. But with some fiction and all poetry (and even the novel I wrote for NaNoWriMo), I just start typing and let the ideas flow. Longer projects may include note taking, but these projects have a free and creative flow, so I make sure the process I use is free and creative too.

Writing processes are methods we can use to improve our writing. The reason so many writers develop these processes is to be more productive and produce better work. Writing processes and other techniques and strategies can be helpful, but it's our responsibility to know what works for us personally as individuals and as creative writers.

Questions:

- Are you aware of a writing process that you use? Does it vary from project to project? Do you have different processes for different types of projects?

- What are the steps you take to get a creative writing project completed?

- If you develop or fine-tune your writing process, what benefits do you think you will gain? How will it affect your writing?

Chapter 7:
Feedback

"Criticism may not be agreeable, but it is necessary. It fulfills the same function as pain in the human body. It calls attention to an unhealthy state of things." - Winston Churchill

There are two schools of thoughts about whether critiques of your work are beneficial.

One school of thought says that art is subjective; a critique is nothing more than someone's opinion, and critiques might harm the artistic integrity of your work by interjecting someone else's ideas and visions into it.

The other school of thought says that art may be subjective, but other people's opinions matter and can actually be helpful. Writers may be too close to their own work to view it objectively, so a second opinion reveals strengths and weaknesses that the author simply can't detect.

In my experience, when approached thoughtfully, critiques do far more good for your writing than harm. In fact, a critique can harm your work only if you let it, and let's face it: ultimately, you're the one who's responsible for what you write.

It's true that a critique is mostly someone else's opinion about your work. But critiques also include ideas to improve your writing—ideas that may not have occurred to you. Additionally, a good critic will point out mechanical errors—grammar and spelling mistakes that slipped past you.

If you're going to submit or publish your work, you'll get feedback anyway. Agents and editors might respond to your submissions with their own critiques of your work, and once your work is published, there's a chance it will get reviewed. Critics, reviewers, and readers are eager to rate and review books and other pieces of writing online. So you might as well get advance feedback to get an idea of how your writing comes across to other people.

Most writers say they want someone to read their work and provide feedback so they can make their writing better. Trouble is, many writers want nothing more than praise. When they hear their writing could actually use some work, some writers freeze up. Others go through the feedback and argue it point by point. A few will even launch into a tirade of sobbing or screaming.

Critiques are designed to help writers, not to offend them or make them feel incapable. But the human ego is a fragile and funny thing. Some folks simply can't handle the notion that despite all their hard work, the piece they've written is less than perfect.

As a writer, you have to decide whether you truly want to excel at your craft. If you do, then you need to put your ego aside and learn how to accept critiques graciously. If you can't do that, there's a good chance your writing will never improve and your work will always be mediocre.

Critiques are not tools of torture. They are meant to help you. If the critique is put together in a thoughtful and meaningful way, it should lift your spirits by pointing out strengths in the piece, but it should also raise some red flags by marking areas that need improvement.

Usually, critiques sting a little. That's okay. Sometimes, you'll get lucky and your suspicions about what is weak in your writing will only be confirmed. Other times, you'll be surprised that the critic found weaknesses in parts of the work that you thought were the strongest.

Whether a critique will be beneficial or harmful depends entirely on you. Obviously, nobody can make you change what you've written; it's up to you to pick and choose what you revise.

Tips for Accepting Writing Critiques and then Writing Better

With practice and by following the tips below, you'll learn how to overcome your own ego; how to obtain a beneficial critique, evaluate it objectively, and apply it to your writing thoughtfully; and for all that, you'll be a better writer.

- Find someone who is well read, tactful, honest, and knowledgeable about writing. If you can find a critic who possesses all these traits, then you have overcome the first hurdle, because such persons are not easy to find.

- Polish your work as much as you can before handing it over. Do not send a rough draft to someone who will be critiquing your work, otherwise much of the feedback you receive may address problems you could have found and dealt with yourself. The point of a critique is to step beyond your own perspective and abilities. Note: Some writers get developmental edits or use alpha readers who read the rough draft and then give general feedback on the story or idea.

This is not a critique in the traditional sense. It's more for bouncing ideas around.

- Don't harass the person who is critiquing your work by calling them every day, especially if they're doing you a favor. If you are working under any kind of deadline, plan accordingly.

- If possible, do not review the critique in the presence of the person who prepared it. The best way to first review a critique is to set aside some time alone. In some cases, you'll do critiques in workshops or writing groups where you have to be prepared to hear live feedback. In these situations, there is usually an instructor guiding the critiques to make sure they are presented and accepted graciously.

- You may have an emotional reaction. Some of the feedback may make you angry or despondent. Know that this is normal and it will pass.

- After you review the critique, let it sit for a day or two. In time, your emotions will subside and your intellect will take over. The reasonable part of your brain will step in and you'll be able to absorb the feedback objectively.

- Revisit the critique with an open mind. Try to treat your own writing as if it were someone else's. As you review it, ask yourself how the suggestions provided can be applied, and envision how they will make your work better.

- Figure out what is objective and what is personal in the critique. Critics are human. Some of their findings may be technical—mistakes that you should definitely fix. Other findings will be highly subjective (this character is unlikable, this dialogue is unclear, etc.). You may have to make judgment calls to determine where the critic is inserting his or her personal tastes.

- Decide what you'll use and what you'll discard. Remember, the critic is not in your head and may not see the big picture of your project.

- Thank your critics. After all, they took the time to help you, and even if you didn't like what they had to say or how they said it—even if the critique itself was weak—just be gracious, say thanks, and move on. Don't argue about the feedback.

- Now you can take the feedback you've received and apply it to your work. Edit and tweak the project based on the suggestions that you think will best benefit the piece.

- You can apply the feedback to future projects too. Take what you learned from this critique and use it when you're working on your next project. In this way, your writing (not just a single project) will consistently improve.

In some cases, you may not have control over who critiques your work. If it's published, anyone can assess it, and they can assess it publicly. If you're taking a class or workshop, peer-to-peer critiques may be required. In cases like these, it's essential that you keep a cool head. Even if someone is unnecessarily harsh or rude in their (uninvited) delivery, respond tactfully and diplomatically.

If you can obtain useful critiques and apply the feedback to your work, your writing will improve dramatically. Critiques are one of the most effective and fastest ways of making your writing better.

How to Deal with Difficult Critiques of Your Writing

"But instead of spending our lives running towards our dreams, we are often running away from a fear of failure or a fear of criticism."
- Eric Wright

You've worked hard on a piece of writing. You poured your blood, sweat, and tears into the prose. You bared your soul through the characters. You rewrote, revised, and polished it until you felt it was worthy of publication.

Then, you brought it to your beta readers and they tore it apart.

Getting critiques is never easy. After all, the critic's job is to find ways for you to improve the writing. If they don't point out weaknesses, they're not doing their job properly. But it still hurts. Some writers react to harsh critiques with anger. Others cry. Only a lucky few escape unscathed.

Let's assume you've taken the proper precautions in choosing who critiques your work. After all, you can't hand it off to just anyone and expect to receive helpful feedback. Remember that a good critic is well read, honest, and understands the importance of emphasizing both the strengths and the weaknesses in your work.

But even the best critics, the ones with the most tact, might take a red pen to your manuscript and cut it to shreds. They'll tell you the characters are lifeless. They'll find plot holes and inconsistencies. And they'll say some of the scenes and passages that you thought represented your very best work should be cut.

Constructive critiques are hard to swallow. But they are essential to your development as a writer, especially if you're just starting out. So here are some tips for how to deal with critiques that hurt.

- **Tell your ego to take a nap:** When you're on the receiving end of critiques, your ego is your number-one enemy. It will get defensive, angry, and offended by even the slightest suggestion that your work is less than perfect. Your ego wants to argue with your critic and defend your work. Diffuse it before you read or receive the critique, and you'll be able to deal with whole affair more objectively.

- **Detach emotionally:** You poured your heart into your writing, and now someone's going to attack it. That doesn't feel good. In fact, even if the critic says a bunch of nice things about your work, the negative comments are going to sting. You have to emotionally detach yourself from your writing, even if only temporarily. That doesn't mean you stop loving it, but you need to shift into the tough-love place.

- **You are not your writing:** You are a person, and your writing is something you made. It might be an extension of you. It might even represent you. But you are not your writing. Critiques are about your work, not about you. Yes, it's hard not to take the feedback personally, but it's not personal.

- **You're only human:** Nobody's perfect. Not a single soul on this earth is perfect, including you. The sooner you accept that, the better your life will be, especially your writing life. Since you are flawed, your work will be flawed too. If you can not only accept but also embrace this fact, critiques won't be painful. They'll actually become enjoyable.

- **Put it aside:** When you first get feedback, it's natural to have an emotional reaction. All the willpower in the world may not be enough to stop you from feeling a little angry or sad. This is not the time to respond to your critic (other than to say *thank you*) and it's not the time to make any decisions about how you'll apply the feedback to your next revision. Always put critiques aside for a few days before you start analyzing them and using them to improve your writing.

- **Look for the good:** Any decent critic will say something good about your writing. If this isn't the case, get another group of beta readers or join some other writers' group. Always look for the good in the critiques of your work. Even if it's something minor, recognize it as a compliment and as an accomplishment.

- **Find the subjective:** Critics are human too. Often, they inject sheer opinion into their critiques. This is a good thing. Art is subjective and learning that some people just won't like your work is a lesson best learned early. The trick is to figure out which parts of a critique are based on taste and which are objective assessments. For example, your critic might have a problem with the futuristic technology in your story, but then again, she does not like science-fiction stories (your story is not to her taste). On the other hand, she might be a die-hard science-fiction fan who says the gadgets three hundred years in the future should be more evolved than what you've got, which is good, objective feedback that you can use.

- **Get a second opinion:** If you're struggling with a critique, feel free to get a second opinion. This can be particularly useful if you feel most of the negative feedback was based on taste or personal preference, or if you're having a hard time deciding which suggestions to apply and which to dismiss.

- **Devise a plan:** Once you've had time to sift through a critique with an open mind, you can start making decisions about how to apply the feedback to your work. Don't just open your document and start revising. Instead, make a plan. Decide which bits of feedback you'll use and which you'll disregard. It's a good idea to keep track of feedback; store it in a folder or some other place in case you need to refer to it later.

- **Improve your work:** Here's where all the pain and suffering of receiving critiques finally pays off. You get to sit down with your writing project and make it even better. After you apply the feedback through revisions, you'll see how drastically critiques can help you improve your work, and it will become a rewarding experience.

If you're looking for ways to strengthen your writing, you can do no better than critiques, especially a professional-quality critique that highlights the strengths in your writing while underscoring the weaknesses. Through this process, you'll learn to see your own work more objectively, as a reader rather than as a writer, and you'll acquire the skills to make meaningful revisions. In time, critiques get easier to bear, so stick it out the best you can, and in the meantime, keep writing.

Finding Helpful Critique Partners

If you approach critiques with the goal of truly improving your writing, then these tips will provide some guidelines that you can use when you put your work up for review.

- Find an experienced critic. It doesn't have to be another writer, but it can be. It should, however, be someone who is well read in your genre.

- If you want feedback on mechanics, make sure whoever critiques your work has solid grammar, spelling, and punctuation skills.

- Find someone who is objective and diplomatic. It won't do you any good if you give your writing to your mother and she gushes over it. Look for someone who will reveal what's good and bad about your piece.

- Hiring a writing coach or developmental editor is a great way to get professional feedback.

- Workshops are similar to classes, but instead of lectures, they consist of students sharing and critiquing one another's work.

- You can find writing groups online and off, or you can start your own.

Tips for Providing Critiques

"When virtues are pointed out first, flaws seem less insurmountable." - Judith Martin

There's a good chance that at some point, you'll swap work with someone and find yourself not only receiving a critique but also providing one.

In essence, your job is to deliver a judgment, but don't bring the gavel down too hard!

- Don't provide a critique unless you've been invited to do so. This is also a good rule to follow online.

- Read the piece in its entirety before making any comments or taking any notes. Once you've gotten the initial reading out of your system, you'll be prepared to revisit it with a critical eye.

- Work your way through the piece carefully, taking notes about what's good and what's not so good.

- If possible, avoid working through a critique on the spot. Ideally, you won't be in the same room as the writer when you're first reading or evaluating a piece, although this isn't always possible.

- Mark up the copy with underlines and highlighting. Don't forget to highlight the strong sections—appealing images, effective dialogue, and descriptive scenes. And don't forget to pay attention to grammar.

- Look for areas where the writing is consistently successful. Are all the characters realistic? Is the grammar tight? These are the writer's overall strengths.

- Also look for spots where the writer seems to have gotten lucky. Maybe most of the images are clichés, but there's one really strong, original piece of imagery. Call this out, so the writer can build on it.

- You have to look for weak spots too. Are there lots of great descriptions with just one scene that doesn't quite make sense? Point it out so it can be fixed.

- Likewise, look for consistent weaknesses. This is essential since persistent problems indicate an area where a writer needs the most improvement. Is the punctuation all wrong? Does the plot go nowhere? Take note!

- Once you've established the good, the bad, and the ugly, it's time to prepare your critique. Organize your thoughts and your notes.

- Always start with what's good. First tell the writer what works, where the strengths are. Kick off the critique on a positive note.

- Ease gently into the negative feedback. It's necessary, but you don't have to slap a writer across the face with it.

- Use positive language to express areas that need work. Try phrases like the following: This would be even more interesting if…That character would be more realistic if…I like the image you've created, but it would be even stronger if…

- Avoid using negative words like the following: don't, never, terrible, weak, boring, doesn't, etc. Instead use positive, action-oriented words. In other words, instead of telling the writer what's wrong with the piece, tell the writer what actions they can take to make it better.

- Never criticize the writer. Avoid language such as "You should..." "Your wording..." or "You didn't..." Instead, talk about the writing: "This could be clearer..." "The wording isn't..." or "This doesn't..." Keep the work and the writer separate and only critique the work.

- If you're working with a new or inexperienced writer, hold yourself back. Focus on problems that are consistent throughout the piece and call out only a few issues. You don't have to address every single detail—the idea is to show a writer how to improve bit by bit. Never hand back a manuscript so marked up that it's solid red.

- As you deliver your feedback, pay attention to the writer's reaction. Grateful? Annoyed? Shocked? Angry? Upset? Heartbroken? You may not be able to do anything about it, but you can always ask if there was anything offensive about your delivery.

- If you are going to give a critique in person, make sure you've listed all the points you want to make so you don't forget anything. Go the extra mile, and give the writer a copy of your notes.

- If you're providing a written critique, make sure your feedback is clear and consistent. Provide a copy of the writer's original material with your comments and markup, and also provide a separate document containing detailed feedback.

- Know that some writers want nothing more than praise. Some people mistake a critique for a personal insult. Others simply can't handle that their work is imperfect. If you're looking for someone to build a partnership with, avoid writers who go on the defensive when you make objective, thoughtful, and honest observations.

- After you've provided your critique, check back with your writer friend to see if your feedback was helpful. Find out which, if any, suggestions they used. Offer to take a look at the revision.

- Stick to your guns. Some writers will try to argue points that you've made. Maybe they just wanted praise, or maybe they're emotionally attached to a particular passage. The writer should not defend his or her work or attempt to convince the critic of its merit.

- Even though you're not budging, let the writer know that your critique is not law. Some feedback is subjective. Each writer is free to apply or discard suggestions within a critique.

Constructive criticism requires compassion. If writers care enough about their work to show it around and invite feedback, then it's probably something in which they are emotionally invested. If you are the person they feel is qualified to provide that feedback, then embrace the invitation as an honor, and approach it with respect.

It can be awkward at first—after all, who wants to be the bearer of bad news (and almost every critique contains at least a little bad news)? After you do a few critiques, you'll get the hang of it, and it will become natural and easy. Just keep these basic tips on how to critique in mind.

Coping with Public Criticism

In the world of art and entertainment, criticism is par for the course. And with the advent of the Internet, where everyone has a voice, the din of criticism has become deafening. Everyone has an opinion, everyone wants to be heard, and the Internet makes that possible, easy, and anonymous.

And there are still professional critics at major magazines and newspapers. It's their job to scrutinize a piece of art.

As writers, we're lucky if we learn how to deal with criticism early on, before strangers get a chance to review our work publicly. Those early, private critiques give us a chance to improve our work, so hopefully the later, more public reviews won't be so difficult to deal with.

But eventually, most published writers receive a bad review or have to scroll through one-star ratings. Reviewers can be harsh, but readers can be harsher, and they can also issue negative reviews for ridiculous reasons.

I've seen readers give books one star out of five because there was a problem with the formatting, because they were expecting something different, or because they loved most of the story but hated one part or character, which ruined everything for them. Readers will give five stars and then explain how they didn't like the story or give one star and say what a great book it was (yes, their rating might contradict their review). They are ordinary people—most of them are not trained in the art of critique or in the craft of writing.

As a writer, if you have a long and prosperous career (and I hope you do), you'll inevitably be confronted with harsh statements about your work. Don't take it too hard. Think about a book or movie you hated but that most of your friends enjoyed. Or think about a movie most of your friends hated but you loved. There is an audience for every book, and there's also a group of people who won't like that book at all.

The fact of the matter is this: not everyone's going to like your work.

I've read tons of reviews that I disagreed with. I've seen critics rave about books and movies that I thought sucked. And I've seen them tear books and movies apart that I thought were great. Yes, critics are experienced in their medium, and theoretically we should be able to trust their analysis. Sometimes we'll find a critic with tastes similar to ours, a critic we can count on. But for the most part, it's just opinion, and opinions vary.

Your goal should be to find your readers, the ones who will love your book. Don't worry about the haters. Ignore them. Do what you love, love what you do, and let everything else flow from that.

Chapter 8:
Tools and Resources

"It's best to have your tools with you."
- Stephen King

Where would we writers be without our tools and resources? From cheap pens and notebooks to expensive word-processing software, from thick reference books to online databases packed with facts and information, our tools and resources are both bane and boon. Love them or hate them, one thing is certain: if you're a writer, you need them.

When we are striving to improve our writing, the act of writing and all the skills that go into craftsmanship are just one piece of the puzzle. We need a place to write, tools to write with, writing references to consult, and research material to cite.

Every writer will develop personal preferences—a favorite writing spot, preferred writing instruments, and a host of trusty resources. These things might not directly improve your writing, but they will make your experience and your process more enjoyable and more efficient.

When you are fully equipped with the writing tools and resources you need to get your job done, you'll do your job better.

A Place to Write

"You want to be a writer, don't know how or when? Find a quiet place, use a humble pen."
- Paul Simon

Many books I've read on the craft of writing say that you should start by creating a special place where you can write. It can be an entire room or just a desk in a corner. Maybe you like to write at a local café or park.

It's not a bad idea. A dedicated writing space can be free of distractions. If you can manage an entire room (some writers set up in a closet), you can keep others out when you're doing your work (just put a sign on the door: "writer at work, do not disturb"). You can fill your space with the tools and resources you need (pens, notebooks, laptop, reference materials, etc.) and it can be decorated with whatever inspires you.

But that's not realistic for everyone. Personally, I've never been able to set up a place just for my creative writing. When I write in a notebook, I usually curl up on the couch or sprawl out on my bed. When I work on the computer, I sit at my work desk, which is where I perform my day job and do lots of other things, from paying the bills to watching my favorite TV shows.

A dedicated writing space is nice but limiting. You'll end up writing in a single location to the exclusion of all other places you could write. You might even become dependent on your own special writing space. If you're ever away from it or if you have to give it up, it could negatively affect your productivity. You'll be far more creative and productive if you train yourself to do the exact opposite: write anywhere and everywhere—on the bus or train, at your desk, or in a bustling café.

You can set up a special space too, but try to avoid relying on it for all your writing sessions.

- A busy, crowded café might seem distracting, but maybe you'll be inspired by the people you see there.

- A quiet room may sound ideal, but is it too isolated? Some writers work better with some background noise.

- Think about your writing environment. Are there things to look at when you're thinking through a problem? Do these things distract you, inspire you, or help you focus?

As you experiment with writing in different locations, pay attention to how each location affects your work. You might do your best work when you're riding the bus or relaxing on the front porch.

Your Writing Tools

Writers' tools may seem obvious: a pen, notebook, computer, and writing software like Microsoft Word are the basics.

But technology has opened up a wider range of tools that we can use, and not all of them are designed just for writing.

Lots of modern products cater to personal preferences. You might prefer a thick pen with a sturdy grip and steady ink flow, or maybe you'd rather work with disposable pens so you don't have to worry about losing them. Maybe an expensive notebook with archival-quality paper forces you to put more thought into your writing, or perhaps you're more comfortable with a cheap notebook so you don't have to worry about making mistakes or messing up an expensive blank book.

Your preferences might be based on your budget or your personal taste. As with most things we do as writers, you have to find what works best for you.

Here are some basic tools that most writers use:

- **Pens:** Choices include ball-point pens, fountain pens, pencils, highlighters, and markers. I like to keep a few red pens around for editing.

- **Notebooks:** Blank books, journals, and notebooks come in various sizes and with a range of quality in the paper. You can also get hardcover or softcover, spiral or perfect bound, blank pages or lined pages.

- **Office supplies:** You might need supplies to help you organize your writing notes and materials: binders, file folders, labels, tab dividers, staplers or paper clips, and binder clips (for securing large manuscripts) are just a few examples of office supplies that might come in handy.

- **Hardware:** The typewriter gave way to the computer. Now we also use tablets, smart phones, and e-readers.

- **Software:** Microsoft Word is the industry standard, but Scrivener is the writing software preferred by most of today's authors. Other popular software includes Pages (by Apple), text programs (like TextEdit or Notepad) and online, cloud-based software such as Google Drive (formerly Google Docs).

- **Apps:** There's a huge range of apps for writers, including dictionaries, thesauri, encyclopedias, e-books, voice-to-text, and recording apps, plus apps for ideas and inspiration. One of my favorite apps is Scapple, a brainstorming app created by Literature and Latte, makers of Scrivener.

Whatever tools you use, if you're writing electronically (and you probably are, otherwise you will eventually), make sure you have a backup system in place. An external hard drive is ideal for backups and there are online backup systems you can purchase as well. Ideally, you'll store backups off-site (keep a backup at a friend's house or store it online).

Be judicious when shopping for your tools. One great way to preview various writing tools is to shop online. You can read reviews by other customers and get a sense of the product's features and flaws. It's also easier to do price comparisons online.

Don't put too much pressure on yourself about collecting tools. Some people will use their lack of the proper tools as an excuse not to write (*I can't afford this expensive software right now, so I can't start my novel*). All you need to get started is a pen and notebook. You probably already have access to a computer. Remember that, ultimately, writing is about getting the words down. The tools we collect just make the process easier or more comfortable.

Recommended Writing Reference Materials

There will inevitably come a time when you need to look up a word to check its definition and make sure you're using it properly. You'll come across a word you've used too many times and need a replacement.

You'll find yourself staring at a sentence, totally perplexed about whether or not you should use a comma.

Writing reference materials help you solve these problems quickly and easily so you can get back to writing. These are look-up books (and websites); you use them to look up facts and information related to language, grammar, and writing.

Dictionary

If you've ever caught yourself using a word only to realize you're not sure whether you're employing it correctly, you know what a lifesaver the dictionary can be. In a situation like that, you have three choices: use another word, look up the word to verify its meaning, or take your chances and pray for the best.

Every time you open the dictionary, you're adding to your vocabulary. You might be learning a brand new word, verifying what you thought you knew, or simply gaining greater understanding of a word's meaning. You'll also build your vocabulary by making good use of the dictionary's close cousin, the thesaurus.

The *Oxford* line of dictionaries are the most prestigious, and they are available in both print and e-book formats. Websites like dictionary.com make looking up words fast and easy, plus many dictionaries offer apps you can install on your smart phone or tablet, making this essential resource mobile.

Your choice of dictionary might be based on the kind of writing you do. If you're doing business, academic, technical, or scientific writing, you'll want a reputable, even prestigious, dictionary, but these can be pretty expensive. These areas of specialty in professional writing may require the use of industry dictionaries as well.

Thesaurus

When you need a replacement word, there's no need to break your brain trying to come up with synonyms. Just take a peek inside any thesaurus to find alternatives that will keep your writing fresh.

I haven't used my paperback *Roget's Thesaurus* in years because I rely on thesaurus.com now. You can access it online and download the app for free.

Grammar and Style Guides

Grammar and style guides ensure that you're writing correctly and consistently. Most style guides include rules for grammar and orthography.

In many cases, the matter of which style guide to use is not up to a writer. Publishers usually provide guidelines explaining which style guide is required.

Most newspapers adhere to *The Associated Press Stylebook on Briefing on Media Law* (*AP Stylebook*), whereas a small-press publisher might ask you to use *The Elements of Style* (often referred to as Strunk and White). Professors and teachers generally require students to use the *MLA Handbook for Writers of Research Papers*.

What about freelance writers, bloggers, fiction writers, and everyone else?

The most popular style guide for general use is *The Chicago Manual of Style*, and this is also the style guide commonly used for manuscripts (i.e., novels and anthologies). Many other style guides are based on *Chicago* or will defer to it for any areas of style they do not specifically address. It covers formatting, includes rules for good grammar usage, and provides a roadmap that helps you ensure your work is consistent.

For general use, *Chicago* is by far one of the best writing resources on the market, and it's been one of the best investments I've made for my own writing career.

Craft-of-Writing Resources

Craft-of-writing resources are any other resources that you use to inspire, inform, and guide your writing.

These are generally books and articles you read rather than refer to on an as-needed basis. They impart writing ideas, methods, and techniques. You'll find lots of books that address the craft generally as well as others that address particular forms, such as fiction or poetry. You can even find specialized resources that deal with genre or specific elements of form, like dialogue or character development.

Books filled with prompts, activities, and creative-writing exercises will stretch your limits and give you fresh writing ideas while imparting useful writing methods and techniques. The gains to be made by working through writing exercises and other creative challenges are immense and will pave the way toward better writing.

For those of us who aspire to become published poets and fiction writers, these creative writing resources may become the most powerful weapons in our arsenal because they give us specialized training. Make sure you start building your own collection of such books.

Here are a few of my personal favorites:

General:

- *The Elements of Style*, Strunk & White: It's also a style guide and a manual on clear, concise writing.

- *On Writing*, Stephen King: King's memoir on his writing life and career plus a treasure trove of his personal writing tips.

- *Writing Down the Bones*, Natalie Goldberg: Tips, ideas, and insight for writing creatively.

Fiction:

- *Wired for Story*, Lisa Cron: Find out what makes stories and characters captivate and compel readers.

- *No Plot? No Problem!*, Chris Baty: Anyone can write a book, and you don't even need an outline.

- *What If?*, Anne Bernays and Pamela Painter: An excellent collection of fiction writing exercises.

Poetry:

- *Sound and Sense*, Thomas R. Arp and Greg Johnson: The ultimate book on poetry and poetry writing, which will enhance all writing skills, not just poetry skills.

- *A Poetry Handbook*, Mary Oliver: A simple but comprehensive guide to reading and writing poetry, perfect for beginners.

- *The Practice of Poetry*, Robin Behn: Jam-packed with poems, poetry-writing exercises, and insights on the art of writing poetry.

When you're shopping for books on craft, do your shopping online, even if you plan to buy in person. Most online retailers display similar items and products that customers "also bought" when they bought the item in question. So if you go to the product page for a writing resource that you enjoyed, you'll find a list of items purchased by other people who bought it, and this is a great way to get leads on quality resources. You can also check the reviews to see what other writers thought of these books.

Have a little fun with your writing resources, and treat yourself to one or two new ones each month until you have a fully stocked library of such works, which will contribute to improving your writing.

Magazines, Journals, Blogs, and Online Resources

It's a good idea to check out literary magazines and journals, especially if you're a short-form writer. These publications often publish short fiction, poetry, and essays. Though not craft-of-writing resources, these publications are great for familiarizing yourself with the market and can present opportunities for submitting and publishing your work.

You'll find these publications in both print and electronic format. Some are even exclusive to the Internet.

The Internet is home to a plethora of blogs and websites dedicated to the craft of writing. A few simple searches will turn up plenty of online resources, and many of them are free.

However, be cautious when scouring the Internet for resources or references you intend to use professionally. While there is lots of quality information out there, there is just as much misinformation online. Review websites and blogs with a critical eye, and be judicious with the resources you use and trust.

Conducting Research

"'Research' is a wonderful word for writers. It serves as an excuse for EVERYTHING."
- Rayne Hall

Almost all writers rely on research for facts and information. Even fiction writers and memoir authors, whose work is either made up from imagination or based on personal experience, will turn to research to fill in holes and answer questions.

We use encyclopedias, reference books, and articles from scholarly journals, and we rely on historical facts and data collected by researchers so we can write truthfully and honestly. We also use Google, Wikipedia, and a host of other material found online. All of this research is supposed to strengthen our work and lead to better, more credible writing.

We absorb this information and then spit it back out in the words we write. Then people come along and read our words. Maybe they go off and repeat what they've read. Maybe they rehash our material in a blog post of their own. Maybe they use it in an academic paper, or perhaps it inspires a poem or a short story. The information itself is constantly making the rounds, getting processed, filtered, and regurgitated. How are we to sift through it all to find reliable facts? How do we tell the truth from the lies?

And telling truth from lies is essential in conducting research. Misinformation is widespread, especially on the Internet.

We are currently bombarded with information. It's more accessible than ever before in history. Millions of facts can be yours with a few keystrokes and the click of a button. Yet, oddly, the spread of misinformation seems more rampant than ever. It's becoming less common for sources to be cited and more likely that the so-called facts you read online are just somebody's beliefs or suspicions.

I find the spread of misinformation grossly irresponsible (it's one of my pet peeves). There are so many ways to get the facts straight, there is really no excuse for it. I'm not talking about misunderstandings or unintentional mistakes—I'm talking about either knowingly repeating things that are untrue or willfully failing to get facts straight before reporting or repeating them.

But what does this have to do with you as a writer? How does responsible research (or lack thereof) reflect on a writer's credibility, and how does solid research and the use of legitimate citations lead to better writing?

It can be difficult to know when research is required to back up the facts. There are some things that we know from life experience or from working in a particular field over a long period of time. Other things are simply common knowledge. And much online writing (especially in blogs) involves doling out advice based on personal experience.

But when you're presenting historical data, citing statistics, or quoting sources, you have a responsibility to get the facts straight and in some cases, you should also cite them, especially in nonfiction writing.

Citations are important for a few reasons. First, a citation gives your readers an opportunity to look further into the topic. Second, you are giving credit where credit is due, to whoever compiled the facts for your use. Third, by citing your sources, you are showing your own work to be responsibly researched and therefore accurate and credible.

How do you know when research or citations are required or warranted? Use common sense and foster a little curiosity. Start by asking questions. If you're writing fiction, you don't need to cite your sources. If you're writing an academic essay, you do. In fiction and poetry, there is room for make-believe. You can use artistic license and bend reality, but beware of readers with high standards. For example, many science-fiction readers will harp on a book with faulty science. If you know your audience and publishing medium, they should guide how you approach research and citations.

Tips and Questions

Here are some questions you can ask and tips you can use to determine whether research is necessary:

Creative-Nonfiction Writing (Memoir, Biography, etc.)

- Did this really happen? Is it true?

- How can I be sure? Is the source reliable?

- Who compiled this research and are they credible? What are their qualifications?

- Could the source be mistaken? How can I be sure?

- Are there any potential conflicts of interest in the reporting?

- Is there any corresponding research to back this up?

- Is there any conflicting research that provides contrast?

Fiction

- If you're writing about a real place, make sure you get the geography (like street names) correct.

- Be aware of the climate, culture, and language you're writing about.

- Make sure you research your characters' professions. If possible, consult with an actual professional who does the same job as your character.

- You may need to do medical research to understand illnesses, traumas, and other experiences your characters have.

- If your story includes science or technology, make sure it's factual or at least plausible. Fiction is about making stuff up, but it still has to be believable.

There is no limit to what you might have to research for a fiction project. If your character is an actor, you may need to research how movies are made, who works on a film set (job titles and descriptions), and what happens behind the scenes. If there is a war in your story, you may need to research branches of the military and learn the lingo and various positions and rules within the armed forces. You may need to research trees and flowers, animals, foreign countries, history, science…The list goes on and on.

Poetry

Poetry probably requires the least amount of research, but that doesn't mean you won't ever have to look things up or check facts. For example, in a poem about nature, you might need to make sure flowers are blooming in the proper season. You might want to research which flowers grow in a particular area. Could the flower in your poem be poisonous? Does it attract or repel animals? Is it an annual or a perennial?

Research isn't limited to looking up facts and information. For example, if your poem rhymes, you might use a rhyming dictionary to find appropriate words.

Research Tips

Here are some final thoughts to consider when you're conducting research:

- Books aren't the only research materials you can use. Watch documentaries, conduct interviews, and check newspaper and periodical archives.

- Check your work for claims or statements that are debatable or that warrant proof. Are you quoting a person or a text? Are you citing statistics? Are you making a claim?

- Be smart about the research you conduct. Confirm the credibility of all your sources.

- Double-check your facts (and their sources) to see if claims have been countered. Try not to be one-sided.

- Cite your sources in the text, in footnotes, or in a bibliography (for books). On a blog or website, you can include a list of sources at the bottom of your article.

Chapter 9:
Creativity and Inspiration

"You can't use up creativity. The more you use, the more you have." - Maya Angelou

As a creative writer and as someone who wants to become a proficient writer, understanding creativity will be a great advantage for you. While it will certainly help with your writing, it will also show you how to see the world and people in it from new perspectives, and it will strengthen your problem-solving skills.

There's an old myth floating around, which suggests that creativity is inherent. You're either born with it or you're born without it.

But creativity can be learned and developed over time. Some people may have a more natural inclination toward creative thinking, but anyone can foster and nurture creativity.

Artists throughout the ages have gone to great lengths and sunk to fathomless lows in pursuit of inspiration. The ancient Greeks personified inspiration in the muses. When they needed inspiration, they invoked these supernatural entities, calling on them for artistic help. Artists have set out on journeys, pursued spiritual and religious activities, and engaged in painful or unhealthy experiences in order to feed their imaginations.

Indeed, there are famous examples of authors drinking themselves to death or committing suicide and, of course, there is the well-known tale of Vincent Van Gogh cutting off part of his own ear. And finally, there's the ever-present stereotype of the starving artist.

Despite these tales of suffering and tragedy among authors and artists, the most successful creative people tend toward more practical measures, choosing lifestyles and habits that are healthy and conducive to creativity.

Unfortunately, these destructive myths about creativity persist.

Ten Myths about Creativity

- **Drugs and alcohol:** One of the worst myths about artistry is that drugs and alcohol promote creativity. That's a lie. What drugs and alcohol do is promote dependence. It is ineffective and inefficient to rely on these substances in order to make art. It's also unhealthy and, in fact, it can be deadly.

- **Misery:** Another common myth is that pain, sorrow, and anger are the best conduits for creativity. Sure, when we are unhappy, writing can provide a healthy, therapeutic outlet. But this has nothing to do with creativity and everything to do with the need to express oneself. While misery may indeed inspire us, we can be just as inspired by happy or emotionally neutral experiences. Relying on a depressive state of mind for inspiration is just as dangerous as relying on drugs and alcohol. And like drugs and alcohol, such thinking is unhealthy and can be deadly.

- **Suffering:** This myth is based on the idea that artistry is won through suffering. Some people actually believe that artists should suffer, and suffer hard, before they get to succeed. What you have to do to succeed is work hard. You shouldn't have to suffer.

- **Divinity:** There are less dangerous myths about creativity and inspiration. Some people believe that creativity makes a divine appearance only when they are supposed to create, and the rest of the time, they shouldn't bother. We all have moments of great inspiration. They come and go and are rare for most of us. The most successful writers don't wait for inspiration, they work for it. Regardless of our religious or spiritual beliefs, we can learn to control our own creativity just as we control other aspects of our lives. It's called free will.

- **Talent:** Lots of people believe that creativity is inherently tied to talent. Talent just means you have a knack for something. Lots of creative people may not be especially talented, and there are plenty of talented individuals with no interest in pursuing the arts.

- **Two kinds of people:** Some people are artistic; everyone else is not. That's definitely not true. Everyone is creative, and the more we nurture and foster creativity, the more creative we become. Creativity is closely associated with the arts, but artists aren't the only people who are creative.

- **Life of poverty:** Many people believe that it's practically impossible to succeed or make a living as any kind of artist. They mistakenly believe that an artist's life is one of poverty and struggle. All kinds of people experience poverty—not just artists—and artists who do experience poverty don't do so just because they are artists, as is proven by the many artists who never struggled with poverty.

- **Fame and fortune:** Conversely, some people believe that artists will enjoy great fame and fortune. While it's possible that you could write a wildly best-selling novel and become rich and famous, it's not likely, although the odds are better for you than for someone working in a cubicle eight hours a day who doesn't make any art at all. At least you have a shot at fame and fortune.

- Creative people are weird: Everybody's weird.

- **Creative people are creative all the time or whenever they want to create:** Once you've shown yourself to be creative, some people will think you're capable of doing anything that requires creativity or that you're a constant fountain of ideas. While many creative people have more ideas than they know what to do with, some have to work hard at finding inspiration.

The truth is that creativity is different for everyone and possible for anyone. You just have to want it and you might have to work for it.

Truths for Promoting Creativity

"Inspiration exists, but it has to find you working." - Pablo Picasso

The myths about creativity are not totally untrue. Like most myths, they are based on certain truths but not absolute truths. The truths about creativity are far more interesting and useful than the myths. They offer sound methods and lifestyle choices that we can use to attract more creativity into our lives.

Stay Healthy

The single best way to keep creativity flowing is to stay fit and healthy. You don't have to become a health nut, but you should eat a balanced diet and exercise regularly. Make sure you get plenty of protein, go easy on the carbs, and don't overdo the caffeine. If you feel good, creativity will come more easily.

It's also important to manage stress. While stress is unavoidable, it is manageable. A balanced diet and regular exercise will help with stress, as will stress management techniques and exercises.

Lots of writers suffer from sleep deprivation. If we already have busy lives and lots of responsibilities, sleep is often sacrificed to make time for writing. While skimping on sleep occasionally won't hurt you, the long-term effects of sleep deprivation will damage your health and ultimately kill your creativity.

Staying healthy is the first rule of success for just about anything, and writing is no exception. Make sure to take care of yourself and see a doctor when you need to.

Be Curious

Curiosity is my personal best creativity technique. I'm inquisitive about everything and full of questions, and I've always been that way.

But you don't have to be born curious in order to stimulate creativity. You can cultivate curiosity.

Remember how curious you were as a child? Everything you encountered spawned a series of questions, because you were trying to learn and understand the world around you. Bring that childlike curiosity back, and you'll never need to look far for new, inspiring writing ideas.

Ask questions about everything and everyone you encounter. That doesn't mean you should pummel a new acquaintance with personal questions, but you can certainly make lists of questions about people, places, and things that you encounter.

Throughout time, many great thinkers have used questions to prompt creative thinking. Sometimes, one question will simply lead to the next, and that's fine. As long as you keep your curiosity well oiled and let those questions flow, you'll never be at a loss for writing ideas.

Show Up

If you are serious about writing, you can't sit around waiting for ideas to fall out of the sky. You have to get to work, write through the dry spells, and be at your desk when inspiration strikes.

Although it sounds counterintuitive, you can train yourself to be creative. A regular writing routine will do wonders for your creativity. Always remember this: the more you create, the more creative you become. By engaging in creative work every day, you'll promote more creativity.

Find a nice chunk of time in your schedule, anywhere from twenty minutes to a couple of hours, and use that time to write. If you write at the same time every day, your body, including your brain (which is where creativity originates), will become accustomed to it, and then writing and creative thinking will become habitual. Inspiration is infinite, but it has to find you willing and ready to work.

Be Open Minded

Creativity gets stifled when you close your mind, and that includes all the things you could close your mind to, from ideas and beliefs that differ from your own to lifestyles and personalities that are beyond your personal experience.

It's normal to be wary or even afraid of the unfamiliar and the unknown. But when you open your mind and allow yourself to explore all possibilities, positive and negative, you invite myriad ideas into your creative thinking.

It's worth noting that fiction writers especially need to be open minded, since their work requires them to get inside the heads of many different kinds of characters. If those characters are to be believable, writers must learn to truly empathize with people (real or imagined), including people who are different from them.

Be an Observer

Sometimes I imagine the artist's mind as a food processor. You put lots of good stuff in, it all gets mixed together, and something new and delicious comes out.

As creative people, it's essential for us to take everything in. We have to observe the world around us; ask thoughtful questions about what we see, hear, touch, taste, and smell; and then put our experiences into words.

Quite simply, the more you take in, the more you can put out.

Make an effort to become an active observer with everything you do and experience. Pay attention to people when you're out shopping. How would you describe them? Take mental notes when you're in a new environment. What does it smell like? Even when you're going through your daily routine, there's opportunity for observation. What do you feel when you're exercising? What do you think about while you're brushing your teeth?

All of your observations will make you more perceptive and will ultimately enhance your creativity and improve your writing.

Explore the Arts

It is of utmost importance for writers to engage with art, including books, music, and film. Especially books. Read, attend concerts, visit museums, and go to the theater. You'll find that every art form informs your writing, no matter the medium.

Movies and theater will enrich your storytelling skills. Music will make your writing more rhythmic and fluid. Dance will help you appreciate how people move. When you are an observer of other creative works, you nourish your own creativity.

You'll also discover yourself in the art you're most drawn to. I started writing poetry because of my love for music. Many fiction writers I know came to storytelling through their love of film and television.

You don't have to immerse yourself in the arts, but do make some time to regularly experience art and learn to appreciate a wide range of art forms.

Focus on Process

It's a shame when writers become obsessed with the end product. We all want to finish a book, but what's the point if we don't enjoy the path we take to get there?

Writing is hard work, but it's also rewarding. It can be tedious and exhausting, but it can also be energizing. I'm taxed after a lengthy writing session, but it's a good kind of tired in which I am filled with a sense of accomplishment.

At the same time, the more I write, the more energized I become. If I slack off and don't write for a few days or weeks, I get mopey. I start dragging my feet and my spirit dampens.

But when I'm writing every day, I'm consistently in a good mood. When I get lost in the process and stop obsessing over the goal (which is to finish the project), my writing is at its peak and so am I.

That doesn't mean I take my eyes off the goal. I'm always working toward a specific objective, but I don't rush and I engage with the work, which makes the completion of it that much sweeter.

Be Yourself

Most of us grow up with funny ideas about what it takes to make it in the world of art and entertainment. So many successful people make it look easy, and we assume they found success overnight. And while some people are born prodigies and some get immensely lucky, most people who succeed in this world do so because they've put in the hours. They've done the hard work.

But there's more to success than hard work. You have to know yourself. You have to know what kind of writer you want to be. Forget about what's popular or what sells. Don't worry about what kind of books win prizes or get loads of loyal fans. While you may indeed find success steering yourself toward these goals, your experience may be soured because you didn't earn it through artistry or passion, but through calculation. There's nothing wrong with success via calculation, but it makes some artists feel like sellouts. That's why it's important to know yourself and be yourself. How do you define a sellout, and where do you draw the line for selling yourself out?

When you write with passion and inspiration, it bleeds into your writing, making the work more charismatic. Find what speaks to your heart and chase after that. Write what's inside you.

Play

When you play, you are relaxed and engaged. If you make time for play, you'll enter an optimal creative state.

Think about what kids do: they play dress up and roll cars and trucks around on the floor. They pretend, either by playacting or using their toys (this can be a great technique for working out scenes in a piece of fiction, by the way). They run, jump, spin, and dance. They paint with their fingers, climb jungle gyms, and swing on swings. They do these things for the sheer enjoyment, and they do them without inhibition. Adults, on the other hand, tend to do things with purpose. Even our leisure activities are built around social norms and social circles.

Maybe you like going to theme parks and riding the roller coasters. Maybe you feel free when you're sailing. You can go to the beach and build sand castles, or stay home and play with your pets. Do something fun, and do fun things on a regular basis. That's what weekends are for!

Live a Little

You have to embrace life and live a little. You'll gain experience by trying new things, traveling to new places, and meeting new people, but more importantly, all these experiences will provide you with ideas and inspiration for your writing.

Practical Techniques for Creativity and Inspiration

"Fill your paper with the breathings of your heart." - William Wordsworth

Here are some practical techniques you can use to boost creativity:

Combine Contrary Elements

Think of two things that don't go together: rap and country music, ice cream and vegetables, westerns and fairy tales. Then, go against the grain and put them together.

I'm not saying you should go to your fridge and literally dish up a bowl of ice cream and broccoli, but the western-fantasy idea has some potential.

When we combine seemingly disparate elements, we make something that is fresh, something that feels original, even if it's completely based on things that already existed.

Did you know that Disney's *The Lion King* was based on Shakespeare's *Hamlet*? That's what happens when you combine seventeenth-century drama with animated animals. Who would have thought? I'll tell you who: Disney's Imagineers.

Save Your Ideas

As you practice being creative, you'll find that creativity sometimes strikes at the most inopportune times. Nothing is more frustrating than coming up with a brilliant idea as you're lying in bed, exhausted and half asleep.

Some writers don't bother to keep records of their ideas, and I've heard some pretty good reasons. For one thing, you'll find that you often remember ideas that are truly worth remembering, so you don't need to write them down. You'll also learn which ideas you're likely to forget. For example, if I come up with a great name for a character, I have to write it down because I know if a day goes by, I'll forget the name. But if I come up with a scene or a series of actions for my characters, I'm unlikely to forget them. I've learned, mostly through trial and error, what I need to write down and what I'll remember on my own.

It's a good idea to create a system for saving ideas as they come to you, especially when you're intentionally fostering creativity. You'll especially want to save ideas if they are not directly related to a project you're currently working on. For example, if you're working on a novel and you get a flash of inspiration to write a short story, you can jot down the idea and come back to it after you finish your novel.

There are lots of ways you can record your ideas. Of course, an idea notebook is obvious and most writers do carry a notebook and pen at all times. But these days, technology makes tracking ideas easier than ever. You can create files and folders on your computer (great for saving ideas you find on the Internet). If you're driving when an idea strikes, you can voice record it on your phone.

As time goes on and you better understand your own creativity, you can hone and refine your process for saving ideas. Figure out what works best for you, then put it into practice.

Stop Trying to Be So Original

Some writers are obsessed with a desire to be original. For some reason, they think that greatness and originality go hand in hand, or they think that a truly original idea will catapult them to the top of the best-seller list.

Actually, the most original works tend to be experimental, and they garner little attention except from elite literary circles.

The more you read and watch movies, the more you'll see that there are no original ideas. Everything is based on something that came before. It might have a new twist, but it's not one hundred percent original.

Let go of the idea that you're going to produce some groundbreaking, original piece of writing. Don't throw away an idea just because it's been done before. Instead, find a way to give it a fresh twist. Putting your own spin on something is original enough.

Keep a Dream Journal

Dreams are a great source of inspiration for some writers. You can promote dream inspiration. Start by remembering and recording your dreams. As you fall asleep, tell yourself that you'll remember your dreams and write them down as soon as you wake up. It might take a few nights, but eventually you'll remember your dreams and be able to capture them in writing. Later, you can harvest your dream journal for writing ideas.

Use Writing Prompts and Exercises

You can find writing prompts and exercises on websites, blogs, and in books. They are excellent tools for inspiration, and they are the most straightforward way to get ideas for writing projects.

Some writers worry that if they use a prompt or exercise, their work could be similar to that of someone else who used the same prompt or completed the same exercise. It's almost impossible for two people to end up with the same story based on a prompt. Two writers will execute the exact same concept in different ways.

Harvest Ideas from the World around You

Inspiration is everywhere. Read the news, talk to people. You'll come across stories and experiences happening all around you that could inspire your next piece of writing.

Coping with Writer's Block

It happens to all of us: we're a few pages in, the words are flowing, and we know what we're going to write next—then all of a sudden, we hit a wall. A moment ago, it seemed as if we were coasting toward the end of the project, but now we're lost somewhere in the middle, with no idea what to do next.

Most writers know what it's like to sit there, staring at the screen. The minutes tick by. Hours pass. Nothing happens.

We all know this can happen when we set out to start a project, but what about when we're in the middle of it? The weirdest thing is that we can have a pretty good idea about what's supposed to happen. We might even be working off an outline. But for some reason, the words don't come. What's a writer to do?

Sometimes writer's block occurs at the word-and-sentence level; you know what you want to say, but you can't find the right words to explain it. Other times, it occurs on a much broader level; you lose your train of thought and the entire concept falls apart.

Here are some techniques you can use when you're writing and run into a brick wall:

- **Push through it:** When I encounter a creative writing block, the first thing I usually do is try to push my way through it. Sometimes, if you keep going over the last few sentences or if you review the assignment, the words will start to flow again. Sometimes reading the piece again, from the beginning, helps.

- **Skip ahead:** If it's a longer project and you're stuck in one particular spot, skip ahead. If you're writing a book, jump to the next scene or chapter. If you're working on an article or essay, jump to the next paragraph. When I skip ahead, I usually make a temporary note in the document with all caps. This makes it easy to find the spot later and serves as a reminder to come back to it. I get the sense that when I skip ahead, the gears in the back of my mind keep working on the problem. Sometimes, I come back to the trouble spot a short time later to find that I know exactly how to handle it.

- **Do some research:** Most of us have had to stop in the middle of a project to conduct research because we just don't have the facts we need to get the writing done. But when we hit a creative writing block, pausing for research is a great way to stay on task and get some work done when we can't do the actual writing.

- **Take a side trip:** As with research, taking a side trip is a way to get work done without writing. This works best with bigger projects like long articles, essays, and books. Work on character backstories, world building, and other details ranging from themes and symbolism to naming characters and places.

- **Plan and brainstorm:** Sometimes we just run out of ideas in the middle of writing. The best way to build up more ideas is with a brainstorming session. I usually get out colored markers and a big sheet of paper and start jotting stuff down. I list various problems with the piece and then work out solutions. Sometimes, I'll also write an outline of what I've written so far and brainstorm to figure out what needs to happen next.

- **Reevaluate:** The worst-case scenario is that you're stuck because something is wrong with what you've already written. Sometimes, we need to stop and reevaluate a project. Have we gone off on a tangent? Was that last scene out of character? If you're stuck because you've taken a wrong turn, stop to reexamine what you've written so far and do a little revising.

- **Check your health:** If you're not physically or mentally up to writing, your body might tell you by erecting a road block that prevents you from writing. Are you hungry? Tired? Do you need to stretch or get a glass of water? This can also happen if we write for too long (I used to have a bad habit of forgetting to eat all day because I got too absorbed in my work). Your writing will be much stronger and smoother if you take good care of your health.

- **Be disciplined:** If I'm working on an especially tedious project, I often take five- or ten-minute breaks when I need respite (usually once per hour). I don't ever turn to social media, games, or other distractions that can eat up longer chunks of my time when I'm blocked. That leads to procrastination, which is something else altogether. If you haven't written anything in weeks, but you've managed to spend forty hours surfing the web or playing video games, then you don't have writer's block. Get back on task!

Creativity Resources for Writers

Below are some tips and resources to help with creativity. These are great whether you're creative by nature and want to enhance your creativity or whether you think you lack creative skills and want to build them so you can produce better writing.

- Head over to the Creativity Portal (http://www.creativity-portal.com), where you'll find tons (and by tons, I mean TONS) of creativity articles, resources, and project ideas.

- You'll find an entire category of my blog dedicated to writing ideas. You can check them out at writingforward.com/category/writing-ideas.

- The Brainstormer was created by artist Andrew Bosley. It's an electronic spinning wheel with random words that you can use to inspire any creative project, but it lends itself especially well to writing (http://andybosley.wix.com/bosleyart2#!brainstormer/c3ys).

Creativity Exercises

Here are a few exercises you can do to get your creativity flowing:

Scribble-Doodle

Spend ten or fifteen minutes doodling. You don't need to be able to draw to do this exercise. If you're not sure how to start, begin by drawing a line anywhere on a sheet a paper. Then draw a circle. As with the line, draw it anywhere you want. Draw a triangle, then a squiggly line, then a spiral, then a square. Let the shapes overlap. Keep drawing shapes and lines, until the entire page is filled. Then shade or color in sections of your scribble-doodle. Use solid shading, hatched lines, even polka dots. You can do this exercise with a regular pen or pencil, or get out some markers or color crayons.

Minute Words

Set a timer for one minute and write down every word you can think of, any word that comes to mind. In fact, try to come up with odd or rare words. When the minute is up, reset the timer for five minutes and use the words from your list to create word art. Don't worry about making sentences or even phrases. You might put some words together because they rhyme. Other words might form an interesting image.

What's Your Superpower?

This exercise is adapted from my book, *101 Creative Writing Exercises:*

What if you could fly or make yourself invisible? What if you could heal with a touch or read minds? Superpowers like these are the stuff of science fiction. Create a new superpower. Stay away from overdone powers like flight, invisibility, and super strength. Avoid psychic powers like telepathy and telekinesis. Think up something fresh: for example, someone who can breathe in outer space. Write a clear description of it, and make sure you include the following:

- Explain how the superpower is obtained.

- Note that anyone with that superpower also has a specific weakness (like Superman's kryptonite).

- Describe how someone might use this superpower for good or evil.

Chapter 10:
Community, Industry, and Audience

"All that I hope to say in books, all that I ever hope to say, is that I love the world." - E.B. White

Writers are notorious for spending hours in solitude, bent over our keyboards, laboring over prose and poetry. And when we're not absorbed in our own writing, we've got our noses wedged deeply into someone else's, because if there's one thing we love as much as writing, it's reading.

We're known as eccentrics, loners, and introverts. Of course, we're not all eccentrics, loners, or introverts. Lots of writers are conventional, social, and extroverted. But we all have to spend lots of time alone doing our work.

Yet none of us does it alone. Whether we realize it or not, writers are part of a much larger community that includes fellow writers, readers, and the entire publishing industry.

Fostering relationships with readers, other writers, and a broader range of people who make up the writing community has immense benefits. From learning the craft and developing skills to keeping creativity alive and staying motivated, this community can be essential in a job where the vast majority of your work is self-directed and done in isolation.

The writing community is immense, and there is a place in it for you.

The Writing Community

At the heart of every community lies a common, shared experience, and it's no different for writers. Other writers understand our unique struggles. Whether we're tangled up in a messy plot, trying to form a poem into a publishable work of art, or working through a stressful revision on an article or essay, the challenges we encounter as writers are particular to our craft.

When we surround ourselves with other writers, we enjoy camaraderie and make new friends—people who sympathize with our writing struggles and lend a bit of writerly advice.

Your fellow writers will relate to small accomplishments and celebrate them with you. When I finished the first draft of my first book, the non-writers in my life wanted to know if I'd already sent it out to get published. My writer friends said, "Good for you! When are you going to start revising?" The stark difference in their responses punctuated why the writing community is so important to me as a writer. The writers understood how meaningful it was to finish a book and knew that a draft is the first step of many. Their understanding filled my heart with appreciation.

Throughout our lives, we'll find ourselves involved in various communities. I've found that writers tend to be warm, supportive, and generous people. Whether I'm sitting in a live workshop, interacting with writers online, listening to interviews, or reading books full of writing tips, I always sense kindness and compassion from other writers.

Plus, writers come in all shapes and sizes. There are fiction writers, poets, novelists, and a slew of nonfiction writers. Some consider their writing an art. Others view it as a livelihood. Some writers are introverts—solitary, shy, and withdrawn. Others are socially active and extroverted.

Getting involved in the writing community is fun and it can be exciting, especially when you meet other writers that you really connect with. Like all passionate people, writers generally love to talk about their passion and are glad to engage in conversations about grammar or swap writing tips.

As with any career and perhaps especially with creative or artistic careers, involvement with others does wonders for strengthening one's connection to the craft. The writing community will help you master the craft, keep you focused and motivated, and provide a safe place for sharing ideas.

You can harness the power of this community for whatever you need. For example, I used to have a hard time staying focused on a writing project. I'd start it and then become distracted by some other project or even a completely different interest. My blog, *Writing Forward*, forced me to commit to writing on a regular basis because it became a space where I interacted with other writers and discussed the craft in meaningful ways. Those interactions, along with my sense of duty to my readers, kept me going and I was finally able to write regularly.

The writing community strengthened and intensified my passion for writing, and it will do the same for you.

Connecting with Other Writers

With the Internet, connecting with the writing community is a snap. It may take a while to find exactly the type of community you're looking for, but rest assured, they're out there. You can find writers blogging, podcasting, chatting on social media, hanging out in forums, and participating in community projects like NaNoWriMo (National Novel Writing Month).

Looking for an offline writing community? Check with your local community center and bookstores in your area to see if there are any local writing groups you can join. One of the best places to meet and mix with writers is in a workshop or class, so see if any creative-writing classes are offered at a nearby community college.

You can form or join small writing groups, intimate circles that meet regularly to discuss writing and share ideas and projects, or you can find a writing partner, someone you can bounce ideas off, swap work for critique, or even write projects with, in a partnership.

I encourage all writers to engage with the writing community on some level, but in a way that is comfortable for you. Some people do best in a formal setting, so classes and workshops are ideal. Others thrive on deadlines and competition: NaNoWriMo is perfect for this. If you'd like to lead a smaller online community, start a blog. If you'd like to make watercooler conversation with other writers, get on social media, find other writers, and chat them up. You might find lots of casual acquaintances, or you may form a few close friendships. You might choose to engage with a community online or in the real world. It doesn't matter. The point is that you engage on some level.

Whether you join a writing community or start your own, you will reap incredible benefits and pleasures from mingling with other writers, and by simply being a writer, you are already part of the larger writing community, so why not get a little more involved?

The Industry

There's also an industrial writing community—people making a living from writing. Writers are the most obvious members of the writing industry, but it also includes agents, editors, publishers, book-cover artists, layout designers, booksellers, marketers, and many others. It takes a lot of people to keep the publishing industry going, and that's true of both traditional publishing and indie publishing.

If your intent is to become a professional or published writer, you'll find many advantages in learning about the industry and networking with industry professionals.

For example, let's say your goal is to become a novelist. You have some story ideas, and you're thinking about starting your first novel. Do you know what to do with it once it's done? Will you try to get a traditional publisher to pick up your book or will you self-publish? Either way, you're probably going to need some help. At the very least, if you self-publish, you'll want to work with an editor and cover designer.

There are three steps to getting a book to readers: writing, publishing, and marketing. Publishing and marketing a book takes a lot of time and effort, and the work is fairly involved. It doesn't hurt to plan the publishing and marketing phases while you're writing.

Start studying the industry now. Set aside a little time to research what steps authors must take to publish a book.

Questions to ask:

Here are some questions you should ask about the publishing industry. Do some research and try to connect with people in the publishing and marketing world as you pursue the answers:

- What's the difference between big publishers and small presses? What's an imprint?

- What are the steps to getting a book published with a traditional publisher (or big publishing house)? Are the steps different if you go with a small press?

- What kind of advance and royalties can you expect from a publishing contract? Does it depend on the genre? Do first-time authors get different deals than established authors?

- If a publisher buys your book, what steps occur between signing the contract and getting the book on shelves?

- How will readers find my book? Will the publisher market it? How are interviews and book tours arranged? Does the publisher handle that or do you have to do it on your own?

- If you self-publish, will you need to hire an editor and a proofreader? How much will that cost?

- Can you make your own book cover? Should you make your own book cover? If not, how do you find someone who can make a professional cover, and how much will it cost?

- With self-publishing, what's involved in formatting and uploading the files? How hard is it? How long will it take? Can you do it yourself?

- You'll need your own website and marketing campaign, whether you self-publish or publish traditionally. What does that involve?

- How do you let the world know about your book? How do you find readers?

While these questions certainly take you way past writing and into another phase of a writer's career, they're worth considering early on. For example, if you are planning to write nonfiction, you'll need to establish expertise in your subject matter and develop a platform (an established audience) before proposing your book to a big publisher. The steps you take to self-publish are different from the steps you take to traditionally publish a novel. Some of what's involved might influence your writing, especially if you're interested in various forms and genres.

It's good to be prepared, so start familiarizing yourself with the industry sooner rather than later.

Your Readers

"I can't write without a reader. It's precisely like a kiss—you can't do it alone." - John Cheever

It's an old adage for writers: know your audience. But what does that mean? How well must we know our audience? And does knowing the audience increase our chances of getting published or selling our books?

Some writers insist that the best way to write is to write for yourself. Sit down and let the words flow. It's true that sometimes a freewheeling approach will result in some of your best work. And writing that way is immensely enjoyable. But there are times when a writer must take readers into consideration.

So, we have these two contradictory writing tips: *know your audience* and *write for yourself.*

In business, academic, and other types of formal writing, the audience is a consideration from the very beginning. You wouldn't write a business letter peppered with Internet shorthand (LOLs and OMGs), and you shouldn't use casual language in an academic paper. In instances like these, it's easy to see why you must keep your reader in mind throughout the entire project, but what about poetry, creative nonfiction, and fiction writing? Should the work be influenced by its intended readers? At what point does the audience begin to matter? And who is the audience anyway?

Some writers know they want to write children's books, so they keep a young audience in mind. After all, it wouldn't do to write a children's book laden with adult language and steamy love scenes. Other writers want to publish a memoir, hoping their own personal story will inspire others. And if you're hoping to inspire people, you should have a good idea about who you want to inspire. That's your audience.

These types of writers have a specific audience, and their writing must cater to it.

That's why, in some cases, it's essential to know who your audience is before you begin writing. But there are other situations in which the goals aren't clear and, therefore, neither is the audience. In cases like these, does a writer need to think about readers?

When you write for the sheer joy of writing or love of the craft and you do so without any particular goal in mind, the creative magic can sweep you away. When I wrote my novel for NaNoWriMo, I started with nothing more than a few characters. My only goal was to write at least 50,000 words. I didn't give a thought to the audience. And I'm certain that approaching the project this way, with an open mind and without any particular goal in terms of content, is what enabled me to actually complete the first draft of my first novel. It felt like quite an achievement.

When I finished my novel, I knew instantly who the audience was. I had written a young adult novel! If I ever decide to revise and polish that (very rough) first draft, knowing that the book is geared toward young adults will be helpful and will inform the way I approach revisions. I'll pay attention to the language to make sure it's age-appropriate and I'll also make sure the characters, themes, and everything else are suitable for the target age group.

Knowing the audience will also drive which agents and publishers we reach out to, because agents and publishers often specialize in specific forms and genres. They cater to clearly defined audiences. If we self-publish, knowing the audience will guide the decisions we make as we build a platform and develop a marketing campaign. Therefore, as a writer, it helps to know the audience by the time we are polishing our work and looking for publication opportunities.

If you write in a journal and nobody ever sees your work, then you don't need to think about an audience. Readers come into play when you decide to share your work, to get it published. There's a point when you decide that you want to cross over from writer to published author, and it's at that point that the audience starts to matter in a big way.

Publication is the point where your art shifts into business mode. It's the stage when you say, "I want to do this for a living and make money doing it." That means you're going to have to sell your stuff, and any time you're selling stuff, you need to know to whom you're selling.

Finding Your Readers

At some point, you'll probably need to identify and understand your readers. If you're writing about something you believe in, are passionate about, or are interested in, then your readers will be a lot like you. That should make it easy to find and connect with them.

Most writers find their readers through genre channels. For example, science-fiction fans attend conventions. The biggest science-fiction convention in the United States is Comic-Con, which takes place in San Diego every summer. This is where science-fiction authors, game creators, and filmmakers connect with the most loyal science-fiction fans in the nation.

Whatever your genre, there are places where fans and readers hang out, online and off, to share and discuss the art and entertainment they love.

If you write nonfiction, you'll find your readers by topic rather than by genre. Let's say you write a memoir about growing up in a military family. You'll find your readers wherever military families gather. If you write a book about the year you spent backpacking abroad, you'll find your readers wherever travelers hang out.

Finding your readers shouldn't be too difficult. First you identify your target audience, then you figure out where they gather, what they read and watch, and how you might be able to reach them.

Your Future in Writing

"Writing is a hard way to make a living, but a good way to make a life." - Doris Betts

A good piece of writing holds your attention. It flows smoothly and everything makes sense. It's interesting and a pleasure to read.

Great writing, on the other hand, doesn't just hold your attention: it commands your attention. You become lost in it. You can't put it down, and when you do, you want to read it all over again.

Great writing doesn't happen overnight. It takes years of study and practice, dedication and commitment to the craft. You've taken the first steps toward great writing by beginning your study and practice. If you remain dedicated and committed, writing will become an integral part of your life and your writing will shine.

The Writing Life

The writer's life is unique. We spend a lot of time alone, with only our words and ideas to keep us company. We are immersed in word counts and submissions, manuscripts and notebooks. We work under tight deadlines, constantly on the lookout for typos. When other people are enjoying their favorite television shows or a day at the beach, we're busy at our keyboards, doing our writerly work.

We are idea seekers—always looking for the next topic, poem, or plot. Every moment is an experience that could lead to a masterpiece, so every moment is a masterpiece. We live as observers, taking in the world around us so we can share the best parts of it with our readers.

We are communicators, using words to forge connections. It's not enough to tell a story. We want to show readers what it was like to be there, to live it, even if it never really happened.

We get excited over things that other people find only mildly entertaining—a passionate voice, a riveting scene, a complex character. We delight in office supplies, stationery, and writing instruments: tools that other people see as mere necessities.

And the most ambitious writers, those who are driven to make creative writing not just a way of life but a career, must also look at themselves in a way few other people do. We must see ourselves as authors and learn how to brand and market ourselves. We have to be self-promoters, and we have to be brave enough to put our work, which can be highly personal, out there for all the world to see.

The writing community is a tight one. Outside of literary circles, when two bookworms or writers bump into each other, they're sure to forge an instant bond because such a person is a rare treasure. There may be some competition among writers, but most of what I've experienced is goodwill and support.

We find ourselves outside of social norms. Our day jobs are simply a means to pay our bills. The real work happens early in the morning, late at night, and on weekends, when the rest of the world is playing. But our work is play. We breathe language. We engage in make-believe. We search for stories that beg to be told. We wrap ourselves up in words and images, grammar and structure, the historical and the fantastical, fact and fiction. And while we may be concerned with ordinary living, we ourselves live rather extraordinary lives.

Moving Forward with Your Writing

Some writers will never finish a book. Some will finish a book, but will never publish it. Some will finish and publish a single book. Some will write and publish many books. There are writers who write slowly and thoughtfully, and there are writers who write quickly and prolifically. Some writers write for several hours a day. Some carve out time whenever they can. A few write in binges, writing fervently for months at a time then not writing at all for weeks—or years.

There is no single road to success in this business. If you want to make writing your career, you will experiment and persist and figure out what works for you. Maybe you're a one-book-a-year author. Maybe you can do three, four, twelve books a year. Maybe you'll write short stories or serials. Maybe you'll self-publish. Maybe you'll get an agent and a traditional publishing deal.

However you get there, I hope you'll get there by being true to yourself. Write what's in your heart. Don't worry about what's hot or what sells. There is an audience for just about anything, and if you write what you love, you'll eventually find your readers.

Enjoy the adventure, and don't worry so much about the destination. Just keep writing.

Book Three
1200 Creative Writing Prompts

Introduction

Have you ever wanted to write but weren't sure where to begin? Maybe you wanted to write a story, but you couldn't think of a plot. Maybe you wanted to write an essay or an article, but you couldn't think of a subject to write about. Maybe you wanted to write a poem, but you couldn't find the words.

Writing prompts provide helpful starting points when you're not sure what to write. Prompts can be used for a variety of situations:

- When you need to take a break from a larger project, you can use writing prompts to work on a shorter project. This allows you to take the break you need but maintain your writing practice and routine.

- Prompts can help you get unstuck. Sometimes a prompt will trigger a solution to a problem you've encountered with a writing project that's giving you trouble.

- Creative writing prompts are perfect for writing classes, groups, and workshops.

- Prompts provide ideas and starting points when you want to experiment with new forms and genres of writing.

How to Use This Book

This book includes three parts, each geared toward a different form of creative writing: fiction, poetry, or creative nonfiction.

The prompts within each section cover a range of genres and topics:

- The fiction section includes storytelling prompts in the following genres: literary, mystery, suspense, thriller, science fiction, fantasy, horror, romance, historical, humor, satire, parody, children's, and young adult.

- Poetry prompts include a mix of starters, subjects, words lists, and images.

- Creative nonfiction prompts cover journaling, memoir, articles, personal essays, and topics related to reading and writing.

Each section contains a list of numbered prompts. You can use the prompts in any way that works for you. Use a poetry prompt to inspire a story. Use a nonfiction prompt to inspire a poem. Mix and match the prompts. Change the details provided in any prompt. Do whatever is comfortable for you and inspires you to write.

The prompts are meant to spark ideas. Review the prompts until you find one that resonates, and then start writing.

You can even use the prompts to inspire a list of your own writing prompts, which you can then share with others or use whenever you need fresh writing ideas.

Whether you're using these prompts to trigger ideas for your own writing projects or to push your writing in new directions, I hope you'll find them fun and useful.

Good luck and keep writing.

Sincerely,
Melissa Donovan
Founder and Editor of *Writing Forward*

Fiction Writing Prompts

1. While at summer camp over a decade ago, five teenagers' lives became irrevocably intertwined. Now their paths have crossed again, and they must all come to terms with what happened that summer.

2. Someone is sitting on a park bench reading a news article about a recent string of crimes. This person knows who did it.

3. As passengers disembark from a transatlantic flight, they start to experience amnesia—all of the passengers except one. The farther they go from the plane, the more severe their amnesia becomes. Will they risk forgetting everything?

4. A writer loses the ability to distinguish reality from the fantastical worlds of his or her stories.

5. The protagonist is obsessed with serial killers and decides to make a documentary film reenacting their most horrific crimes.

6. Some relationships aren't simple enough to be classified as toxic or healthy. Writing about a complex relationship is, well, complex. Give it a shot.

7. In a country that rants and raves about freedom, the government decides that its people should not be allowed to drink liquor. Write a story set during Prohibition in the United States.

8. The setting is a festive party honoring the holiday of your choosing. Something unexpected happens, and the guests are drawn into a weekend of pranks and hijinks.

9. One kid in a big city is bored. School won't be out for a couple of months. There are no holidays to look forward to. He or she wishes the family lived in the country. (Where do kids get these ideas?)

10. On the first day of school, two best friends discover a frightening secret about one of their new teachers.

11. Some stories rhyme. "'Twas the Night Before Christmas" is one example. Shakespeare's plays are another. Try writing a story that is also a rhyming poem.

12. It's a cold, rainy night. A man and woman stand beside a car outside a convenience store, arguing. One of them pulls out a gun.

13. Four friends on a nature hike discover a deep cave, complete with running water. As they go deeper and deeper into the cave, they find strange objects—human skeletons, an old computer from

the early eighties, a gas mask, and strange mango-sized orbs that emit a glowing blue light.

14. What if you discovered a portal to another world? Where is the portal? How does it work? What's on the other side?

15. Everyone is getting tired of the cold and eagerly anticipating summer. But this summer is going to bring more than sunshine and easy days at the beach because something terrifying and unimaginable is lurking in the water.

16. An elderly couple traveling through the desert spends an evening stargazing and sharing memories of their lives.

17. Write about a historical natural disaster that caused death and destruction to a small number of people and therefore never received national or international attention.

18. The protagonist is about to drift off to sleep only to be roused by the spontaneous memory of an embarrassing moment from his or her past.

19. Write a children's story about a bird and squirrel who live together in the same tree (like *The Odd Couple*).

20. All the kids are looking forward to their winter break. There's a school-sponsored ski trip, and one girl is aching to go so she can try snowboarding for the first time.

21. While shopping in a department store, a middle-aged man comes face to face with the guy who almost certainly kidnapped his child ten years earlier.

22. The protagonist wakes up in a seemingly endless field of wildflowers in full bloom with no idea how he or she got there.

23. A con man who convinces people they've been abducted by aliens and takes their money...is abducted by aliens.

24. A school of dolphins is too trusting and approaches a boat whose crew is intent on capturing the dolphins and bringing them to a theme park for a swim-with-the-dolphins attraction. Write the story from the dolphins' perspective.

25. Vampires, werewolves, and mummies are classic monsters. Create a classic monster of your own, and then write a story about it.

26. Neither of them wants to marry a total stranger, but arranged marriage is the custom. Their lives will change dramatically on their wedding night, but will it be for the better or for the worse?

27. The entertainment industry boomed in the twentieth century. Technology changed entertainment from an attraction you paid to see in a theater or other public setting to something you could enjoy from the comfort of your home.

Every home had a radio. Black-and-white silent films evolved into Technicolor talkies. Now we have the Internet. Write a story centered on entertainment technologies of the past.

28. An arrogant businessman hits a car full of old ladies. He gets out and approaches their vehicle, blaming them for the accident. Hilarity ensues when those old ladies show him what's what.

29. Puppies and kittens aren't always born in spring. This winter, a special puppy is born, one that will change people's lives. Write this story for children.

30. A young man on his first hunting trip has a deer in his sight and suddenly remembers the day his dad took him to see *Bambi*.

31. Write a story about a character who walks away from the life he or she knows and the people he or she loves. Why would a person give up everything he or she holds dear?

32. A small team of graduate students is conducting research at sea when they are overtaken by a wild storm.

33. The earth has been ravaged by war, famine, disease, and devastating natural disasters. In less than a decade, the population has dwindled from seven billion to less than 42,000. There is no law or order. The grid is gone. Everyone is struggling to survive.

34. There is a magic talisman that allows its keeper to read minds. It falls into the hands of a young politician.

35. The protagonist turns the key in the lock and opens the door. Beyond, he or she discovers untold horrors.

36. A high society engagement threatens to fall apart when one of the betrothed falls in love with an outsider. Businesses, lives, and old family relationships could be destroyed forever.

37. Write about characters living before *Homo sapiens* evolved or during a time when humans existed simultaneously with the species they evolved from.

38. Write a satirical story about an orphanage that is managed as if it were an animal shelter, or write about an animal shelter that is managed as if it were an orphanage.

39. Children are delighted when a mama cat gives birth to a litter of five orange tabbies and one little gray runt.

40. A single mother leaves her two teenage children home alone for the summer.

41. A woman has three children, all of whom are soldiers in a military that is at war. Within the span of three days, she learns that two of her children were killed in combat. Six weeks later, there's a knock at the door. When she opens it,

she finds her third child standing there—the same child who convinced the other two to enlist.

42. The protagonist is raking leaves on the lawn. He or she pauses for a breath and glances at the neighbors' lawn. *They never rake their leaves*, the protagonist thinks, *and their dog is always using my yard as a latrine*. The protagonist decides to do something about these inconsiderate neighbors.

43. The year is 1623. A visitor arrives in a small, tribal village in Nigeria. The visitor is wearing blue jeans, an old rock-band t-shirt, and a fedora and is carrying a pack that contains a solar-powered laptop computer.

44. The protagonist walks into his or her house and it's completely different—furniture, decor, all changed. It doesn't look like the same house anymore. And nobody's home.

45. Scientists have figured out how to create hybrids: dog-people, cat-insects, and bird-fish. One of their experiments goes terribly wrong and unleashes a swarm of hybrid predators on the population.

46. Two athletes competing (either at an individual sport or on opposing teams) get stuck somewhere together (broken-down bus in a remote location, elevator, etc.) and fall in love.

47. The Great Depression filled the space between America's Prohibition (which was still in effect during the Depression) and World War II. The Depression affected the entire world. Well-to-do people lost everything and found themselves standing in food lines. Ordinary people went to extraordinary measures to get a meager meal. Meanwhile, someone, somewhere profited.

48. It's the most wonderful time of the year! Wait—no, it's not! The holidays are cheesy. Bah humbug!

49. Two siblings capture a butterfly and a moth and proceed to argue over which insect is superior.

50. Write a story about two teenagers who are on their first date.

51. A family of five is driving across the desert on their way to vacation in California. They get lost, and then the car breaks down in the middle of nowhere. Their cell phones are dead and the sun is setting. The kids are hot, tired, and hungry. Mom is scared and frazzled. Dad, an office worker with no survival skills, is frustrated and angry. An animal howls in the distance.

52. In a highly competitive and lucrative industry, one executive squashes competitive young upstarts by murdering them. Will the detective on the case ever be able to prove it?

53. Two children, a boy and a girl, decide to make a time capsule and bury it at the edge of a farm under a big oak tree. While digging, they unearth a metallic object the size of a shoebox. It's shaped like a bullet and has the number eight engraved on it. It appears to be a container, since it rattles when they shake it, but there is no obvious way to open it.

54. A woman is working in her garden when she discovers an unusual egg.

55. Write a horror story about a family in which one of the family members slowly becomes creepier and crazier until he or she turns into a full-blown hellhound wreaking havoc on everyone else.

56. An old-fashioned couple struggles with their child's decision to marry—a marriage that defies tradition and their bigoted beliefs, which have been passed down for generations.

57. The Industrial Revolution changed the world for everyone. Write a story about a character who had a hand in the Industrial Revolution—for example, someone working on the development of the railways.

58. Politics is serious business, so try turning it on its head and making a comedy out of it. Start with an unlikely candidate running for office.

59. Write a children's story about people who are hiking in the woods when they are suddenly surrounded by hundreds of butterflies.

60. Two best friends make a pact. When they get to junior high, they grow apart, but the pact haunts them. Will they fulfill the pact they made as children?

61. A couple met in high school and married as soon as they graduated. Life wasn't easy. They had five kids and money was tight. One worked as a domestic servant and the other worked in a factory. Every day was a financial hardship, but they loved each other. Three years after their youngest child leaves home, the couple wins the lottery—and wins big.

62. Write a story about a detective solving a crime that was committed against his or her partner or a crime that his or her partner committed.

63. A deadly virus hits a highly populated metropolitan area, killing thousands of people. After it passes, those who survived realize they have acquired bizarre talents and abilities.

64. Fairies, unicorns, and elves are usually depicted as benevolent. Write about fairies, unicorns, or elves that are evil.

65. A biological engineer sets out to create a superhuman, but something goes wrong, and instead, the scientist creates a vicious, all-

powerful monster that cannot be controlled or stopped.

66. Trapped in a stale marriage, the protagonist finds companionship outside of marriage and in the most unlikely of places.

67. Write a story about a European monarchy in which siblings are willing to kill each other for the throne, or there's a child heir who will inherit the crown but doesn't want it.

68. Suffering from amnesia, the protagonist is thrust into a strange and hilarious life that he or she has no memory of.

69. Children's stories sometimes try to help kids solve difficult problems. Write a story about children overcoming nightmares, getting potty trained, wetting the bed, losing a pet or grandparent, or attending the first day of school.

70. A teenager who is obsessed with celebrities experiences conflict with his or her parents, who want to see more focus on academics.

71. A little girl loses her sister to a rare terminal illness. The girl vows to become a doctor and find a cure for this disease. At the age of forty-two, she successfully develops a treatment.

72. Someone is murdered and the only viable suspect is one of the victim's close family members (parent, child, spouse, or sibling), but the

detectives on the case are certain this suspect did not commit the crime.

73. A traveler picks up a souvenir, a colorful rock with one side that is completely flat. As she goes about her travels, she realizes that when she has the rock with her, she can understand any language that people are speaking but can only speak her native language.

74. After a car accident and a minor head injury, a teenager starts having precognitive dreams. Initially, family and friends insist the dreams are coincidences, but the proof becomes undeniable when a government agency steps in.

75. A cult is formed by a small group of people who are obsessed with death. In one ritual, an individual must commit suicide so that the other members can bring him or her back to life.

76. The protagonist is nearing the age of fifty. After a lifetime of living single, childless, and focused on his or her career, the character has a sudden change of heart.

77. The setting is the American Dust Bowl. Write about a family that decides to stay put as all their neighbors emigrate to the West Coast.

78. Hilarity ensues when a group of friends from the big city sign up for a one-week survival course in a remote mountain setting.

79. Three children are sitting on a log near a stream. One of them looks up at the sky and says...

80. The kids were raised on the mantra "Family is everything." What happens when they find out their parents aren't who they pretended to be? Will the family fall apart?

81. A ten-year-old boy comes home from school and heads out to the backyard to play with his beloved dog, but he finds the dog lying dead underneath a big, shady tree.

82. Several high-profile research-and-development labs have recently been burgled, and trade secrets that could be dangerous to the public have been stolen.

83. While on vacation on a tropical island, a young couple spots a strange bird that speaks their names. When the bird takes off, they decide to follow it.

84. In ancient times, there were five portals to another world carefully hidden on Earth's five largest continents. Those portals have since been buried, but their discovery is inevitable.

85. A team of archaeologists is studying ancient caves that have been buried over the millennia when they are suddenly trapped deep underground. Terror ensues as the team faces earthquakes, rockslides, and monstrous creatures.

86. One character is a soldier, and the other is a citizen in a country ravaged by war. They are on opposite sides, but their love could change the tides for everyone.

87. Write a story set at the point in history when Christianity split from Judaism. Write the story from the perspective of an ordinary person—in other words, not from the perspective of someone who was involved but from the perspective of an outside observer.

88. The protagonist is digging in the garden and finds a fist-sized nugget of gold. There's more where that came from in this hilarious story of sudden wealth.

89. Halloween is just around the corner, and the protagonist has a lot do this year: candy, costumes, and pumpkin carving. The house smells like apples and caramel. While making preparations, he or she looks outside and sees something astonishing.

90. Two adolescent siblings are visiting their relatives' farm and witness a sow giving birth.

91. Write a story about someone with a debilitating condition, illness, disorder, or handicap. The story starts on the day the character is diagnosed.

92. The protagonist is obsessed with another person. When the object of the protagonist's obsession is

found dead, the protagonist becomes the prime suspect.

93. A sixteen-year-old growing up on a ranch is out in a storm, gets hit by lightning, and survives. After that, the kid can hear other people's (or animals') thoughts.

94. At first, they think a strange visitor is selling snake oil, but over time, they come to realize the magic is real…and it could be dangerous.

95. Castaways on a deserted island find themselves stalked by ferocious wildlife.

96. The protagonist has a plan: go to college, start a career in a demanding and highly competitive field, and retire with wealth and accolades. But then the protagonist falls in love, and the relationship threatens to derail all those carefully laid plans.

97. Think back to the decade in which you were born. Now write a story about an adult protagonist living during that time.

98. Try your hand at parody: choose any serious dramatic film or novel and retell the story as a comedy.

99. A young girl and her mother walk to the edge of a field, kneel down in the grass, and plant a tree.

100. Write a story set in juvenile hall.

101. There's an old man sitting in a rickety wooden chair, fishing through a hole in the ice on a frozen lake. A loud cracking sound reverberates across the lake's surface, and he feels the ice shift beneath him. He scurries, but the hole expands too quickly, and he goes into the icy water. What happens next?

102. When his or her commanding officer is found dead, one young soldier goes AWOL and launches a personal investigation to find out who did it.

103. A surgeon who does not believe in miracles is diagnosed with an aggressive terminal illness and is given six months to live. Three years later, the surgeon is alive and perfectly healthy.

104. At the height of human technological development, a special child is born who can communicate telepathically with computers and other mechanical and electronic devices.

105. A teenager becomes obsessed with books, movies, and video games that depict graphic violence and murder, and the teen's parents are not pleased about it.

106. Two ambitious coworkers want the same promotion, and they're both willing to do just about anything to get it. Then they fall in love. Does the competition heat up or die down? Will their romance survive office politics?

107. Choose a period of history and a place that interests you, and write a multigenerational saga about a family that lived during that era.

108. Write a comedy about a rural, salt-of-the-earth family moving to a big city and trying to get along with city folk who are sophisticated and refined.

109. While shopping in a department store during the holidays, a child is separated from his or her parents and discovers a portal to a winter wonderland.

110. A teenager's beliefs are not in line with his or her parents' religious system. Can we control what we believe? Can we control what others believe?

111. Most of us have had a nemesis of some kind, whether it was a bully on the playground, a nasty coworker, or someone who caused us or our loved ones pain and suffering. These people make great models for villains in our stories. Fictionalize an antagonist from real life in a story.

112. When marriage becomes a living hell, the protagonist attempts to kill his or her spouse by bringing on depression and encouraging overeating and other unhealthy lifestyle choices.

113. Scientists discover that the galaxy itself is a living organism.

114. All over the world, there are secret societies of people who have magical abilities. They've kept

themselves hidden for centuries, but now something threatens to make their existence known to the public.

115. An old man or woman confesses a lifetime of secrets—many of which involve violence, torture, and murder.

116. A protagonist is forced to choose between family (or culture) and the one he or she loves.

117. Write a story set in an orphanage anytime in history.

118. In the 1970s, someone started putting rocks in boxes and selling them as Pet Rocks, complete with care and training manuals. The business made millions. Write a story about an inventor or businessperson who comes up with a ridiculous product.

119. Children love to pretend and play grown-up. Write a story about a child playing grown-up and pretending to have a particular career: teacher, veterinarian, artist, etc.

120. In the midst of a natural disaster, a classroom is locked down and everyone inside is trapped until they are rescued three days later.

121. A woman is walking alone on a beach in the summer twilight (or at dawn) when something happens that completely changes her life.

122. The protagonist is blamed for a murder but doesn't remember committing it—even though every shred of evidence along with a hazy memory suggests otherwise.

123. A young girl starts having recurring dreams about a dragon. In one of the dreams, the dragon says, "You made me." The girl becomes obsessed with dragons and decides her life purpose is to become a genetic biologist so she can, indeed, make a real dragon.

124. A man who sees ghosts checks himself into a mental institution, oblivious to the fact that the facility has been closed for almost thirty years.

125. The protagonist wakes one morning gagged and tied to the bed, and there's a maniac sitting in the bedside chair.

126. Love saves the day when the protagonist is helped out of dire circumstances by falling in love with someone wealthy and powerful. But when the relationship falls apart, the protagonist realizes that it's better to rescue oneself and build a relationship on companionship instead of dependency.

127. Write a story about an interracial relationship set in a time and place where such relationships were scandalous or even illegal. The relationship could be a romance, friendship, or a business partnership.

128. Fed up with being bullied by coworkers, the protagonist plans a series of pranks to embarrass his or her colleagues.

129. After learning his or her parents are struggling to make ends meet, a child prodigy decides to fix the family's finances.

130. They were a normal, happy family until one of the parents was injured in a terrible accident and became severely disabled. Write the story from the perspective of one of the children.

131. It's the season of snowmen and sleigh rides. Children are out gallivanting on snowy slopes and making snow angels in their backyards. One child longs to join them but cannot, so he or she watches from a lonely upstairs window. Why can't the protagonist go outside?

132. A group of young adults gets together to rent a cabin for a weekend. They drink and party, and the next morning one of them is found murdered. In the months that follow, the friends suspect each other and question themselves. Who did it? Will they figure it out before the police do?

133. In a thousand years, Earth is controlled by nanobots that live in the blood of world leaders. Write the story from the nanobots' perspective.

134. You probably have beliefs about what happens to human consciousness after death. Write a story

about a protagonist who dies, showing what happens after death.

135. A physicist who's ridiculed by scientific colleagues discovers a parallel universe, a universe where the beasts and creatures of human mythologies and folklore actually exist. Horror ensues when the physicist opens the portal between the two worlds.

136. Romance stories are usually about someone looking for love or avoiding it and falling into it anyway. Write a love story that takes place after the search for love is over.

137. Nowadays people go to college or trade schools to prepare for a career. But there was a time when most careers required apprenticeship. Go back in time and write a story about a mentor and his or her apprentice.

138. Survival stories are often gritty and tragic. Write a survival story that is funny. Start your story by bringing the characters into a situation they must survive: a natural disaster, for example.

139. During a field trip to a museum, a group of kids (who are not friends with each other) gets lost and goes on a grand adventure through time and space.

140. There are lots of stories about parents who pressure kids into law, medicine, and sports. Write from the perspective of a kid whose parents

are pressuring him or her in a less conventional direction (music, art, etc.).

141. Write a story in first-person point of view from the perspective of someone who is your complete opposite physically, politically, spiritually, or in some other significant way.

142. The protagonist buys an antique trunk from a junk shop and discovers a mummified body inside—a body that was murdered.

143. An asteroid and a meteoroid collide near Earth, and fragments rain down onto the planet's surface, wreaking havoc. Some of those fragments contain surprising elements: fossils that prove life exists elsewhere in the galaxy, for example.

144. In the fantasy genre, sometimes all the wizards seem the same. Write a story about a wizard who doesn't have a long white beard, doesn't wear robes, and is not a mentor or guide.

145. The protagonist wakes up one morning in a parallel universe that is similar to our own but much darker and more terrifying.

146. One man or woman is nearing the age of sixty. Decades after giving up career aspirations to focus on family, he or she suddenly has a change of heart and decides to go for the dream abandoned years ago.

147. Spaceships, planes, and men on the moon: We started out traveling around on foot. Then some clever Neanderthal invented the wheel. Now, we soar through the skies and tear through space. Write a story about a long journey set in an era when planes, trains, and automobiles weren't readily available.

148. Two characters who loathe each other get locked inside a department store overnight. Hijinks and hilarity ensue.

149. A child pretending to be a spy discovers incredible secrets while surveilling his or her parent, who conducts top-secret research for the military.

150. The story starts when a kid comes out of the school bathroom with toilet paper dangling from his or her waistband. Does someone step forward and whisper a polite word, or do the other kids make fun? What happens in this pivotal moment will drive the story and have a deep impact on the main character.

151. A doctor puts his hand on his patient's arm and says, "You or the baby will survive. Not both. I'm sorry."

152. A newlywed receives word that his or her spouse was killed in action. A few months later, the widowed protagonist starts receiving

communications that could only be from his or her dearly departed spouse.

153. A team of researchers in a submarine is caught in a deadly sea storm. The instruments on board go haywire. The submarine submerges deep into the ocean in search of calm waters until the storm passes. Afterward, the submarine surfaces, but the instruments are still not functioning properly. They can't get a fix on their location or find land, which should be nearby. When night falls, the researchers realize there are two moons in the sky and the constellations are completely unfamiliar.

154. We've seen cute and cuddly dragons, mean and vicious dragons, and noble dragons. Write a story about a different kind of dragon.

155. A scientific experiment meant to give animals the ability to communicate with humans goes wrong. The animals gain the power of human speech, but their intelligence also skyrockets, and they are determined to take the planet back from humans.

156. After three failed marriages and countless broken hearts, the protagonist has given up on love. It's been years since he or she so much as considered going on a date.

157. Revolution could be defined as a war between a state and its people. Revolution often occurs when people are oppressed to the point of mass suffering. Choose one such revolution from

history and write a story about the people who launched it.

158. Some of the funniest stories have simple plots that are humorous because the protagonist figuratively (or literally) gets gum on his or her shoe every step of the way. Ideas: the protagonist wakes up by rolling off the bed, spills coffee on his only clean shirt, realizes he is wearing two different shoes after arriving at work, etc.

159. Write a story about a child and his or her imaginary friend.

160. Kids start realizing their identities around junior high. That's often when the friendships of elementary school fade as kids forge bonds and form into cliques more suitable to their personal interests and social status. Write a story about best friends from grammar school who are drifting apart in junior high.

161. A person who lives in a metropolitan apartment connects with nature through the birds that come to the window.

162. The world of politics is fraught with shady deal making. How far will a career politician go to save his or her job? Is framing someone for murder too far? Is committing murder too far? Or is that just how it's done?

163. Will humans ever settle on another planet? Write a story about interstellar colonization.

164. You're flying somewhere—anywhere—but when your plane lands, you and the other passengers quickly realize you didn't reach your intended destination. In fact, you've arrived in a strange, wondrous (or terrible) world that you never knew existed.

165. Write a story about a kind, loving protagonist who blacks out and commits heinous crimes, which he or she cannot remember later. Be sure to provide a scientific or fantastical explanation for this odd phenomenon.

166. The protagonist is desperate to get married and have kids and employs every tactic imaginable to meet his or her mate. Write a story about these adventures in dating.

167. Sometimes it seems like real-world villains never get what's coming to them, especially when heroes are taken down by madmen, including political or religious zealots and revenge seekers. Write a story that contrasts what happens to a benevolent historical figure with one who is seen as evil.

168. Write a funny story about a dysfunctional family that has just won the lottery.

169. The protagonist is only two or three years old but all he or she cares about is candy. What do you want for your birthday? Candy. Where do you want to go for vacation? Candy store.

170. Write a story about a youth who is about to age out of the foster care system.

171. A group of college students launches a project to grow their own food because they think it will earn them good grades in their science class.

172. Over the course of one week, five high-profile CEOs go missing. Were they abducted? Killed? Did they all run off to escape their high-pressure lives?

173. A spaceship is hurtling through the galaxy in this tale of adventure. Write a story about its crew. Are they civilians? Are they lost, or do they have a destination? Do they visit various planets or stay aboard their ship?

174. An elderly patient with dementia is whisked back and forth between the real world and a magical world where anything is possible and people live forever.

175. Horror stories often deal with monsters and maniacal killers. Write a horror story in which the villain is nature and the characters are being killed off by storms and other natural phenomena.

176. A young teenager falls in love. His or her parents disagree with each other about the relationship and whether it should be allowed to continue. Could a child's love tear a family apart?

177. Can you imagine what it would have been like to live during a time when humans hadn't yet started

building huts—let alone houses? Write a story about ancient humans living on the land and in caves.

178. A family of five from a large, urban city decides to spend their one-week vacation camping. Hilarity ensues.

179. Write a story about sibling rivalry from the perspectives of two to four small children.

180. Write a story about a teen struggling with poverty. A tragic ending would have the teen growing up and staying in poverty. An uplifting ending would show the teen finding a way to make a good living.

181. A misfit teenager is seduced by a cultlike church. Can this impressionable protagonist be saved?

182. The protagonist is the star of the police department, someone who solves every murder that comes across his or her desk, until a killer unleashes a series of mastermind murders that seem unsolvable.

183. Write a story about how humans could breathe in space without having to wear bulky, uncomfortable space suits.

184. The real oceans of Earth are a fantasyland in their own right. Most fantasies set in the sea focus on mermaids. Write a story that includes sirens, serpents, and other fantastical water creatures.

185. Lots of horror stories are about a group of teens in the woods or some other remote location. What if horror was unleashed at a business conference or fan convention?

186. They say that rebound relationships are doomed to fail. Write about a protagonist who enters into a new relationship shortly after a difficult breakup.

187. There was a time when most people believed the earth was flat. Write a story set during the time when the idea of a spherical earth was spreading.

188. Write an adventurous comedy about a group of friends on a hunting trip.

189. Every day at preschool, a group of friends plays a game of make-believe in a magical wonderland of their own invention.

190. It's not easy being an adolescent. Write a story about an adolescent protagonist whose friends are growing up—dating, partying, and thinking about college—while the protagonist would still rather play with toys and watch cartoons.

191. Write a story about two people who care deeply for each other but who, for whatever reasons, move on and away from each other.

192. Write a story about a lawyer who must defend a heinous criminal, even though everybody knows the suspect is guilty.

193. Scientists finally master DNA and human genes, and they invent a treatment that fundamentally changes people, making them smarter, more energetic, less violent, more beautiful, etc. It can even change people's beliefs. Write about a scientist who takes it upon himself or herself to secretly unleash this treatment upon the population.

194. Write a story from the perspective of a banshee or the Grim Reaper.

195. The closest most of us get to a real-life horror story is a nightmare. Write a story about nightmares leaking into the characters' real lives either literally or figuratively.

196. Two candidates for the Senate, embroiled in a nasty campaign leading up to a close election, fall in love.

197. Think about some famous historical animated films (for children), especially the Disney princess movies. Most of those stories are based on old legends and fairy tales. Reimagine any of them with a more realistic take (no magic!).

198. Write a story about four elderly people who were once tough and wild party animals.

199. The protagonist is a child who likes to solve mysteries around the house, at school, and in the neighborhood. Who ate the last cookie? Why was there a substitute teacher for over a month? Who

keeps letting their dog use the next-door neighbor's lawn as a bathroom?

200. The protagonist is driven to finish school, get a scholarship and an education, and eventually achieve a stable career. But there are many distractions in high school.

201. The story starts at the end of a trial when the defendant is declared guilty and is sent to prison.

202. An archeologist who is bored and tired of digging up meaningless fragments of ancient civilizations stumbles upon an ancient text that could change the world's understanding of history—and the future of humanity—forever.

203. A scientist discovers a source of free, unlimited energy that has no negative effects. Wealthy and powerful people do not want this energy source made available to the public.

204. Write a story about a protagonist with psychic abilities: clairvoyance, telepathy, or telekinesis. What challenges does he or she face? How does the protagonist use these powers?

205. A series of simultaneous natural disasters occurs all around the planet, leaving governments disabled, rescue workers incapacitated, and ordinary people alone to face the horrors of the aftermath.

206. Write about a man and woman who are friends— just friends—and who are both happily married to

(or involved with) other people. Show their romantic relationships with others through the lens of their friendship with each other.

207. In 1989, the Berlin Wall came down. Write a story about people who climbed the wall and chipped it away.

208. A bunch of clumsy thieves attempt to pull off the heist of the century but make a mess of things.

209. Write a story about children who go to see a magic show.

210. Most teenagers can't wait to become legal adults so they can make their own decisions. Write a story about a teenager struggling with parental rules and the desire to become autonomous.

211. The protagonist is an introvert who is suddenly thrust into a workforce that insists on extroverted behavior through office policies that require speeches, networking, and business trips where the protagonist has to share a hotel room with coworkers who are practically strangers.

212. While out for a morning walk, the protagonist finds a child drugged and left for dead in an old well. Nobody knows who the child is and nobody steps forward to claim the child.

213. We humans are a divided species. Write about a worldwide event that brings a fractured Earth together, unifying humanity.

214. Epic fantasies and quests through lands filled with dragons, elves, and fairies—these stories are staples in the fantasy genre. What's your take on the classic fantasy tale?

215. In horror stories, we usually don't get to know the killer or the monster very well. Write a story that reveals the villain's full history and personality.

216. Love at first sight: some say it's a mirage; others say it leads to marriage. Write a story that shows what you think about it.

217. The 1960s gave us Civil Rights, Woodstock, and the space race. What happens when a nation's people are divided? What happens when minorities of people are oppressed? What happens when ordinary kids decide they don't want to grow up and become just like their parents? Mix in the fact that there's a war nobody understands and most people don't believe in. Add drugs, flowers, and peace signs and you've got the sixties. Write a story set during this iconic decade.

218. First dates can be filled with awkward moments. Write a funny story about a first date.

219. Write a story for children explaining where food comes from. A good setting would be a ranch or a farm.

220. High school lasts only four years but it feels like an eternity. Write a story that follows a group of

four friends through high school with each year depicted through the perspective of a different character.

221. The protagonist finds himself or herself stranded on a deserted island. But this island wasn't always deserted. An abandoned village and a lighthouse, which may be the best chance for getting rescued, become the protagonist's new home.

222. Decades after reneging on an important political deal—a choice that destroyed a colleague's career—a retired senator is murdered, and the Secret Service agent who had protected the senator for years is determined to prove who did it.

223. Time travel goes crazy when people from history and the future start arriving in the present. What happens when unusual people from the past and future all show up in the here and now, and why have they come?

224. Archaeologists discover an ancient city buried deep underground, filled with bones and artifacts that prove mythical beasts and magical creatures once roamed the earth.

225. Turn ordinary animals into monsters that prey on humans: dog-sized rats, killer rabbits, or a pack of rabid mountain lions. Give the animals intelligence and set them loose.

226. Write a classic romance story about two young lovers from different—even enemy—worlds. Will it be a tragedy? A comedy? Drama? A little of everything?

227. In Nazi Germany, Hitler managed to get ordinary citizens to support his evil actions against Jews and other groups he deemed unfit for society. Write about one such ordinary citizen. Did this character go along with Germany's actions out of fear? Loyalty? Was the character convinced by Hitler's rhetoric?

228. A couple decides to spend their honeymoon in a tropical paradise, but everything imaginable goes wrong.

229. Children's stories often impart ethical lessons. Write a story for kids that teaches a lesson in values.

230. Write a story about two teens who get separated because one moves far away. Do they stay in touch or grow apart? A story like this could partially be told through e-mail correspondences.

231. Unable to have children, one couple turns to the foster care system, believing they can fill their empty home and make someone else's life better. They take in a troubled twelve-year-old youth.

232. A bounty hunter is caught between a rock and a hard place when he or she finds out there's a price on the head of someone he or she loves.

233. Aliens are often depicted as either ferocious and terrifying or cute and cuddly. Write about aliens who are more complex, aliens from a culture more like our own.

234. Werewolves are probably the most common shape-shifters in literature. Come up with a shape-shifter of your own, and write a story about it.

235. A defining feature of horror is a tragic, disturbing ending. Write such a story about a virus that breaks out all over planet Earth.

236. Write a story about a character who finds love later in life. Is it his or her first love? Third marriage?

237. Write a story that is set around the assassination of an important, benevolent, historical figure: for example, Gandhi, Martin Luther King, JFK, or John Lennon.

238. There's a contest for the world's ugliest dog every year in Northern California. Write a funny story about the competition, one of the contestants (and its human companion), or the winner.

239. Write a story about a child who draws or writes stories and who believes his or her stories are real in some other world.

240. Kids at the bottom of the social hierarchy in school get ignored, bullied, and picked on. What

happens when one of those kids dies? How does it affect the other students, especially the ones who did the bullying?

241. In a typical first-world suburb, one family struggles with poverty while trying to hide their dire financial circumstances.

242. Two siblings who haven't spoken for years are reunited when their widowed parent is found dead of unnatural causes.

243. Science fiction often explores what would happen if robots or artificial intelligence (AI) surpassed human intelligence and then decided to take over the world. But what if they decided to take over in an effort to ensure the survival and betterment of humanity because they were programmed to do just that?

244. An artist who sculpts and carves figurines learns he or she has magical powers that bring the figurines to life.

245. Write a story about the Middle Ages with a horror twist (just think about all those horrifying torture devices they used).

246. Some people look for love in all the wrong places. Write about someone who finds love in the wrong place.

247. Write a story about a person, couple, or family who operates a lighthouse during the 1800s.

248. The kids are grown, off to college, or married and having kids. But all of them fall upon hard times—at the same time—and move back into the family home. Laughs ensue.

249. Write a story about a little kid who talks all the time, even when alone, playing in front of adults, or with other children.

250. Write a story about a student in junior high or high school struggling with a bigoted teacher.

251. Mysteries and crime stories often include protagonists who are cops, detectives, or special agents. Write a story about one of these people but focus on their personal lives rather than their work.

252. A team of FBI agents is assembled to take down a human trafficking ring. They do not get along with each other very well, but they have to learn to work together in order to save the victims and see justice done.

253. Humans discover they are compatible with an alien parasite that offers benefits: prolonged life, higher intelligence, and other desirable abilities.

254. It's not easy to get into the heads of animals— whether they're farm animals or wild animals. Write a story about animal culture from the perspective of the animals themselves.

255. A bunch of happy-go-lucky vacationers are horrified when their cruise ship returns to port to

find that they are the only remaining survivors on Earth.

256. What happens when two characters fall in love online? Is it real? Will they ever meet in person and find out? If so, are they who they claimed to be when they were safe behind their keyboards and monitors?

257. Write a story set in a historical era when men and women's roles were dramatically different than they are today.

258. Write a comedy about a well-to-do family from the city that has lost all their wealth except an old, run-down farmhouse in the country. They are forced to move into it and learn to live humbly.

259. Write a children's story about a kid who struggles with nightmares.

260. It's not easy being the new kid. The protagonist has just moved to a new town, and if that weren't bad enough, the people there are nothing like the folks back home.

261. While their spouses are deployed overseas in a war that has no end in sight, a young man and woman meet and strike up a friendship that is centered around the struggles they're facing as newlyweds with absent spouses.

262. A young sports or entertainment celebrity known for partying and promiscuity is linked to a murder of passion. Only an experienced, top-notch

lawyer can crack the case and prove the star's guilt or innocence.

263. Write a story set a hundred years in the future. What is the population of the planet? How far into space have we gone? What are we using for energy? Are we still separated by borders, race, and religion?

264. A child living on a farm or ranch can hear the thoughts of animals—both the livestock and the local wildlife.

265. Some say torture doesn't work and is morally wrong. Others say it does work and is a necessity. Write a story about torture from the perspective of the tortured or the torturer.

266. Write a story about a protagonist who has hallucinations and is in love with someone who doesn't really exist.

267. During the Crusades, people were brutally murdered because they did not follow the religion of the land. Write about someone who pretended to subscribe to Christianity in order to survive.

268. One of the easiest ways to inject humor into a story is to make one of the characters funny—either because the character is naturally funny or is always saying and doing things that others laugh at. Write a story about one such character.

269. Stories often teach children how to resolve issues. Write a story demonstrating how to solve conflict at school (preschool or kindergarten age).

270. Write a story about a teenager frustrated by a younger sibling who copies everything and always wants to tag along.

271. Two siblings are separated at a very young age when their parents decide to have nothing to do with each other ever again. Many years later, an unexpected event forces the siblings, who hardly remember each other, together again.

272. One of the most sought-after assassins in the world is known for his or her ability to hunt down and kill wily targets. What happens when this assassin is hunted by a younger but equally talented assassin?

273. A disgraced starship captain is kicked out of the interstellar military. He or she buys a run-down passenger ship and starts a business transporting people (including aliens) across the galaxy.

274. Demons and monsters are, by definition, evil. But what if the demons and monsters are actually the good guys and humans are the bad guys?

275. Write a story about a group of kids who are writing and filming their own horror film.

276. The protagonist grew up sheltered in an overprotective family. What happens when he or

she goes out into the world as a young adult and starts dating for the first time?

277. Write a story about a character living in the American South during the Civil War.

278. Three friends are retired and either single or widowed. They're elderly and each one lives alone, but then they decide to share a house.

279. Write a children's story about siblings whose parents are getting a divorce.

280. Kids these days—and their gadgets! Write a short story exploring how the next generation is plugged in all the time. Does technology cut them off from the real world, or does it allow them to connect with a larger circle of other people?

281. A wife and husband have spent the last twenty years of marriage immersed in their respective careers. Other than the occasional dinner or romp in the sack, they've been living separate lives. When they both retire, they are forced to spend almost every waking hour together. They realize how far apart they've grown and try to remember what brought them together in the first place.

282. What starts out as an ordinary investigation into the murder of a street criminal (a drug dealer or prostitute) evolves into a whirlwind mystery of white-collar crime.

283. Imagine that violence on Earth is at an all-time high. By merely leaving your house, there is a 35

percent chance you will be killed. The farther you go from your house, the higher the odds that you will be murdered. A team of investigative scientists discovers that humanity's violence is being driven by microchips that were secretly implanted in a large portion of the population at birth. Who did this? Why? And how can it be stopped?

284. Write a story about a protagonist who discovers the fountain of youth and gains the gift of immortality.

285. Some horror authors say they write to exorcise their worst fears or inner demons. Write a story that exorcises your worst fears or inner demons.

286. The protagonist is married to his or her high school sweetheart—they've been together since they were fourteen. But a terrible accident leaves the protagonist widowed. How hard is it to find love again when you've only loved (and lost) one person?

287. A passionate, dedicated history teacher inspires students to take an interest in his or her classes by telling vivid stories about the course material.

288. A group of mean kids pulled a prank on another kid in junior high—a prank that made the target the laughingstock of the school all the way through high school. Now it's time for their ten-

year reunion—and it will be filled with laughs and retribution.

289. The kids in the neighborhood are convinced there's a monster that comes out and roams the streets at night. Some mornings, the garbage cans are turned over. Other mornings, the lawns are trampled. And then there are those weird noises they all hear when they're trying to fall asleep...

290. A brother and sister are only one year apart in age. What happens when they are teens and dating each other's friends?

291. While sorting through a three-month old pile of junk mail, the protagonist finds a handwritten letter—a letter that changes everything.

292. When a federal judge is murdered, a team of investigators must find out if the murder was political or personal.

293. Write a story set in the distant future when humanity is at a fork in the evolutionary road. Some humans are evolving; others are not.

294. Most dragon tales take place in far-off lands, but what if a dragon somehow ended up in the here and now? How did it get here? Is it dangerous? What is its goal?

295. What's more horrific than a creepy, evil child? Write about a child who traumatizes everyone he or she comes into contact with.

296. Write about a protagonist with a condition that causes him or her to fall in love with inanimate objects.

297. What was it like before humankind traveled into space, before we landed on the moon? Write a story set just before or during the time we made these momentous advances.

298. A charming street magician uses tricks and illusions to con people out of their money in a gritty metropolitan comedy.

299. While digging in the garden, a child finds a magic ring that makes any wish come true.

300. Write a story about a group of teens working at their first jobs. One is earning money to help his or her family. One is saving up for a car or college. One wants extra spending money. One wants an excuse to get out of the house.

301. Write a story about someone who is about to lose his or her job because of technology.

302. An ego-driven preacher decides the best way to combat sin and terrorism is to build a religious army by radicalizing his congregation.

303. When aliens finally come to Earth, it turns out they want to use our solar system as an outpost because it's in a strategic location for the war they're fighting with another alien species.

304. Write a story about a character who travels through time whenever he or she falls asleep.

305. Horrific events often occur inside the walls of a prison. Your story could be about what happens among the prisoners and the guards or it could be about a group of prisoners who take over the prison and hold the guards hostage.

306. Write a story about a protagonist who falls in love with a character he or she created for a story or video game.

307. Throughout history, people have emigrated across land and ocean. Choose a time period of heavy human migration. Then choose a starting place and a destination and write the story of a character or group of characters who take the voyage. Focus on the journey, not the place of origin or the destination.

308. Write a story about the shenanigans in a place of business where lots of young people work: a fast food restaurant, theater, or retail store.

309. There's a crazy new teacher at school who dresses funny, says things that don't make sense, and always makes silly faces.

310. A misfit teenager discovers a bookstore that nobody else can see. Every book in the store takes the reader on an adventure—a real adventure!

311. It's the weekend of a twenty-year high school reunion. A group of old friends decides to get together the night after the reunion at a restaurant where they spend a long evening sorting through the baggage and secrets of their past.

312. A serial killer has clipped every instruction and rule from the Bible and is now killing people who violate its tenets—many of which are contradictory. The detective on the case is forced to work with a biblical scholar to solve it.

313. In the distant future, the one-world government uses logic and statistics via technology to control everything: the education that people get, whom they marry, how many children they have, and even the genetic makeup of their children. But there's also a population of outsiders—people who use technology but still live naturally and make their own decisions.

314. Imagine a world where humans weren't the only animals to evolve into intelligent beings.

315. Scientists are developing a serum that would give humans superpowers, but the serum accidentally falls into the hands of a maniac who's putting together a mob of crazed criminals.

316. Write a story about a wealthy character who is tired of being used for his or her money and has stopped dating.

317. During the witch burnings, many midwives and healers were burned as witches, and male doctors slowly took over their duties. Write a story about a woman healer who is accused of witchcraft by a male doctor who wants to take her business.

318. Write a comedy about a writer who is struggling with writer's block.

319. Fed up with life, a little kid runs off and tries to join the circus. He or she spends a full day with the circus folk, working and learning about what it means to belong to a family.

320. What happens when a teenager discovers a note in his or her locker from a secret admirer?

321. When a young family from overseas moves into the apartment downstairs, a grumpy, elderly neighbor is annoyed by all the noise they make, the smell of their foreign cooking, and their otherness.

322. After a long and harrowing workweek, the protagonist is pulled over for what seems to be an ordinary speeding violation, but things go from bad to worse when the protagonist is arrested for murder.

323. What happens in the future when humans are settling in space among a diverse group of aliens and are confronted with cross-species culture wars?

324. Create a monster. Write a vivid description of it and make it as vicious as possible. Then write a story about a protagonist who tames the monster.

325. It's the classic murder mystery with a twist of horror: A group of guests are invited to spend a weekend at a mansion. Terror is unleashed when they realize there's a killer on the loose and they cannot leave the property.

326. One couple has an enticing and thrilling sex life, but they can't make their relationship work outside the bedroom.

327. Write a story that is set around the death of a historical figure who was deemed evil: Hitler, Mussolini, etc.

328. Paris is the city of lovers, but what happens when a group of tourists descends on the city, marring it with their ogling and unromantic ways?

329. Write a story about a child who attends day camp. It can be any kind of camp (art, science, sports, etc.). The protagonist makes friends, encounters conflict, and learns a new skill.

330. Some teenagers dare one of their friends to venture into a creepy place that everyone says is haunted (it could be an abandoned warehouse, a haunted house, or a graveyard).

331. There are people we see every day—our best friends, immediate family, neighbors, and coworkers. And then there are people we only see

occasionally but who are constants in our lives. Write a story set at a wedding, funeral, or other life event where people who have strong ties but don't see each other very often come together.

332. A small-town police chief attempts to cover up a murder because the prime suspect is a member of the chief's family.

333. In an attempt to curb the effects of global warming, scientists develop a way to control the weather—they cause or cease tornadoes, hurricanes, earthquakes, tsunamis, and other natural disasters. Will the governments of the world now use weather for warfare?

334. Seven angels are each assigned to a different sin: lust, gluttony, greed, sloth, wrath, envy, and pride. The angels' job is to steer humans away from these sins.

335. There are lots of stories about killers that are people, robots, aliens, animals, and supernatural monsters. Write a horror story about killer plants and trees.

336. What happens when a serial heartbreaker falls in love with someone who's just not interested?

337. The 1950s are often painted as a simple and idealistic time in American history. One income could support an entire family. Jobs were plentiful. Moms stayed home with their kids. Divorce was scandalous. Write about a

protagonist who didn't fit the mold, whose life was difficult because of the cultural and societal conventions of the time.

338. Write a comedy about the bartenders and patrons of a dive bar on the wrong side of the tracks.

339. Write a story about a little girl who wants to grow up and become a ninja or a little boy who wants to grow up and become a nurse.

340. When a teenager is diagnosed with a life-threatening illness, friends, family, acquaintances, teachers, and even enemies step forward to show their support.

341. When he was sixteen, he spent a summer out of state with his grandparents while his parents sorted through their marital problems. That summer, he hung out with the fifteen-year-old girl next door. When one of his grandparents dies five years later, he returns for the funeral and finds out the girl has a child—his child.

342. The protagonist has a semi-successful career ghostwriting mystery novels. When a close family member is murdered, the protagonist gets caught up in solving a real-life crime.

343. Almost all of humanity is wiped out in a single day—by plague, aliens, or war. But a few dozen humans survive. They can use technology to communicate but are separated by land and sea.

Now, they'll each embark on a dangerous journey to unite and rebuild.

344. Write a story about a protagonist who leads a double life, coexisting in two different worlds or times, and who constantly travels back and forth between them.

345. The protagonist is paranoid and believes that people are watching and trying to kill him or her. Friends and family—even the psychiatrist—says these are delusions, but in the end, they are wrong.

346. The royal monarch, who is young and widowed, falls in love with a servant in the castle.

347. Many historical revolutions were started to gain independence from colonial overlords. Choose one such revolution from history and write a story about ordinary people living in those times.

348. In a poor, rural area, a treasure map is discovered. All hell breaks loose when a bunch of locals get their hands on copies of the map and embark on a race to find the treasure first.

349. The protagonist is a child whose parents run a candy store or bakery. All the other kids in the neighborhood always expect the protagonist to give them free treats. Some even make threats!

350. Almost all teenagers have difficulties with parents: Some parents ignore their kids; others berate them. Some parents push their kids too

hard; others spoil their kids rotten. Write a story about teens who come together and learn about each other's familial struggles.

351. An elderly person lives a rather lonely life that changes when he or she finds a puppy on the doorstep. But the puppy is a pit bull, and soon the neighbors demand that it be destroyed by animal services even though it hasn't harmed anyone and has a sweet disposition.

352. The protagonist is abducted and imprisoned by a psychopath. Write the story from the protagonist's point of view while he or she is held captive, or write it from the abductor's point of view.

353. Write a story set in a world where the Internet is a virtual reality that is almost indistinguishable from the real world. Some people are plugged in all the time. Others won't plug in at all.

354. In our world, war is bloody and violent. But what if war was fought with wits and magic, and nobody got hurt?

355. Write a story about a clairvoyant who can communicate with ghosts and other supernatural beings—but only beings who are dark and disturbed.

356. The protagonist is a wild wanderer and avid traveler who never wants to settle down. But

then, while on a trip, he or she gets stranded in a small town and falls for one of the locals.

357. History is peppered with inventions that changed the course of human progress: the wheel, the wagon, the printing press, the train, the airplane, the computer, and the Internet. Write a story set during a time when one such invention was taking hold. How did it change culture, and how did it affect the marketplace?

358. Write a story about a thirty-something bachelor or bachelorette who is perfectly happy with every aspect of life except the fact that friends and family keep trying to play matchmaker.

359. There's a child who wants nothing more than to grow up and become an astronaut. What kinds of things does the child do? End the story with a bang—admission to space camp or a meeting with a real astronaut.

360. The teenage protagonist is wild—dabbling in sex, drugs, and stealing.

361. An agoraphobic protagonist has not left his or her apartment in over a dozen years. But now the apartment building has been declared condemned. Staying there is no longer an option.

362. Write about a protagonist who is a detective or agent and who chose that career because of a crime against a loved one many years ago.

363. An interpreter or translator in the far-off future specializes in alien languages.

364. What happens when a group of friends plays around with magic and gets it to work?

365. The protagonist was born with a physical deformity that causes others to view him or her as evil (horns, mark of the devil, etc.). But the real cause of the evil that consumes the protagonist is having been shunned and treated like a leper his or her whole life.

366. A clean-cut conventional character who follows all the rules falls in love with an edgy, tattooed punk rocker.

367. Write a story about a young couple heading out west hoping to strike it rich during the California gold rush of the 1840s.

368. Pets and animals are always good for laughs. Write a comedy set in a veterinarian's office.

369. Mom and Dad are delighted because they are expecting. How does their firstborn feel about acquiring a sibling?

370. Write a story about a teenager who is working hard and getting good grades because he or she desperately wants to go to college but whose family doesn't have enough money to pay for an education.

371. Every morning, the same customers show up at a quaint and cozy small-town diner. Some are great friends, some loathe each other, and some barely know each other. One day, a stranger comes to town and becomes a regular at the diner, shaking up old relationships and rivalries.

372. What happens when a top government official (president, senator, judge) becomes the target for an assassin? Is the motive personal or political? Make it surprising!

373. Write a survival story about one person or a group of people stranded on a distant planet, having lost all contact with Earth. How will these technology-reliant characters adjust to life without gadgets?

374. In a magical world, it might be difficult to keep prisoners behind bars. Write a story about a group of prisoners living in a land of magic.

375. Demons are usually horrific monsters, but what if a demon was living in the body of a human being? What if a human being was a demon?

376. The protagonist is agoraphobic, never leaves the house, and falls in love with the package delivery person.

377. Western stories tend to get rolling when a stranger comes to town. Write a western without the token stranger. Instead, explore the lives of the people who lived in the Wild West.

378. Write a comedic story about a nuclear family living in the modern world, but write the father as king, the mother as queen, the daughter as princess, and the son as prince. Dad's chair in front of the television is the throne, the family dog is the court jester...You get the idea.

379. It's important for children to learn the alphabet. Write an ABC book. You can write a separate vignette for each letter, write a story linking them all together, or write a nonsense rhyme for each one.

380. Write a story about a teenager who is forced to spend a weekend at a big family reunion but who would rather stay home and hang out with his or her friends.

381. The protagonist is a dedicated grad student with no social life. He or she finally caves in to peer pressure and sets studies aside for one night out on the town. It turns out to be a night filled with danger and adventure.

382. Most mystery stories are written from the perspective of whoever solves the crime—a hero. Write a story from the perspective of the criminal, the villain.

383. The protagonist is special. He or she can control electronics remotely, using the power of the mind. What happens when the protagonist finds

out he or she is a prototype—an experiment in biotechnology?

384. The two-thousand-year-old protagonist is finally about to die but will first tell the story of his or her life to a disbelieving journalist.

385. Turn your favorite fairy tale, myth, or legend into a horror story. Make sure there's plenty of terror and gore.

386. What happens when a conservative lobbyist falls in love with a liberal politician?

387. Write a story set in your hometown one hundred years ago.

388. When a string of petty robberies sweeps across middle-class suburbia, the residents band together to try and snare the culprits. Include a surprise ending revealing who the culprits are and what they're really after.

389. Write a children's story about siblings who have lost one or both of their parents and have to go live with relatives.

390. The teenage protagonist is a misfit who works very hard to be invisible—sitting in the back of class, spending lunch in a dark corner of the cafeteria, and generally blending in so nobody will notice.

391. After being convicted of a serious white-collar crime but making a deal to avoid prison time, the

protagonist is shunned by colleagues, friends, and family. It's a long, hard fall from the penthouse to the poorhouse.

392. The military handles crimes within its factions internally. But when a series of violent assaults extends beyond the confines of the military, a public prosecutor exposes crime and corruption in the military justice system.

393. Two people from the distant future time-travel back to the present day with a dire warning for humanity. While here, they are as shocked by how we live as we would be if we traveled back to the Middle Ages.

394. Literature is full of stories about witches—all kinds of witches. Some of them have become rather stereotypical. Create a witch of your own—aim for creating a unique witch unlike any we've seen before, and then write a story about him or her.

395. Write a story about a cult or underground organization that is actively working to bring about the apocalypse.

396. Write a story about two characters who fall in love while staying in a hospital for the mentally unstable.

397. World War II gave rise to what journalist Tom Brokaw called "the greatest generation." Create a cast of compelling characters and write a story

showing how circumstances forced them to become great.

398. The worst day ever starts when the protagonist wraps up the job interview of a lifetime—only to realize as he or she is exiting the building that there was toilet paper hanging out of his or her pants during the entire interview.

399. Write a story about a child who loves to do something (dance, draw, play sports, etc.). One adult in the child's life keeps saying it's a waste of time or the child is no good at it. Another adult provides support and encouragement.

400. A student is found murdered on a high school campus. Will the victim's friends solve the murder before the cops do? Is one of them next?

401. The main character is a big-league sports star complete with a chauffeur, a cook, a gardener, and an entourage that includes bodyguards. An unexpected family death rips into the athlete's life and brings him or her home to humbler roots.

402. They're both married, so they meet in discreet locations to carry out their affair. During one such tryst, they witness a horrific murder. If they come forward, their affair will be revealed. If they don't, the killer will be free to murder again.

403. A young citizen journalist joins the military in order to work his or her way into special ops. While there, he or she discovers that not only is

the military aware of aliens, the Air Force also has spaceships that can travel to the far reaches of the galaxy. What happens when, years later, the journalist publishes a tell-all book or produces a documentary revealing the truth to the world, complete with irrefutable proof?

404. Write a story about two characters who switch bodies. What would a man think of being in a woman's body? What if they were from different parts of the world? What if one of them was an animal?

405. The protagonist wakes up alone in a cold stone room, chained to the floor. The abductor enters. It's someone from the protagonist's past— someone who is very angry and deeply disturbed, and it's all the protagonist's fault.

406. One character is a thief. The other is a cop. If their relationship is going to succeed, someone's going to have to give up their career. Who will it be?

407. Write a story about a group of European settlers coming to the New World and discovering native tribes. Show how different characters in the group respond to the natives' culture in different ways.

408. You can write comedy in any genre; Western, science fiction, romance, and even horror stories can be packed with laughs. Take a serious story from any genre and retell it as a comedy.

409. Write a story for children about animals that live together: cats and dogs, mice and rabbits, deer and butterflies.

410. Write a story about two siblings or best friends. One is obsessed with a rock star or a band. The other is obsessed with politics, a world leader (past or present), or a historical figure.

411. In Nevada, where prostitution and gambling are legal, an ambitious college graduate starts up a business enterprise that would be illegal in most other states.

412. Shortly after moving into a home and beginning renovations, the protagonist discovers a collection of journals that belonged to the original owner— journals that open over a dozen cold cases at the local precinct.

413. In the middle of the twenty-first century, artificial intelligence (AI) is about to reach singularity— the point at which it becomes smarter than humans. This development changes the face of politics when a movement is born that seeks to stop all development on AI. But another faction believes AI will save humanity.

414. How are monsters and fantastical creatures made? One becomes a vampire through the bite of another vampire. One becomes a ghost through death. How does one become a werewolf, a witch, or a wizard?

415. If one has an up-close vantage point, the most realistic horror story imaginable takes place within a war. Write a war story with a twist of horror.

416. The fair's in town for a week and the protagonist, who has deep roots in the community, falls in love with one of the workers, who lives a nomadic life traveling from town to town.

417. Write a story about a family living during a time when people grew their own food and slaughtered their own meat—before refrigerators, bathrooms, cars, and phones existed.

418. After working at a bank (or some other high-end job) for ten years, the protagonist throws it all away to do something crazy (become an artist, sail around the world, etc.). Write it as a comedy.

419. It's important for children to learn their numbers. Write a counting book that covers numbers, at least up to ten. You can write separate vignettes for each number, write a story linking all the numbers together, or write a nonsense rhyme about each number.

420. The protagonist was raised by one parent and never knew the other. Write the story of how he or she finds this missing parent and the first time they meet.

421. After living in captivity as a slave for over a decade, a twenty-two-year-old attempts to integrate back into family and society.

422. Four siblings live in fear of their abusive parent until they start planning for the time when they will be old enough and strong enough to seek revenge.

423. Imagine a time in the future when robots don't look like humans but can do almost anything humans can do, even though their personalities are a little dry. Their most popular use is in children's hospitals, retirement homes, orphanages, and other assisted living facilities. Write about one human's relationship with a companion robot in such a facility.

424. Superheroes are fun and exciting. The superpowers! The supervillains! The costumes! The gadgets! Write a superhero story.

425. What happens when the makers of a horror-genre video game find themselves trapped inside the world they've created?

426. Write a story about two friends. Each one thinks the other is heterosexual and struggles to keep romantic feelings at bay.

427. Ancient Egypt was rich with culture: hieroglyphs, pyramids, and pharaohs. Write a story that includes ancient Egypt—either use characters

who are interested in it or set the story in ancient Egypt itself.

428. A day of laughs and hijinks kicks off when a group of housemates wakes up to discover that the water, electricity, and cable have been turned off.

429. Children love stories about inanimate objects that come to life: computers, stuffed animals, and toy trains. Write a story starring an inanimate object.

430. A teenage protagonist has to cope with public and political life because his or her parent is president or prime minister.

431. Write a story about people who live in the same neighborhood or apartment building. Explore their similarities, relationships, differences, and conflicts.

432. A family's world is turned upside down when a corpse is discovered in their backyard and the parents become the top suspects in a murder case.

433. Ordinary civilians find an alien device that is a portal to another world, solar system, galaxy, or universe.

434. The protagonist is the last in a long bloodline that dates back millennia. What happens when he or she returns to the motherland and discovers there is magic in his or her blood?

435. Start with a monster that consumes humans—make up your own monster or use a vampire or a werewolf that subsists on human flesh. What happens when circumstances require the monster to work closely with a human because they share a common objective or enemy?

436. A journalist conducts a series of interviews with a prison inmate and becomes convinced of the inmate's guilt—but develops a romantic interest in the inmate anyway.

437. During the fourteenth century, the plague (Black Death) devastated Europe and other parts of the world. Write a story about characters who lived through the plague.

438. Slapstick comedy is silly and ridiculous: people falling down, getting hit in the face with pies, and goofing off. Try your hand at writing slapstick.

439. If you plant an acorn today, it won't grow into a mature oak tree for about sixty years. Write a children's story about doing something today that will pay off in the future—maybe even after we're long gone.

440. A group of teenagers gets locked inside an amusement park overnight.

441. At age thirty, the protagonist has done everything that was expected, including finishing college and finding a spouse. Now the pressure is on to start a family. This character comes to realize this is not

the life he or she wants. It's a life of someone else's design.

442. Soldiers returning from the war are being picked off by a new kind of serial killer. The murders happen miles apart, indicating there is more than one suspect involved. Military officers, agents from the CIA and FBI, and officials from other government agencies must work together to find the killers and bring them to justice.

443. Write an alternate-history, science-fiction story set in the present day by eliminating or introducing technologies at different points in time. What if the atomic bomb had been available during World War I? What if television had been invented a century earlier? What if we'd achieved deep space travel by the late 1970s?

444. There have been many takes on ghost stories: romance, horror, even comedy. Write your own ghost story.

445. The protagonist is a demented time-traveling serial killer hunting down saints and martyrs to erase them from history.

446. What happens when a devout believer in (any) religion and an atheist develop feelings for each other?

447. There are always casualties in war, but there are always survivors, too. Choose any war in history

and write about the survivors, people whose lives were forever changed by war.

448. The protagonist, a former fun-loving free spirit, has become a workaholic who rarely leaves the house. Friends step in with plans for a makeover and a weekend getaway in a story packed with laughs.

449. Why do kids love things that creep and crawl? Write a story featuring bugs, lizards, snakes, and mice. It could be an adventure or a story about an animal family.

450. A teenager or college student has dreams and ambitions, and taking over the family business is not one of them.

451. Write a story about two high school sweethearts who reconnect in their old age.

452. Government spies keep their eyes on other countries, but what happens when they start spying on each other? The CIA watching Homeland Security, the NSA watching the FBI...

453. Fantasy stories often concern themselves with magic. Science fiction sometimes addresses similar concepts but explains their workings through science. Write a story about science or technology viewed as magic by a primitive species (alien or human).

454. The veil between the ordinary world and the magical world has grown thin. Creatures from the

other side are slipping through. Write a story about a bounty hunter who is hired to round them up and return them to their home world or dispose of them.

455. Situated on a long and lonely stretch of desert highway are a run-down gas station and convenience store. Some of the patrons who stop there never come out again.

456. After the protagonist learns his or her significant other is a crazed killer, he or she vows to never get involved in a romantic relationship again.

457. Write a story set in Hollywood around the time when silent films were giving way to talkies. This technological advance changed things for a lot of people, including actors, directors, and writers.

458. Write a list of the funniest things that have ever happened to you or that you've ever witnessed— including your most embarrassing moments. Use all those funny moments in a fictional story.

459. One of the best ways for children to learn language is through rhyming. Write a story that rhymes for kids.

460. Write a story packed with all the things teenagers struggle with: their changing bodies (hair, pimples, etc.), hormones, conflict with parents, difficulty focusing on studies, and trying to get through high school in one piece.

461. It may be controversial but it happens every day: write a story about a teenage couple who find themselves dealing with an unplanned pregnancy.

462. In a small town, every member of the community works for a factory owned by the wealthiest family in town. Friction between the people and the family eventually leads to murder.

463. Within a few decades, people will start embedding microchips and other technologies into their bodies. What happens when a shady corporation uses this technology to control people and make them do the corporation's bidding?

464. A photographer who collects and uses old cameras acquires one that takes pictures through time. He snaps a picture in one time and place, and what comes out in the darkroom is from the same place but another time.

465. Cemeteries are great settings for creepy stories. What happens when a group of teens hanging out at the graveyard find themselves stalked by a terrifying night walker?

466. The protagonist's significant other is a musician—always on the road. When rumors of trysts with groupies arise, the protagonist decides to follow the tour bus and see what's really going on.

467. Apartheid in South Africa was a political system of racial segregation that oppressed the rights of

the majority, which was the native black population. Write about characters living during apartheid.

468. Kids are always good for a laugh. They ask the funniest questions, or they ask serious questions that fluster parents into giving funny answers. Write a dialogue story (or a script) about adults answering children's questions.

469. Kids love stories that play with language. Write an ABC book and come up with a single sentence for each letter—but here's the catch: each sentence must be a tongue twister featuring the letter it represents.

470. Write a story about a teenager struggling with depression.

471. A phobia is a persistent, irrational fear. Write a story about a protagonist who is coping with a phobia or paranoia. Explore how the condition prevents the character from living a full or normal life and how the character is affected by the stigma attached to the condition.

472. A brilliant but evil scientist unleashes a biologically engineered virus that targets people with specific ideologies, as identified by their genetic makeup.

473. One scientist is out to prove that there is an energy field resonating through the entire universe—a field that connects us all and that we

can use for miraculous purposes if only we can learn to access it.

474. There have been lots of stories about characters with supernatural abilities who work with law enforcement. Write a story about one such character who works in a hospital.

475. A journalist researching a book about serial killers finds himself or herself hunted by one of the killers he or she wants to interview.

476. They've known each other for years because they have a close friend in common. They've hung out at parties, even gone on trips with the group. But they've always been in other relationships. Now they're both single.

477. Write a story about a character who discovers a safe house where Jews hid in Nazi Germany.

478. When an aunt or uncle unexpectedly has to babysit, everything goes topsy-turvy—from a hilarious trip to the grocery store to trying to put together a decent meal with sugar-infused kids running around.

479. Authors often use stories about baby animals to teach children about life. Write a story about a baby animal that experiences something difficult: getting separated from a parent, struggling for food, or finding it difficult to make friends.

480. For reasons entirely up to you, a young teen becomes a ward of   the foster care system.

481. Write a story about a family struggling to adjust to a child that has a serious or difficult condition (autism, ADHD, etc.).

482. While on a sky tour over Africa, a helicopter crashes, depositing a group of wealthy first-worlders into the heart of the African wilderness.

483. In the future, another branch will be added to the militaries of Earth: the space branch. Write a story about a protagonist enlisting, going through training, and becoming a space-faring soldier.

484. Humans are not real. They only exist in stories that parents tell their children in a world of fairies, elves, unicorns, etc.

485. A chemical spill releases toxins into the environment, resulting in mutant humans who must consume human flesh in order to survive.

486. Practice writing a steamy scene: a gourmet meal, a bottle of wine, a crackling fire, and candlelight set the stage for a romantic evening in a remote cabin in the woods.

487. Write a story about a runaway teenager.

488. Write a comedy about a protagonist who is seeing a therapist for sleepwalking.

489. Write a story about a couple of children who are exploring a garden together. What do they see, smell, hear, taste, and touch?

490. A teenager has a birthmark in an unusual but distinct shape. This protagonist meets someone else with the same birthmark. What does it mean?

491. A teenager dreams of being an artist (musician, dancer, etc.), but the teen's father puts his foot down and pushes the teen toward academics and sports. Just before the teen's high school graduation, his or her mother and brother die in a car accident. The father and teenage child must rebuild their relationship to save what's left of their family.

492. People are getting sick, and officials are concerned that the new disease might be the beginning of a bio-terror attack.

493. The protagonist appears to be slipping in and out of reality—one day a normal, functioning, successful person, and the next day believing he or she is living on another world full of alien species and other wonders. This keeps happening over and over. What is real?

494. Thousands of years ago, creatures of magic roamed the earth: fairies, unicorns, sorcerers, elves, and dragons. As humans inherited the earth, the magical creatures died out until only a few remained. Now, they have learned how to grow their numbers and are planning to retake the earth from the humans who are destroying it.

495. When a military or scientific research submarine malfunctions, the team is stranded at the bottom of the ocean. They fight over food and water. Medical supplies are limited. And someone—or something—on the sub is killing people.

496. A car accident shatters the protagonist's life but at the same time brings a new love (paramedic, doctor, physical therapist, fellow member of a counseling group) into it.

497. Write a story about a character running a safe house where slaves hid during the American Civil War.

498. A group of friends from suburbia, determined to see their favorite band in concert, embark on a hilarious adventure in the big city.

499. Children love stories about animals. Write a story about talking animals living in the jungle. Include a lion, zebra, parrot, snake, hippo, giraffe, elephant, and monkey.

500. The protagonist is a teenager who will do anything to get and stay popular, including giving up everything he or she loves.

Poetry Writing Prompts

1. Write a descriptive poem about a banana split: three scoops of ice cream with banana halves on either side and a big mound of whipped cream on top laced with chocolate sauce and sprinkled with chopped nuts—all topped off with a plump red cherry.

2. Use all of the following words in a poem: tapestry, sings, eye, din, collide, slippery, fantasy, casting, chameleon, lives.

3. Write a poem about somebody who betrayed you, or write a poem about betrayal.

4. Write a poem using the following image: a smashed flower on the sidewalk.

5. The hallmark of great poetry is imagery. A truly compelling poem paints a picture and invites the reader into a vivid scene. Choose an image or scene from one of your favorite poems and write a poem of your own based on that image.

6. Use all of the following words in a poem: scythe, fresh, bloody, dainty, screaming, deadly, discovery, harrowing.

7.   Write a poem about one (or both) of your parents. It could be a tribute poem, but it doesn't have to be.

8.   Write a poem using the following images: a "no smoking" sign and a pair of fishnet stockings.

9.   You're feeling under the weather, so you put the teapot on. Soon it starts to scream. Write a poem about the sound of a whistling teapot.

10. Use all of the following words in a poem: stem, canvas, grain, ground, leather, furrow.

11. The beach, the mountains, the vast sea, and deep space are all great for tributary poems about places. Write about the city you love, the town you call home, or your favorite vacation destination.

12. Write a poem using the following image: a pair of baby shoes.

13. Some poems are more than just poems. They tell stories. Try writing a poem that is also a story, a play, or an essay.

14. Use all of the following words in a poem: elegant, hips, fern, listless, twisting, bind, surprise.

15. Write a poem about the first time you experienced something.

16. Write a poem using the following image: a torn photograph.

17. Although holidays have deeper meanings, we like to truss them up with a lot of decadence and nostalgia. All that food! All those presents! Oh, what fun it is…Write a poem about the holidays.

18. Use all of the following words in a poem: burnt, spacious, metropolis, pacing, fiery, cannon.

19. Write a poem about an inanimate object. You can write a silly poem about how much you admire your toaster or you can write a serious piece declaring the magnificence of a book.

20. Write a poem using the following image: a small rowboat tied to a pier, bobbing in the water under darkening skies.

21. Now that time has healed the wounds, write a poem to someone who broke your heart long ago.

22. Use all of the following words in a poem: deadline, boom, children, shallow, dirt, creep, instigate.

23. Write a poem about streets, highways, and bridges.

24. Write a poem using the following images: a broken bottle and a guitar pick.

25. Write a poem about the smell of cheesy, doughy, saucy, spicy pizza baking in the oven.

26. Use all of the following words in a poem: green, loudly, tub, swim, sultry, sharp, throw.

27. Write a poem about something that scares you.

28. Write a poem using the following image: a rusty handsaw.

29. Imagine you are twenty-five years older than you are now. Write a poem about your life.

30. Use all of the following words in a poem: haunt, long, water, dream, waste, back, push, breathe, chase, where, packed, glass.

31. The most traditional odes extol the virtues of a loved one. Whom do you love? Tell that person why with a poem.

32. Write a poem using the following image: a camel walking across the desert.

33. Think back to the most wonderful place you've ever been. What was the weather like? What did you do there? What did you see?

34. Use all of the following words in a poem: dash, hard, staple, billboard, part, circle, flattened.

35. You don't have to know or love someone to pay tribute to them. Write a poem honoring one of your heroes—someone who has, from a distance, made a difference in your life.

36. Write a poem using the following image: a clearing deep in the woods where sunlight filters through the overhead lattice of tree leaves.

37. Write a poem about the fizzing sound of cola being poured into   a glass full of ice cubes.

38. Use all of the following words in a poem: heart, rose, twisted, stars, fire, nibble, eyes, parched, dance, chaos.

39. Write a poem about the wind or the sky.

40. Write a poem using the following image: an owl soaring through the night sky.

41. There is always anticipation before a first date or an important meeting. Anticipation can even precede watching a movie. Write a poem in which anticipation is the main emotion and include a detailed description of the setting. Don't forget to stimulate the five senses.

42. Use all of the following words in a poem: humanity, hunger, equality, power, greed, redemption, freedom.

43. Write a poem honoring something that can't be seen or touched: honor, passion, curiosity, or loyalty.

44. Write a poem using the following image: a partially deflated basketball.

45. Even though it's freezing outside, people are out and about, bundled up and chattering among themselves. Write a poem about pedestrians in the winter.

46. Use all of the following words in a poem: ball, surf, concert, barbecue, sand, over, net.

47. Write a poem to or about someone you despise or believe is evil. What happens when you look at your enemy and search for his or her merits? Can you see the good in someone you view as bad?

48. Write a poem using the following image: a circus clown removing his or her makeup.

49. You're digging your fingers through a box of hot, buttered, salted popcorn in a dark movie theater. Describe the sensation in a poem.

50. Use all of the following words in a poem: forward, song, dip, along, race, pick, surge.

51. Write a poem about a band on a tour bus after a show.

52. Write a poem using the following image: an oxygen tank.

53. The heat is sweltering and everybody's indoors. The lucky ones have air conditioners. Everybody's trying to stay cool. Write a poem about what it feels like at the height of a scorching summer.

54. Use all of the following words in a poem: curse, manner, impatience, thoughtless, slow, apart, bully, down.

55. Write a poem about a situation that makes you uncomfortable or anxious.

56. Write a poem using the following image: sea life dying in waters that have been poisoned with toxins or littered with dangerous waste.

57. Describe bumper-to-bumper traffic on the throughway during evening commute—it's like a pack of hungry wolves sprinting and braking in their rush to return to the den for their evening meal.

58. Use all of the following words in a poem: car, king, interested, laughing, hit, blame, cup, gold.

59. Has a total stranger ever helped you? Have you ever thought about all the people in this world you've never met but who have affected your life? Write a poem about strangers.

60. Write a poem using the following image: a pile of old, dusty electronics.

61. Write a poem about the taste of medicine: cherry-flavored cough syrup.

62. Use all of the following words in a poem: pathetic, mind, created, overflow, social, deep.

63. Write a poem about a number.

64. Write a poem using the following image: a fishing rod.

65. Write a poem about waking up to the smell of hot, freshly brewed coffee.

66. Use all of the following words in a poem: haunted, lover, visions, mimic, safe, knock-knock, dragging, frills, clever.

67. Write a poem about the end of the world.

68. Write a poem using the following image: a house full of boxes waiting to be packed or unpacked.

69. Write a descriptive poem about a grand feast: the spread of a holiday meal.

70. Use all of the following words in a poem: roots, guard, bags, memories, age, land, eyes.

71. Be a fan. Write a poem about your favorite book, movie, song, or television show.

72. Write a poem using the following image: an empty hospital bed.

73. Sunlight dances on the surface of the water. Waves roll gently against the shore. Seagulls soar above, dipping and diving through the sky.

74. Use all of the following words in a poem: lonely, shine, drop, bloom, hiss, past, rust.

75. Write a tongue-in-cheek, satirical tribute. Tell bad drivers, rude customers, and evil dictators how grateful you are for what they've done. Do it with a wink and a smile.

76. Write a poem using the following image: tumbleweeds blowing across the desert.

77. Write a poem about the sound in your head when you munch on crispy chips or crunchy crackers.

78. Use all of the following words in a poem: equinox, rake, golden, apples, jacket, blow, future.

79. Write a poem about a first romantic (dare I say sexual?) experience or encounter.

80. Write a poem using the following image: a trampled garden.

81. Write a poem about driving alone in your car, radio at full blast, with the wind blowing against your face.

82. Use all of the following words in a poem: team, resentful, jingle, spotlight, rearrange, plans, foresight.

83. Write a poem about a dream.

84. Write a poem using the following image: a glove lying in a puddle.

85. Write a poem about the squishy sensation of kneading dough between your fingers and the smooth texture of it when you pat it and roll it out.

86. Use all of the following words in a poem: measure, signature, staff, key, instrument, notes, band, play, riff, radio, runs, tune, listen.

87. Write a poem about somebody you've forgiven, or write a poem about forgiveness.

88. Write a poem using the following image: a metropolis at night when the power is out.

89. You dip your chip into a bowl of salsa, and when you take a bite, your mouth goes up in red-hot flames. Write a poem about spicy food.

90. Use all of the following words in a poem: feast, fire, modify, squash, robbed, forgotten, understated.

91. Write a metaphorical poem comparing an abstract concept to something concrete.

92. Write a poem using the following image: laundry drying on the line.

93. There's a big bowl of chilled, fresh summer fruit in the fridge. It's colorful, juicy, and sweet. Write a descriptive poem about it.

94. Use all of the following words in a poem: petty, scales, spread, vault, combination, stripes, anchor.

95. Write a poem about school.

96. Write a poem using the following image: a smoking gun.

97. The leaves turned gold and amber, and then they drifted to the ground. We raked them into mounds then leaped and landed.

98. Use all of the following words in a poem: titanic, lure, power, turned, smash, collateral, lengths.

99. Write about something (not a person) that makes you sad. It could be a song, a place, or a memory.

100. Write a poem using the following images: trees bent and broken, dangling branches, and fresh-cut stumps.

101. Wheels spin, racing against the wind. Against the tide. Against the crack of the whip, against time.

102. Use all of the following words in a poem: spades, dripping, waves, crashing, platter, shaved, mobs.

103. Write a poem about something (not a person) that makes you angry.

104. Write a poem using the following image: a red stapler.

105. You're driving through town with your windows down, and you pass that intersection where you can smell all the fast food restaurants.

106. Use all of the following words in a poem: clean, squeak, scoop, gone, morsels, pound.

107. Write a poem about technology.

108. Write a poem using the following image: a highway packed with cars during commute hour.

109. It's Halloween and you're bobbing for apples. You stick your face in the cool water, chomp around searching for purchase, and feel the apples bumping against your face and floating away from you. Then you get a ripe little apple lodged firmly   between   your teeth.

110. Use all of the following words in a poem: telling, rinse, foul, junction, harbor, possessive, horse.

111. Write a poem about being a writer.

112. Write a poem using the following image: the vast emptiness and beauty of space.

113. It's so hot, you can see the heat dancing against the asphalt. So hot, you rub an ice cube against your neck. So hot...

114. Use all of the following words in a poem: lemonade, cotton, fish, taffy, ripe, saltwater, blackberry.

115. Write a poem about a junkyard, an antique store, or a pawn shop.

116. Write a poem using the following image: the back room of a butcher shop.

117. After a light but satisfying meal, you order dessert. It's rich, sweet, and freshly baked. You bite into it and your taste buds explode with delight.

118. Use all of the following words in a poem: womb, harvest, wishes, food, spinning, hands, leaves, lie.

119. Write a poem about the house in which you live.

120. Write a poem using the following image: an office worker sitting in a cubicle.

121. Write a poem about something ugly—war, fear, hate, or cruelty—but try to find the beauty (silver

lining) in it or something good that comes out of it.

122. Use all of the following words in a poem: thunder, blaring, seagulls, fans, children, wrap, span.

123. Write a poem about a restaurant.

124. Write a poem using the following image: a window on the forty-second floor of a high-rise building.

125. Silvery flakes drifted downward, glittering in the bright light of the harvest moon. The blackbird soared.

126. Use all of the following words in a poem: brother, car, flying, animals, rolling, concrete, ice, red.

127. Write a poem about the library or a bookstore.

128. Write a poem using the following image: a grave surrounded by mourners.

129. A twinkling eye can mean many things. Write a poem about a twinkle in someone's eye.

130. Use all of the following words in a poem: snap, spoon, grass, needles, carts, roll, squeeze, crimson.

131. Write a poem about hobos.

132. Write a poem using the following image: bats hanging upside-down in a cave.

133. Two players, two sides, two strategies. They rise with weapons held high—words or swords, law or rebellion. Write a poem about opposition or competition.

134. Use all of the following words in a poem: toes, pale, veins, floor, spiderwebs, dive.

135. Write a poem about an abandoned ghost town.

136. Write a poem using the following image: a prison cell with writing all over the walls.

137. Write a poem about something beautiful—love, birth, a glorious sunset—but find the dark side of it.

138. Use all of the following words in a poem: sisters, duty, floating, give, green, face, found.

139. Write a poem about the sun or the moon.

140. Write a poem using the following image: a courtroom after a trial.

141. A face mapped with wrinkles and years...Bent hands that worked for decades...Write a poem about old age.

142. Use all of the following words in a poem: shift, dynamite, screen, flag, pipes, boots, grime, flailing, spray, grind.

143. Write a poem about gypsies.

144. Write a poem using the following image: a shark nearing a school of fish.

145. Beneath the frost a little green shoot pushes itself up from the soil, through the icy crust, and into the damp, chilly air.

146. Use all of the following words in a poem: whine, crow, gap, black, danger, divide, pithy.

147. Write a poem about hunting.

148. Write a poem using the following image: a mad scientist's laboratory.

149. Write a poem to someone who makes you uncomfortable.

150. Use all of the following words in a poem: ink, hair, banjo, roller, tea, parade.

151. Write a poem about the last day of school.

152. Write a poem using the following image: a penny on the floor of a subway station.

153. Fresh skin, smooth head, and a tiny wailing mouth. Write a poem about a baby.

154. Use all of the following words in a poem: curl, motor, spice, retch, racket, lavender, crumble.

155. Write a poem about fashion.

156. Write a poem using the following image: a vase filled with dying flowers.

157. In the clock shop, the walls are covered with timepieces. Pieces of time. Chimes on the hour. Tick-tock. Tick-tock.

158. Use all of the following words in a poem: fade, slumber, belly, step, magnificent, snip.

159. Write a poem about a place you want to go someday.

160. Write a poem using the following image: blood on the dance floor.

161. The glass house cracks.

162. Use all of the following words in a poem: whistle, low, biting, smooth, stroll, scrape, blast.

163. Write a poem about the ocean, a lake, or a river.

164. Write a poem using the following image: a howl at high noon.

165. They march with their heads high, weapons at the ready, approaching the front line. Write a poem about soldiers.

166. Use all of the following words in a poem: underdog, lambast, prayer, blue, cringe, fall, tense.

167. Write a poem about your favorite sport or athletic activity.

168. Write a poem using the following image: a commuter on the subway wearing headphones and tinkering with a smartphone.

169. Just one kiss is all it takes, and you're barreling like a roller coaster car on the loose. Write a poem about new love.

170. Use all of the following words in a poem: tinker, brass, maple, brush, stomp, fast.

171. Write a poem about vampires, werewolves, or zombies.

172. Write a poem using the following image: a cat sitting on a windowsill looking outside.

173. It smells of disinfectant and medication. Quiet footsteps bustle down corridors and into rooms filled with sorrow and hope. Write a poem set in a hospital.

174. Use all of the following words in a poem: claw, wool, lift, silver, buried, coax, fixed, moving.

175. Write a poem about being chased or hunted.

176. Write a poem using the following image: an old person sitting in meditation.

177. There's a quiet cracking sound, and then an apple falls, twirling to the ground below and bruising itself against the hard earth.

178. Use all of the following words in a poem: dust, gnaw, light, copper, tubes, silent, saw, crash, drip.

179. Write a poem about looking for something or someone.

180. Write a poem using the following image: a group of kids eating together at a table in a cafeteria.

181. Sand. For miles and miles, nothing but sand and dry, scorching heat. Parched throat, sweaty, sunburned brow. Oasis. Mirage.

182. Use all of the following words in a poem: shuffle, back, starts, flat, tug, gone.

183. Write a poem about hope or honor.

184. Write a poem using the following image: someone sleeping in a car.

185. The campfire burns, and marshmallows melt, seeping liquid sugar into the hot flames. The stick is charred, and we smack our lips in the dark.

186. Use all of the following words in a poem: stamp, bail, treat, keel, gray, joint.

187. Write a poem about a photograph.

188. Write a poem using the following image: adults dressed in costumes.

189. The stars wrap themselves around Earth in a celestial embrace.

190. Use all of the following words in a poem: net, brisk, mammoth, oily, pierce, wobbly, young.

191. Write a poem about innocence and corruption.

192. Write a poem using the following image: someone opening a letter near the mailbox.

193. Write a poem to someone who always offends you or makes you angry.

194. Use all of the following words in a poem: drive, clock, sparkle, yellow, palm, dress.

195. Write a poem about corporations.

196. Write a poem using the following image: a lone red balloon floating up into the sky.

197. A politician on the dais, a preacher in the pulpit, and seekers in the stands.

198. Use all of the following words in a poem: bridge, watch, lower, square, faded, bound, shoe, crooked.

199. Write a poem about moving on.

200. Write a poem using the following image: the aftermath of a bar fight.

201. The wind roars and trees pound against the house. In the backyard, a shade umbrella is swept up, swirling into the storm.

202. Use all of the following words in a poem: river, chime, toll, drift, coil, backlash.

203. Write a poem about the house in which you grew up.

204. Write a poem using the following image: a frog sitting on a lily pad.

205. Sticky-faced kids and long lines for broken-down rides.

206. Use all of the following words in a poem: yeah, chip, down, neck, order, room.

207. Write a poem about two people who haven't seen each other in a long time.

208. Write a poem using the following image: a dancer stretching in a dance studio against a backdrop of hardwood floors and a wall of mirrors.

209. A cobwebbed cabin tucked so far into the trees, they're growing though the floors.

210. Use all of the following words in a poem: lake, tick, charge, composed, moss, believe.

211. Write a poem about a sunset or a sunrise.

212. Write a poem using the following image: a child sitting alone on a bench in a schoolyard.

213. Write a poem about civil service

214. Use all of the following words in a poem: slide, aged, bank, jam, lead, permit, stink.

215. Write a poem about a pen, a computer, or a piece of paper.

216. Write a poem using the following image: a large family eating together at a harvest dining table.

217. The dew is fresh and the world is hushed in the breaking light of dawn. Hurried footsteps scamper across the stones in the garden.

218. Use all of the following words in a poem: left, match, pile, row, sign, survey, charge, dear.

219. Write a poem about your favorite meal. What does it look like? How does it smell? Describe the texture and the taste.

220. Write a poem using the following image: a floor covered with torn wrapping paper and discarded ribbons and bows.

221. Pedestrians collide, and a letter falls from a pocket. It tumbles onto the sidewalk, kicked along by passersby.

222. Use all of the following words in a poem: cap, court, back, cobble, sniff, nick, shebang.

223. Write a poem about secrets.

224. Write a poem using the following image: a couple dressed in formal attire sitting on a bench at a bus stop.

225. A tiny scar, a large scar, a break in the bone, and blood. Stitches and pitches and cries and yawns. A tiny pill and the pain is gone.

226. Use all of the following words in a poem: bit, draw, flex, perilous, bubble, corner, rancid, pound, high, open.

227. Write a poem about your body.

228. Write a poem using the following image: a punk rocker covered in tattoos and piercings with a purple mohawk.

229. The snow is freshly fallen and still falling, piling up—mounds   of   cold powder.

230. Use all of the following words in a poem: card, cheating, breathless, fit, pull, sacred, sink, off.

231. Write a poem about trying something new.

232. Write a poem using the following image: a package sitting on a front porch.

233. The sky is laden with dark clouds and the land is buried under a blanket of pale, gray snow. The ground, the streams, and the lakes are frozen and the whole world is eerily quiet and still.

234. Use all of the following words in a poem: mean, rumors, maximum, new, battles, chance, downwind, murmur, skin.

235. Write a poem about a hero.

236. Write a poem using the following image: a child looking up into the sky.

237. The car careens across the meridian, screeches past oncoming traffic, and plummets through the rail on the other side of the highway.

238. Use all of the following words in a poem: nail, bump, flicker, turn, yawn.

239. Write a poem contrasting two opposites (such as fire and ice).

240. Write a poem using the following image: an overgrown front lawn.

241. The heart races. Skin is hot to the touch. Breath comes fast, and beads of sweat dot the forehead. Inhale, exhale. Dizzy.

242. Use all of the following words in a poem: crisis, carry, matter, old, easy, boulder, sound.

243. Write a poem about monsters.

244. Write a poem using the following image: a pair of glasses with a large spiderweb crack covering one lens.

245. Sticky floors, loud music, and the clink of bottles and glasses. Cigarette smoke hovers overhead, swirling beneath the florescent lights. Write a poem set in a bar.

246. Use all of the following words in a poem: space, press, tie, round, case, blow, stones.

247. Write a poem about saying good-bye to someone who is dying.

248. Write a poem using the following image: a bird's nest full of eggs.

249. The stage is set, the cameras are rolling, and nerves are high. Clustered backstage, they warble and stretch beneath the white-hot lights.

250. Use all of the following words in a poem: crush, note, pier, salt, seal, cardboard, link, stand.

251. Write a poem about cheating or lying.

252. Write a poem using the following image: a single blade of grass.

253. Dishes are piled high in the sink, dirty pots and pans are sitting on the stovetop, and broken glass is scattered across the floor.

254. Use all of the following words in a poem: simulation, button, reach, plug, mark, menace.

255. Write a poem about a bicycle.

256. Write a poem using the following image: a person dining alone in a restaurant.

257. A bell rings, and bodies flock toward the chimes, congregating like birds that descend when old people fling breadcrumbs across the park grass.

258. Use all of the following words in a poem: automatic, leaky, scratch, slip, minutes, bug, door, coming, hands.

259. Write a poem about a circus or zoo.

260. Write a poem using the following image: the locker room after a team has lost (or won) an important athletic game or before a team is about to play an important game.

261. Quaint storefronts line the boulevard, but one by one the shops are closing, making way for bigger, cheaper stores.

262. Use all of the following words in a poem: orange, crank, courier, beneath, shouting, breeze, world, make.

263. Write a poem about hiding from something or someone.

264. Write a poem using the following image: a book, a pair of glasses, and an empty teacup sitting on a table.

265. A fox slips through the trees, darting around boulders, dodging the hunter's sight.

266. Use all of the following words in a poem: slam, film, tasty, point, hint, stir, doorway, deadline.

267. Write a poem about poverty.

268. Write a poem using the following image: a rocket soaring through space.

269. Deer bound across the field, breaking delicate blades of grass with hard hooves, pausing to dine on soft flowers.

270. Use all of the following words in a poem: consider, magic, dare, flame, one, cards, elastic.

271. Write a poem about the first day of a new job.

272. Write a poem using the following image: a scruffy kid and a scruffier dog walking through city streets.

273. They beat and holler, tap and howl. Fire in the middle—a circle of drums.

274. Use all of the following words in a poem: coincidence, bus, deal, absurd, letter, fortune, clip, distant, bat.

275. Write a poem about your dream house.

276. Write a poem using the following image: five teenagers sitting in detention.

277. A lizard scuttles over a hot rock, tongue lashing at dried-out beetles.

278. Use all of the following words in a poem: scarce, pilgrimage, tongues, luck, tire, test, alive.

279. Write a poem about the government.

280. Write a poem using the following image: a robot assembling products on a factory line.

281. The halls are filled with notes and chords, the vibrations dancing softly across doors, walls, and hearts.

282. Use all of the following words in a poem: weakness, station, momentum, speak, last, restless, place, choose.

283. Write a poem about one of the four elements: earth, air, fire, or water.

284. Write a poem using the following image: someone sitting on the floor, alone, with a bottle of whisky.

285. A bell rings and children stream out of the schoolhouse, youthful energy unleashed like a thousand bolts of lightning.

286. Use all of the following words in a poem: hang, calling, broken, pine, patriotic, downhill, took.

287. Write a poem about a criminal.

288. Write a poem using the following image: the view outside a submarine porthole.

289. Hips coil, shoulders shimmy. Tap your toes, and move across the floor.

290. Use all of the following words in a poem: trust, dead, pretty, buy, hurray, try, wrong, sleeve, done.

291. Write a poem about working hard.

292. Write a poem using the following image: a driver on the highway flipping off another driver.

293. The old crow swoops into the road—pay dirt! It's a trampled snake. Round up to dine on the wire.

294. Use all of the following words in a poem: late, wise, vice, fill, nowhere, time.

295. Write a poem about language.

296. Write a poem using the following image: a picture of Earth taken from space.

297. They move like swans across the hardwood floor, spinning and leaping and toe-rising.

298. Use all of the following words in a poem: long, waste, handle, asleep, back, wide, decline.

299. Write a poem about something or someone that excites you.

300. Write a poem using the following image: a canvas, a palette, and a handful of paintbrushes.

301. A wall of water, tall as any skyscraper, surfs across the surface of the sea, ready to rain down and wash away every inch of beach.

302. Use all of the following words in a poem: barrel, bode, wear, drink, stalk, cross, sting, reared.

303. Write a poem about someone or something that makes you laugh.

304. Write a poem using the following image: a blue-green lagoon on a tropical island.

305. They roll from town to town, hopped up on beer, lugging amplifiers, drums, and big dreams.

306. Use all of the following words in a poem: stay, factory, breaker, whistle, rich, demand, hurry.

307. Write a poem about growing up.

308. Write a poem using the following image: a bird (or other animal) in a cage.

309. Molten rock and burning earth bubble from the peak then explode, dazzling the sky; the lava rolls down the mountainside and swallows all life in its fiery path.

310. Use all of the following words in a poem: miles, pride, supply, insurgent, silver, downhill.

311. Write a poem about puberty.

312. Write a poem using the following image: travelers waiting for a delayed flight at the airport.

313. The wind curls into a neat funnel, skipping through the city streets, catching cars and lampposts, ripping them up, and spitting them out in the distant countryside.

314. Use all of the following words in a poem: polish, billow, far, divergent, vote, silence, tiger, Zen, rhyme, pitcher, missed, pale, shine.

315. Write a poem about walking around barefoot.

316. Write a poem using the following image: a band playing on stage in front of a disinterested audience.

317. One toe in the water, one toe in the sand. Standing on the precipice.

318. Use all of the following words in a poem: crow, read, leader, mythology, beginning, rent, means.

319. Write a poem about a company of dancers.

320. Write a poem using the following image: a child giving another child a piggyback ride.

321. Dirt under fingernails. Chipped teeth. Rough hands. Bent back. It's a life. It's a living.

322. Use all of the following words in a poem: country, fit, wind, congratulate, approval, itemize, cents, trailer.

323. Write a poem about birds.

324. Write a poem using the following image: a camp for prisoners of war.

325. They huddle around the grave, tossing in flowers, dirt, and memories.

326. Use all of the following words in a poem: sale, fight, hero, fallen, skinned, congress, occupation, top.

327. Write a poem about desire and longing.

328. Write a poem using the following image: a mother or father in the hospital holding a newborn baby.

329. She waves her wand and the music rises and falls—deep lulls and glorious crescendos, trills from the wind section and a deep hum from the brass.

330. Use all of the following words in a poem: hemisphere, sharp, address, hill, crush, renegades, blank, glitter, brace, flex, shrug, crocodile.

331. Write a poem about a marine animal.

332. Write a poem using the following image: a raccoon rifling through a garbage can.

333. Deep inside a dark, cold cave, water trickles down a rock wall, carving a wet trail on the hard slate.

334. Use all of the following words in a poem: earthquake, tournament, pop, lamb, awake, stay, voice, keep.

335. Write a poem about lust, greed, revenge, laziness, gluttony, jealousy, or pride.

336. Write a poem using the following image: a stack of blank journals and notebooks.

337. Snap crackle cool slide. Dip trip big-bass jive.

338. Use all of the following words in a poem: sense, acumen, airplane, pearls, collapse, show, cry.

339. Write a poem about an empty house. Is it new? Old? Is someone moving in or out?

340. Write a poem using the following image: a politician giving a speech to a crowd at a county fair.

341. Vultures descend on a carcass that is rotting on the side of the road.

342. Use all of the following words in a poem: race, confession, fool, move, screw, hungry, incinerate.

343. Write a poem about the many ways love can be expressed.

344. Write a poem using the following image: a dog barking at a passerby through a chain link fence.

345. The trail is covered with footprints—human and animal. The large cat crouches atop rocks watching the hikers below.

346. Use all of the following words in a poem: hours, enemy, grunt, choice, good-bye, hint, always, tide, news, lion, sentimental, number.

347. Write a poem about nudity.

348. Write a poem using the following image: a big bowl of fresh, homegrown summer fruit.

349. She walks down the street wearing nothing but a full-sized flag wrapped around her body. Lady liberty is on the loose.

350. Use all of the following words in a poem: wolf, honorable, hurricane, mad, sing, thought, waking, blinded, rapid, choice.

351. Write a poem about spending time alone.

352. Write a poem using the following image: an empty, unmade bed.

353. Headphones, backpack, smooth moves. Dancing on the street corner. Dancing at the bus stop. Rocking out on the subway.

354. Use all of the following words in a poem: broom, sight, ladder, quiet, century, turned, honey, wasted, pathetic.

355. Write a poem about what it means to be part of a team.

356. Write a poem using the following image: a group of rambunctious kids sitting at the back of the bus.

357. They gather around a steel barrel that is half-filled with coal and douse it with kerosene, and as the flames rise, they drop books in, one by one.

358. Use all of the following words in a poem: bedroom, vested, structure, everything, head, strong, ugly, shame, raw, true.

359. Write a poem about a predatory animal.

360. Write a poem using the following image: a big, shiny red fire engine.

361. A photograph falls from a hand, sailing to the floor, landing facedown.

362. Use all of the following words in a poem: servant, hide, knees, alive, sworn, shook, wasted, deal, capital.

363. Write a poem about an animal you admire—not a particular animal, such as your pet, but a type of animal, such as a penguin or a giraffe.

364. Write a poem using the following image: a unit of soldiers riding in a helicopter.

365. Power: electric, personal, international, and up for grabs.

366. Use all of the following words in a poem: road, gentry, combat, listen, plead, hold, about, ring, heartless, relax, defense.

367. Write a poem about dancing.

368. Write a poem using the following image: a spread of fresh, homegrown fall vegetables just harvested from the garden.

369. Workers swarm into the office. A hundred years ago, they would have worn coveralls, kerchiefs, and stood over a conveyer belt. Today, they wear business casual, drink lattes, and bend over computer keyboards.

370. Use all of the following words in a poem: collar, rationalize, fury, victims, haul, super, achiever, ignore.

371. Write a poem about the cycle of life from birth to death.

372. Write a poem using the following image: a telescope aimed at the night sky.

373. The water is so clear, you can see the bottom. Ten feet below, layers of brightly colored pebbles: blue, green, and amber.

374. Use all of the following words in a poem: junk, population, bigger, hollow, democratic, screamed, straight, waiting.

375. Write a poem about a clown.

376. Write a poem using the following image: people dancing around a bonfire on the beach.

377. The cocoon wobbles, then a tiny tear stretches into a long gap, and out steps a butterfly.

378. Use all of the following words in a poem: turn, work, rapture, not, people, shoes, slump, jam, skinny.

379. Write a poem about a car salesperson.

380. Write a poem using the following image: a fish with its nose against the glass of a small fishbowl.

381. Stand still at the edge of the dock and look out at the gray waves—how they rise and fall. The water, it speaks to you.

382. Use all of the following words in a poem: jelly, pepper, cream, morning, never, reason.

383. Write a poem about a movie theater.

384. Write a poem using the following image: a house with a picket fence and a tire swing hanging from a tree in the front yard.

385. That summer, everybody was listening to that song. It was playing everywhere.

386. Use all of the following words in a poem: cause, tower, dusk, precipice, breathing, travels, rockslide.

387. Write a poem about animals in the wild whose habitats are being destroyed or endangered by humans.

388. Write a poem using the following image: a soup kitchen on the night of a major holiday.

389. The years keep turning over, and we just keep spinning around and around.

390. Use all of the following words in a poem: primitive, burning, miracle, backward, hypnotize, rules, promises, desecrate.

391. Write a poem about a dark, scary place.

392. Write a poem using the following image: a book with a worn cover and dog-eared pages.

393. Have you ever walked through a garden at night? What about a forest?

394. Use all of the following words in a poem: educated, churning, blackbirds, trickle, real, coals, sorry.

395. Write a poem about loneliness.

396. The Great Pacific Garbage Patch is an island of garbage floating in the middle of the ocean. Write a poem about it.

397. Every tooth, every discarded shoe, every grass-stained elbow tells a story.

398. Use all of the following words in a poem: behind, waiting, snakes, engaged, overflow, nation, set.

399. Write a poem about a long journey.

400. Write a poem using the following image: someone standing in a doorway, soaking wet, with rain pouring in the background.

Creative Nonfiction Prompts

1. Write about someone you admire from afar—a public figure or celebrity.

2. Revisit your earliest memories of learning about faith, religion, or spirituality.

3. Write a how-to article about a task, activity, or project you've learned to complete through practical experience in your career.

4. Have you ever had déjà vu—the strange sense that you've experienced something before? Write a personal essay about it.

5. What is the number-one goal you want to achieve as a writer? To reach your main writing goal, what do you need to do?

6. Think about what your favorite holiday means to you. Why do you celebrate it? How does it shape or affect your life for the rest of the year?

7. Heartbreak is part of life and full of lessons. Tell the story of a heartbreak you've experienced.

8. Write a critical review of your favorite book. What made it so good? Could it have been better?

Provide a detailed analysis of its strengths and weaknesses.

9. Remember when you were a little kid and you learned something new about life or how the world works? Write an article for kids about what you learned, how you learned it, and how you felt about it. For example: learning where food comes from.

10. Have you ever felt like you were meant for something, that some event or moment in your life was fated? Have you ever felt an inexplicable call to do something? Where do you think this feeling comes from? Write about it.

11. Read your favorite poem and take a few minutes to contemplate it. Then write a reaction to the poem. Why do you love it? How does it make you feel? What makes this poem so special to you? If you don't have a favorite poem, write about your favorite song lyrics.

12. Write a top-ten article listing your favorite songs or albums with short explanations of why each one earned a spot on your list.

13. Do you believe the existence of a higher power can be proven or disproved? Write a personal essay about it.

14. Art is all around. You can purchase books packed with images of art. You can visit museums and galleries. You can surf the web for photographs

of paintings and sculptures. Choose a piece of art that speaks to you and write about it. Describe the piece. How does it make you feel? What details give it power or make it captivating?

15. They say it's better to have loved and lost than to never have loved at all. Whom have you loved and lost?

16. Think back on some embarrassing moments that you've experienced. Now write a series of scenes depicting those moments.

17. Write a how-to article about something you can do that is not part of your job (for example: how to bake a cake from scratch or how to change the oil in your car).

18. What do you like to wear during summer, winter, fall, or spring? Write about your sense of fashion (or lack thereof). Does it change with the seasons?

19. Tell a story about one (or both) of your parents.

20. Write about your experience with a mentor, teacher, or coach, explaining how working with someone more knowledgeable than you helped you.

21. What determines an action or person as good or evil? Who gets to decide what or who is good or evil? Write a personal essay about it.

22. Think about the last book you read. How did the book make you feel? Were you sad? Scared? Intrigued? What was it about the book that evoked an emotional response from you? Was it the characters? The plot? The subject matter?

23. Write about a sport you play or watch, or write about an athletic activity you enjoy.

24. Tell the story of the first time you earned your own money.

25. Write a personal essay about how music has affected you or shaped your life.

26. Write about how the real world influences your writing, or write about how your personal experiences and beliefs influence your writing.

27. You get to create your very own garden. Will it be a flower garden or a vegetable garden? Maybe you'd prefer a grove of trees instead? Write a descriptive personal essay about it.

28. Write a critical review of your favorite movie. What made it so good? Could it have been better? Provide a detailed analysis of its strengths and weaknesses.

29. Choose a polarizing topic you feel strongly about and write an essay espousing the opposing point of view. For example, if you believe in the death penalty, write an argument against it.

30. It's the last snowfall of the year. What do you do? Go sledding? Build a snowman? Head to the pond for some ice skating?

31. Sometimes, we use common sense and do the right thing or make the best choice. But sometimes, we learn lessons the hard way. Write about a time in your life when you made the wrong choice and learned a lesson the hard way.

32. Most people aren't single-issue voters, but chances are that when you go to polls, there's one issue at the top of your list of concerns. Write an essay about your position through the lens of your personal experiences. What in your life experience has caused you to take this position?

33. Film is one of the greatest forms of entertainment. The audience gets to sit back and snack on junk food while the movie plays and takes us on a wild ride through someone else's life story. We all have our favorite films. What are yours and why? What do you love most about them? The characters? The plot? The special effects?

34. Throughout history, many stories have been told about the origins of the universe. Some people rely on religion to answer this question; others look to science. What do you think?

35. Every once in a while, someone comes into our lives for a short time and fundamentally changes us. Has that ever happened to you?

36. Write an article about your top-ten favorite authors, highlighting the strengths of each one.

37. Write a personal essay about coping with the loss of a loved one.

38. Many dramas use comedic relief to add emotional balance and realism. Write about how this is done successfully and why readers and audiences find it so compelling.

39. Write about animals. How do you feel about them? What is their purpose? Do they have rights? Should they have rights?

40. At some point, we are taught enough science to begin to grasp just how big the universe is and how small we are. Describe the moment you made this realization.

41. Write a personal essay about what you would do with your own personal robot.

42. Think of a book that was a page-turner. What were the hooks or cliffhangers that made you want to keep reading? How did the author build tension?

43. Do you believe in a supreme being or higher power? Are you atheist or agnostic? How did you arrive at your beliefs? Have you always held the same beliefs on this issue, or has your perspective changed over time?

44. Many of us have experienced a terrifying moment in which we thought we were going to die. If you've ever experienced a moment like that, write about it.

45. Here's what sells: sex, money, and articles on how to look your best. Write a splashy article on one of these topics.

46. Write a manifesto: a mission statement that includes your personal and professional goals and philosophies.

47. Music makes the world go round. Listen to your old favorites or explore some brand-new music. Choose a song or album that you have a visceral response to. Maybe it makes you want to dance, laugh, or cry. Write a descriptive essay about it. Is it soft and tender? Hard and brash? Hip and groovy? What moves you? The lyrics? The melody? The rhythm?

48. Fate or free will? Do you believe in destiny, or do you believe that life's outcome is strictly the result of choice and circumstance? What experiences or evidence has led you to your position on fate versus free will?

49. Tell the story of an important long-term goal you have accomplished.

50. Write a critical review of your favorite television show. What made it so good? Could it have been

better? Provide a detailed analysis of its strengths and weaknesses.

51. Write a personal essay about a time when you wanted to escape or run. Maybe you actually did it!

52. Write about nonfiction. Do you read memoir, biographies, or reference books? Which ones are your favorites and what do you get out of them?

53. Think of something you wish you were good at but aren't. Write a narrative about your attempts to do this thing and how you coped with failure.

54. Write an article about your favorite musician. What makes this musician so special? Looks? Talent? The sheer number of fans? Awards and critical acclaim? Sales? Quality of craftsmanship?

55. Go through your photos and choose one that is special to you. Write a personal essay about it. You can also use a series of photos from a single event.

56. What is your favorite genre of books? Why? What makes that genre so special or interesting?

57. Do you believe in absolute good and evil? Are good and evil counterpoints that are constantly striving to balance each other out? Do good and evil both have to exist, or can one eliminate the other for once and for all? Are good and evil nothing more than human-made concepts?

58. Tell the story of a difficult or harrowing period in your life that helped you become a better person.

59. Choose something you're good at—the thing you are better at than anything else. Then write an article including ten to twenty-five tips on the subject.

60. Write a personal essay about your proudest moment in life so far, and don't leave out the events leading up to it!

61. Choose one of your favorite stories. What was uniquely likable about the protagonist? What made the antagonist bothersome or despicable?

62. Are your morals and ethics circumstantial or static? For example, if you believe it's wrong to kill someone, is it always wrong, or are there exceptions? Is it unethical to kill a mass murderer or someone who is attacking you? What other moral beliefs do you hold and what are some exceptions that would cause you to put those morals aside?

63. Think of something important you've learned about human relationships, and write an article describing what you learned, how you learned it, and how it could benefit others.

64. We've all had bad days. But there's probably a day for you that stands out as the worst. Write a personal essay about it.

65. E. B. White said, "All that I hope to say in books, all that I ever hope to say, is that I love the world." What do you hope to say through your writing?

66. Dystopia is an imagined world in which humanity is living in the worst possible (or most unfavorable) conditions. One person's dystopia is another person's utopia. What would the world look like in your version of dystopia?

67. Identify a key theme from your childhood and write about it. For example, perhaps your family spent a lot of time camping. Write a series of stories from the trail.

68. Write a top-ten article listing your favorite films with short explanations of why each film earned a spot on your list.

69. Most of us have had an aha moment, an instant in which we reached an epiphany about something. Write a personal essay about one of your aha moments.

70. Throughout history, books have been banned by governments, schools, and churches. To this day, people will launch campaigns to ban a book. What do you think about book banning? Do you believe in freedom of speech? Who has the right to decide what other people can and can't read?

71. What happens when we die? This is a question many people don't like to think about even

though it's the only certainty in life and the one thing that happens to every single living thing. Do you believe in an afterlife? Is the jury still out? Where did you get your ideas about what happens at death?

72. Write a narrative about how fear has shaped your life—steering you away from some things and toward others.

73. Think about something you were good at or enjoyed when you were a kid: for example, sports, drawing, or academics. Write an article for kids about it.

74. Write a descriptive essay about a gadget, device, or other new technology that you wish someone would invent.

75. Write about your earliest memory. Include as much detail as you can remember.

76. Think of something you're good at—something you taught yourself. For example: cooking, working on cars, gardening, or caring for animals. Write a narrative about how and why you developed these skills.

77. Write an article about your top-ten favorite books highlighting the strengths of each one.

78. Write a personal essay about someone or something that gave you hope when you really needed it.

79. What is your greatest goal in life? Have you started working toward it yet? What is your plan for achieving it?

80. Tell the story of your early childhood up until kindergarten. Recollect stories your family has told you. Interview relatives if necessary.

81. Think of something you've always wanted to learn how to do, and then write an article explaining what steps one might take to learn that thing.

82. Many of us grew up with pets and currently live with pets. Write a personal essay about a special pet who had a profound impact on your life.

83. What is your least favorite genre of books? Why don't you like it?

84. Utopia is the opposite of dystopia. It is an imagined world in which humanity is living in the most ideal and favorable conditions. What does your utopia look like?

85. Tell the story of how you ended up in the career you have now.

86. Write about a flaw or negative trait or behavior that you've overcome. Write it as an article for helping others overcome the same thing. For example, how to stop being a pessimist, how to live a healthier lifestyle, etc.

87. Write a personal essay about a place that has special meaning for you.

88. Write a detailed description of your writing process for a particular project you completed.

89. Write about the happiest day of your life.

90. Choose someone you know well (or used to know) who is unconventional or eccentric, and tell the story of your relationship with this person and how he or she affected you.

91. Write a critical review of your favorite song or album. What made it so good? Could it have been better? Provide a detailed analysis of its strengths and weaknesses.

92. Write a personal essay about something you, as an adult, learned from a child.

93. Write a few paragraphs describing censorship. Include examples of how, when, and where censorship might occur. Is it ever okay to censor a book? Who has the right to censor a book? Is it ever okay for the government to censor its citizens?

94. Think back to the first time you had a best friend. Tell the story of your friendship.

95. Write an article for children titled "Ten Things I Wish an Adult Had Told Me When I was a Child."

96. Write a personal essay about money. How important is it to you? What would you do if you had lots of it? What would you be willing to do in order to obtain lots of it?

97. Literature is where writers live and breathe. Where would we writers be today without our predecessors who, through their artistry, contributed to the literary canon and years of best-seller lists? Which novels or poets inspired you to become a writer? Which authors embody a voice that resonates with you? Which genres are you most drawn to?

98. If you could obtain any superpower, which one would you choose and why? How would you use it?

99. Most of us have plenty of vivid childhood memories. Make a list of some of your most vivid memories from elementary school, and form them into a narrative.

100. Write an article filled with travel tips based on your own travel experiences.

101. If you had to go back to a point in your life and do things differently, what point would you choose and what would you do differently? How would the changes ripple through your life?

102. What if there were world peace? What would the world look like?

103. Think about someone who was mean to you when you were a kid. Write an article for kids with suggestions on how to deal with meanies.

104. Write a personal essay about a book, movie, or television show that fundamentally changed you. The essay should include a thesis statement about how the arts can affect the world.

105. Describe your current writing workspace. Then describe your ideal writing workspace.

106. What if you could go back to school and study anything you wanted? What would you study and why?

107. Tell the story of the craziest thing you ever did, saw, or experienced.

108. Write a personal essay about how art has affected you and shaped your life.

109. What if you had an opportunity to travel to outer space? Would you ever take a trip to the moon? Would you travel aboard an interstellar starship?

110. When you were a kid, you probably had an idea about what you wanted to be when you grew up. Write about what you wanted to be and why, and try to draw connections between your childhood dream and grown-up reality.

111. Write a personal essay about an animal that is important to you. It could be a specific animal,

such as one of your pets, or it could be a type of animal, such as birds or foxes.

112. Write about your favorite comedy book, film, or television show. Who's the funniest character? Is the comedy physical, emotional, or intellectual? Why does it appeal to your personal sense of humor?

113. What if you woke up one day as a world leader? City mayor? State governor? President? Monarch? What would you do for your community?

114. Write your own coming-of-age story. When did you start feeling like an adult?

115. If you could change one thing in the world, what would you change and why?

116. Write an article about what distinguishes poor writing from good writing, or write an article about what distinguishes good writing from great writing.

117. What if you could talk to animals?

118. Write an article that inspires people to do something you've already done successfully.

119. Science fiction and fantasy authors sure have wild imaginations. Think of something that doesn't exist and probably won't ever exist—something you wish were real. Write a descriptive essay about it.

120. What if you had a chance to travel anywhere in the world, but you had to stay in one location for a whole year? Where would you go and why?

121. Junior high is a tumultuous time for many adolescents. Make a list of your most vivid memories from junior high and form them into a narrative.

122. Soft skills include communication, attitude, and empathy. Choose the soft skill you have the greatest aptitude for and write an article about how this skill is beneficial, using your own life experiences as examples.

123. Write a personal essay about the best gift you ever received. Why is it your favorite? Who gave it to you? What made it so special?

124. When you retire, what will you have written?

125. Write down a full account of a dream you've had recently. Include as many details as possible.

126. Have you ever won a contest or an important competition? What did you have to do in order to win? Did you work for it or did you get lucky?

127. During your next job interview, the hiring manager hands you crayons, markers, pencils, and drawing paper. He or she says you have one hour to draw whatever you want. Before leaving the room, the hiring manager advises you to refrain from drawing anything work related. What do you draw and why?

128. Write about poetry. Do you like it? Which poems or poets do you enjoy? Why?

129. What if you could change careers? You get to choose any profession with the guarantee that you will be highly successful at it. What would you choose? Why?

130. Have you ever had to speak in front of a large crowd? Were you nervous? Well prepared? How did this speaking event come about? Write it as a narrative.

131. Think back to your childhood. Did you collect anything? Did you have a hobby? Write an article for kids about it.

132. Write a personal essay describing your greatest strength. Has it ever caused you problems? How do you leverage this strength? Do others ever commend you on it?

133. Think back over some of the dreams you've had and try to identify recurring themes. Perhaps you're often being chased in dreams (or maybe you're the one doing the chasing). Maybe a lot of your dreams are set in nature or feature animals.

134. Do you have children? Tell the story of how you became a parent. Write the stories of your first years as a parent—the joys and the struggles.

135. Write a biographical article about someone you admire.

136. Write a personal essay describing your dream date.

137. What is the first book you remember reading or falling in love with? Why does this book stand out for you?

138. Appreciating little things like a sunset or a delicious meal is important. Write about some of the little things you appreciate.

139. Imagine you've had a long and prosperous career as an author. Describe your legacy. What will you leave behind?

140. High school. It seems like it's going to last forever, but then it's over before you know it. Make a list of some of your most vivid memories from high school and form them into a narrative.

141. Have you ever thrown a big party? Write an article about how to throw an unforgettable bash. If you've never hosted such an event, use your imagination.

142. Think about someone in your life who always gets a giggle out of you. Can you remember some of the funny things that person has said or done that made you laugh? Write them down.

143. Everybody has experienced rejection. Did you give up or keep trying? Why? Would you react differently now? Write a narrative story about your personal experience with rejection.

144. Hard skills are abilities you have acquired—using software, analyzing numbers, and cooking are all examples of hard skills. Choose a hard skill you've mastered and write an article about how this skill is beneficial using your own life experiences as examples.

145. Write a personal essay describing one of your flaws or weaknesses. Does it hold you back? Have you ever used it to your advantage? Does it have a positive side? Do others ever point this flaw out to you?

146. Have you ever felt like a dream was trying to tell you something or send you an important message? What was the dream, and what message did you come away with?

147. Have you ever experienced something that cannot be explained? What happened? Have you tried to come up with an explanation?

148. Everybody has their own way of dealing with fear and anxiety. What works for you? Write an article that helps others cope with fear and anxiety.

149. Write a personal essay describing your house or a room in your house. What makes this room special?

150. Describe your favorite writing tools and resources.

151. Write your bucket list—at least ten (and up to a hundred)   things

you want to do before you die.

152. Do you have nieces or nephews? Tell your story of becoming an aunt or uncle. How did it change or affect your life?

153. Using your own experience as an example, write an article about how to deal with personal conflicts within a family, among friends, or at work.

154. Write a personal essay about your diet. What foods are you likely to consume over the course of a week? A month? Are you eating healthy food, junk food, or a mix?

155. What if you wrote a wildly successful best-selling novel? What would it be about?

156. What do you look for in a good story? Characters you connect with? Action and adventure? A puzzling or riveting plot? Sheer entertainment?

157. If you could construct a full, vivid dream that you would have tonight and remember in full tomorrow, what would happen in the dream? Who would be there? Where would it take place?

158. We've all been sick, and many of us cope with chronic conditions ranging from allergies to diseases. Write a story about an illness you've experienced.

159. Write an article that is a top-ten list of your best tips for managing, saving, or earning money.

160. Write a personal essay about what you hope will be your greatest accomplishment in life.

161. Do you read more print books or more e-books? Which do you prefer and why?

162. Write about one of the best experiences of your life. Why are you grateful for that experience?

163. Think about the first few years after you finished high school. Did you travel? Work? Go to college? Make a list of some of your most vivid memories from those years and form them into a narrative.

164. Write an article about how you use technology in your personal life. Has it made your life easier? Has it saved you money? How would you improve upon the technology you use?

165. Write a personal essay about a bad habit you'd like to eliminate from your life.

166. When did you first become interested in writing? What drew you to the craft?

167. Think back to a time when you gave in to fear. Now think of a time when you overcame fear. Tie these two experiences together in a single narrative.

168. Write a personal essay describing your favorite vacation destination.

169. What was the first thing you wrote on your own (not as a school assignment)? Was it a story? A poem? An essay or term paper? Describe it.

170. Tell a story about a time when you lost an item that mattered to you.

171. If you went to college, write an article about the steps you took to apply and, if applicable, obtain financial aid. Include tips for college freshmen that might help them deal with living in the dorms, choosing classes, or developing an education plan.

172. Choose an inanimate object—for example, a table or a coffee cup. Write an essay describing it in minute detail.

173. Choose your favorite story from a book, movie, television show, or real life. Now write a brief synopsis of the plot. Keep it to 250 words or fewer, and make it catchy. The goal is for the synopsis to make prospective audiences want to buy it.

174. What are five things that make you nervous or uncomfortable? What is it about each of those five things that bothers you? Where does this discomfort come from?

175. Write a narrative telling the story of the first time in your life you acquired (or realized you had) real responsibilities.

176. Write a personal essay describing your childhood home.

177. Choose a word you like. Maybe you like it because of its meaning. Maybe you like the way it sounds or the way it looks on the page. Write about the word.

178. Write down one thing that truly terrifies you. Is your fear of this thing keeping you safe or preventing you from living the life you want? How likely is it that this thing will happen? Why are you so frightened of this thing? If this thing happened, what would happen next?

179. Have you ever taken care of someone who was sick? A child, a parent, even a pet? Tell the story of how you dealt with it and got through it.

180. Write a how-to article explaining how to write something: a book, a poem, an article, etc.

181. Write a personal essay describing your favorite time period in history. What do you like about it?

182. Someone you barely know asks you to recommend a book. What do you recommend? Do you ask the person a few questions first to get an idea of their tastes?

183. Tell a story about a time when you had to let go of someone you cared for.

184. Have you ever had pets? Write an article for kids about how to take care of a pet.

185. You have to choose between spending a month in the desert or a month in the snow. You'll be living outdoors, but you'll have basic camping gear and supplies for survival. Which do you choose and why?

186. Choose your favorite character from a book, movie, or television show. Do a character study describing the character in full detail. Include the character's physical description, goals, challenges, flaws, and inner conflicts.

187. If you could absorb all of the knowledge of any one topic in a single day, what topic would you choose and why?

188. Think about a time in your life when you felt great gratitude. What led up to that moment? Why was it so important? Tell the whole story.

189. Write a personal essay about secrets. Have you ever had a big secret? Have you ever kept one for someone else? From someone else? Did you ever give someone's secret away?

190. Who do you think is the most popular character in all of storytelling? Why is that character appealing to so many people?

191. What are your thoughts and feelings on war? Does it depend on the war?

192. Using your own experience as an example, write an article about how to handle a disgruntled customer.

193. Write a personal essay about whether it's possible to change other people. Will people change for you just because they love you? If they don't change, does that mean they don't love you? Is it acceptable or reasonable to expect another person to change?

194. If you could visit the fantastical or historical world from any story of your choosing, which world would you visit and why? What if you had to live there forever?

195. What are your thoughts and feelings on stealing? Is it ever okay to steal?

196. Nobody does it alone. We all get help from others. Sometimes they actively do favors for us; other times, they help us without even realizing it. Tell a story about someone who has helped you.

197. Write a personal essay about your exercise regiment (or lack thereof). Do you need to exercise more? Could you exercise less and stay in shape?

198. You get to turn any book into a movie. Which book do you choose? Why? Whom do you cast? Whom do you hire as the director?

199. You get to have dinner with one person, living or dead. Whom do you choose and why?

200. Tell a story about a time when you had to let someone down.

201. Write an article that is a top-ten list of your best tips for getting or staying in shape.

202. Tell the story of how you met your best friend or significant other.

203. Have you ever read a book and thought, I wish I'd written that? What book was it? Who wrote it? Why do you wish you'd written it? How can you use it to influence your own work?

204. If you could change one thing about your appearance, what would you change and why?

205. Write a personal essay about what your life would look like if you had it all.

206. Make a list of the ten most iconic characters and write about what they have in common.

207. What are your thoughts and feelings on violence? Is it ever justified?

208. Write a narrative about your first day of school. It can be your very first day of school, your first day at a new school, or the first day starting a new grade level in school.

209. Many of us have, at some point in life, found ourselves in a toxic or unhealthy situation—a bad job or a relationship with someone who drained us emotionally. Write an article about identifying and getting out of toxic situations and/or relationships.

210. Write a personal essay describing the oldest person you know. How do you know this person? What influence does he or she have on your life?

211. What are your thoughts and feelings on big-box stores causing mom-and-pop stores to close? What about online stores causing big-box stores to close?

212. Write a narrative about the proudest moment in your life. What led up to it? How did others respond or participate? Did you celebrate or was it a quiet moment?

213. Write a how-to article about moving (finding a new place to live, packing, etc.).

214. Write a personal essay describing the elementary school, junior high, or high school you attended. Don't forget to include the teachers and staff.

215. Imagine you're a librarian or bookseller. What kind of library or bookstore would you work at? Describe a day at work.

216. Write about your vision of an ideal family.

217. Tell a story about a time when you were let down by someone you counted on.

218. Choose a cause that you feel is worthy and write an article persuading others to join that cause.

219. Write an essay about doing something courageous.

220. Have you ever published a book? Do you plan on publishing a book? Write a list of the steps you'll need to take in order to get a book published. You can write the steps for traditional or self-publishing.

221. You've won a one-month vacation to the destination of your choice, and you get to bring one other person with you. Where do you go and who do bring?

222. Write a narrative about when you did something bad and got away with it.

223. Write a how-to article detailing strategies for playing your favorite game.

224. You get to cure one disease. Which disease do you choose and why? Do you choose the disease that affects the most people or the one that has affected you or your loved ones?

225. Your next house comes with a library. Write a descriptive essay of your personal dream library.

226. If you wrote a weekly advice column, what would it be about?

227. Have you ever experienced a disastrous vacation? Tell the story of what happened.

228. Think about how you use technology in your professional life. What would your job be like without technology? Could it be done at all?

Write an article about how technology is (or isn't) important to your career.

229. Write a personal essay about a good habit you'd like to adopt in your life.

230. Think back to the books you read as a child. Which ones were your favorites? Do you think those books shaped the person you became? How much did they influence you and how did they affect you?

231. Have you ever built anything? Tell the story of what you built, why, and how.

232. Think of a major worldwide problem: for example, hunger, global warming, or political corruption. Write an article outlining a solution (or steps toward a solution).

233. Write a personal essay about a regret from your past.

234. Have you ever read a book and thought, I could write a better book than this? What do you think you could have done better? Were there any elements of the book that you didn't feel you could improve upon? What would you have changed and why?

235. Write about your favorite foods. What is your favorite meal of the day? If you could only eat one dish for the rest of you life, what would you choose?

236. Tell the stories of the first time you drove a car or the first time you bought a car. What other cars have you bought or driven over the years? Connect the cars to your life experiences for a broader, more compelling story.

237. Write an article about how to learn from one's mistakes. The article can be about little mistakes or big ones.

238. Write a personal essay describing your family. What makes them special? What do you love about them? What bothers you about them?

239. Do stories have the power to shape or change people's ideas, or are people drawn to stories that reinforce their existing ideals?

240. Write about your siblings. Describe their appearance, their personalities, and your relationship with them. If you don't have siblings, write about why you would want them, or why you're happy as an only child.

241. Many of us know someone who has coped with a tragedy, or we have coped with a tragedy ourselves. Sometimes sharing our stories can be therapeutic. Tell the story of a tragedy you've coped with.

242. Write an article explaining how to make your favorite meal.

243. Write a personal essay describing your dream home. Where is it? What does it look like on the outside? Inside? Who lives there?

244. Other than entertainment, what do we get out of reading? How do stories enrich our lives?

245. Think of an artistic talent that you don't possess but wish you did (singing, dancing, drawing, etc.). If you had that talent, what would you do with it? For example, if you were a master painter, what would you paint?

246. Write a narrative about when you did something bad and got caught.

247. Think of a time in your life when you were happy. How did you get there? Was it chance and circumstance, or did you bring happiness into your life through the choices you made? Write an article about how to be happy.

248. Write a personal essay describing an exotic animal you'd like to have as a pet.

249. William Wordsworth said, "Fill your paper with the breathings of your heart." What did he mean by that?

250. Have you ever traveled alone? Tell your story. Where did you go? Why? What happened?

251. Let's say you write a weekly advice column. Choose the topic you'd offer advice on, and then write one week's column.

252. You're opening your own restaurant. What do you call it? What's on the menu? How is it furnished and decorated?

253. Think about the last book you read. How was the book structured? Did it have chapters? Were they numbered or named? Was there an introduction, a prologue, or an epilogue? A table of contents? To whom was the book dedicated? Whom did the author thank in the acknowledgments? Who was the publisher?

254. Some people have a problem with authority. How do you feel about authority? Are you authoritative?

255. Write an article about how failure comes before success. What do we learn from failure? How does it build character?

256. Have you ever had a run-in with the police? What happened?

257. Maya Angelou said, "You can't use up creativity. The more you use, the more you have." What is your attitude about creativity? How do you use it? How do you cultivate it?

258. Do you consider yourself conventional or unconventional? Describe both the conventional and unconventional aspects of yourself.

259. Write a scene depicting a huge fight you had with someone you cared about.

260. Writers often support the cultivation of creativity in children. Write an article persuading adults to encourage creativity in kids.

261. Write a personal essay about your views on honesty and dishonesty. Is it ever okay to lie? When?

262. Do you have a friend or family member who is always there when you need someone? String together the stories of the times this person came through for you.

263. Write about something or someone you can't resist. What is it about this person or thing that you find irresistible?

264. Stephen King said, "If you want to be a writer, you must do two things above all others: read a lot and write a lot." How much do you read? How much time do you spend writing?

265. Have you ever fixed something that was broken? Ever solved a computer problem on your own? Write an article about how to fix something or solve some problem.

266. Write an essay about your favorite color. Why is it your favorite? How does this color make you feel? Where do you find this color?

267. You have the opportunity to interview any author, living or dead. Which author do you choose? Write a list of interview questions you'd like to ask.

268. What would you do if you suspected a friend or family member was struggling with addiction?

269. Write a personal essay describing the youngest person you know. How do you know this person? What influence does he or she have on your life?

270. Rita Mae Brown said, "Writers will happen in the best of families." What did she mean by this? What are some of society's attitudes about artists in general and writers in particular?

271. Describe the worst mistake you ever made. How would your life be different if you had chosen differently? Could the mistake have been averted? Did you learn anything from it?

272. Do you have a lucky charm or some other sentimental object that boosts your positive outlook? How did you get it? How do you use it? Where do you keep it? What is it?

273. Take a look at the cover of the last book you read. Did it make you want to read the book? How does it represent the book and compel readers to buy it? Notice the font used for the title and author's name. Notice the placement of text and the composition of images. Write a detailed description of it.

274. Every relationship is its own story. Tell the story of your marriage. If you are not (or have never been) married, then tell the story of a long-term relationship you've had.

275. What do you think the world of technology will look like in ten years? Twenty? What kind of computers, phones, and other devices will we use? Will technology improve travel? Health care? What do you expect to see and what would you like to see?

276. Have you ever read a book and thought, I could never write a book this good? What book was it? Who wrote it? What was it about the book that impressed you? What can you learn from it?

277. You get to give a million dollars to any person you want, but you will not get any of the money. Whom do you give it to and why?

278. Every home has a story. Does anyone you know live in a home that is the gathering place for others? Has the home itself changed over the years? What if its walls could talk?

279. Jodi Picoult said, "You can always edit a bad page. You can't edit a blank page." What did she mean by this?

280. You get to give ten million dollars to the charity or cause of your choice. Whom do you give the money to and why?

281. Have you ever experienced discrimination, bigotry, or harassment? Write a narrative about your experiences.

282. Have you ever found an activity so consuming that you get lost in it and lose track of time? Write a personal essay about it.

283. If and when you publish a book, you'll need to market it and build a readership. Write an outline of the actions you can take to promote your book.

284. Describe the qualities of a good friend. What would their flaws be?

285. Most of us shape our political and/or spiritual beliefs over time. Tell the story of how your life experiences and your perception of the world helped you shape your current belief system.

286. Have you ever defended someone who was powerless? Have you ever stuck up for an underdog? Write an article about helping those who cannot help themselves.

287. You're invited to a fancy costume party and you have an unlimited budget for your costume. What do you dress up as and why? Describe your costume in detail.

288. Robert Frost said, "Poetry is when an emotion has found its thought and the thought has found words." What is poetry?

289. Do you use social media? Have you ever used it for business purposes? Do you use it to meet people or stay connected with friends and family? Write an article about how you've effectively used social media

in your career or personal life.

290. We all have pet peeves. What are yours? Why do they bother you so much?

291. Every family has its own holiday rituals and traditions. Choose a holiday and write a narrative about how your family has celebrated it over the years. Include personal stories whether they are sad, funny, or troubling. As an alternative, write about one particular holiday occasion.

292. Some people think that the number thirteen, walking under a ladder, or breaking a mirror will bring bad luck. Are you superstitious? What superstitions do you hold? Why do you believe in them? Do you think they are cosmic or psychological?

293. Have you ever been close with your neighbors? Did you all get together regularly? Ever throw a block party? Tell the story of you and your neighbors forming a community of friendship (or rivalry).

294. What are your shopping habits? Do you buy recklessly? Do you clip coupons? Do you have any shopping tips that might benefit others? Write an article about shopping.

295. Many people feel their greatest legacy is their children. Besides children, what legacy would you like to leave behind?

296. Dance is one of the most unappreciated art forms. Dancers are stuck somewhere between the arts and sports. But think about this—dancers get out there and do their thing, and the only tools they possess are their own bodies. No pens or computers, no cameras, no paintbrushes, and no instruments. You can watch dance performances on television, in music videos, or simply by searching through YouTube. Watch a few dance performances and then write about them. Discuss how the dance is tied to the music. Make observations about how the dancers bring the choreography to life. Compare dancing to writing. Are there similarities?

297. What is your favorite season? What do you like about it? Write a descriptive essay about it.

298. Our beliefs and attitudes about love change over time as we gain life experience. Write a series of vignettes telling stories about how different experiences in your life changed or shaped your views about love.

299. We've all felt mistreated by businesses. They overcharge, fail to follow through, or can't get our orders right. Write a thoughtful but critical article from the customer's perspective based on a negative experience you've had with a business.

300. Are we alone in the universe? Write a personal essay about your thoughts on whether there is

other intelligent life besides humans in the universe.

Thank You

Thank you for reading *Adventures in Writing: The Complete Collection.* To get more creative writing tips and ideas and to find out when new books on the craft of writing are available, subscribe at Writing Forward:

http://www.writingforward.com/subscribe

Please consider leaving a review for this book on the bookstore website where you purchased it. Reviews help authors find new readers, so we can continue writing books.

You can also follow Writing Forward on social media:

Twitter:	http://twitter.com/WritingForward
Facebook:	http://www.facebook.com/writingforward
Google +:	https://plus.google.com/+Writingforward/posts
Pinterest:	http://pinterest.com/writingforward/
Goodreads:	http://www.goodreads.com/user/show/4944129-melissa-donovan

Thanks again for reading *Adventures in Writing.* I wish you an enjoyable and prosperous writing journey. Write on, shine on!

-- Melissa Donovan

About the Author

Melissa Donovan is the founder and editor of *Writing Forward*, a blog packed with creative writing tips and ideas.

Melissa started writing poetry and song lyrics at age thirteen. Shortly thereafter, she began keeping a journal. She studied at Sonoma State University, earning a BA in English with a concentration in creative writing. Since then, Melissa has worked as an author, copywriter, professional blogger, and writing coach.

Writing Forward

Writing Forward features creative writing tips, ideas, tools, and techniques, as well as writing exercises and prompts that offer inspiration and help build skills.

To get more writing tips and ideas and to receive notifications when new books in the *Adventures in Writing* series are released, visit Writing Forward.

www.writingforward.com

CPSIA information can be obtained at www.ICGtesting.com
Printed in the USA
BVOW06s1122250516

449513BV00027B/368/P